Indian Head Massage

Indian

Head Massage:

A practical guide

Second edition

Muriel Burnham-Airey
and Adele O'Keefe

Australia • Canada • Mexico • Singapore • Spain • United Kingdom • United States

THOMSON

Indian Head Massage: A Practical Guide 2nd Edition
Muriel Burnham-Airey and Adele O'Keefe

Publishing Director
John Yates

Commissioning Editor
Melody Woollard

Editorial Assistant
Thomas Rennie

Production Editor
Alissa Chappell

Manufacturing Manager
Helen Mason

Senior Marketing Executive
Natasha Giraudel

Typesetter
Tek-Art, Croydon, Surrey

Production Controller
Maeve Healy

Illustrations on pp. 16, 19, 114, 116 by
Oxford Designers and Illustrators

Cover Design
Harris Cook Turner, Basingstoke

Text Design
Design Delux, Bath, UK

Printer
Zrinski, d.d., Croatia

British Library Cataloguing-in-Publication Data
A catalogue record for this book is available from the British Library.

Contents

Foreword

In today's busy and stressful world, the therapeutic value of massage is undeniable. In particular, the ancient art of Indian Head Massage has grown in both appreciation and popularity.

This growth is largely due to the fact that Indian Head Massage complements so well both the hairdressing and beauty therapy fields. It can easily be integrated into the range of treatments available, and is something that all hair and beauty practitioners should consider offering as part of their service.

The second edition of *Indian Head Massage* has been updated and extended, and will be of help to those just starting out or looking to extend their skills. The new independent study section is a great addition, as it allows the reader to revise everything learned in previous chapters.

What strikes me most however about this book is the sheer breadth of knowledge and experience that Muriel Burnham-Airey and Adele O'Keefe display.

Muriel has many years of experience in both salons and colleges. As both an educator and a practitioner, her commitment to the industry shows true dedication and passion, whilst her considerable expertise has no doubt proved invaluable in creating this book.

Likewise, Adele is also a qualified therapist, with a background in both salons and colleges. As the head of hairdressing, beauty therapy and holistic therapy at Bolton College and an external verifier for City & Guilds, Adele is ideally placed to develop high quality learning materials.

Collectively, their specialist knowledge has allowed them to create this essential guide.

Alan Goldsbro
CEO
Habia

Acknowledgements

The authors and publishers would like to thank the following people for their assistance in producing this book: photographer Nick Robinson; models Teresa Currie, Cheryl Marsden and Donna McGovern; original massage routine diagrams by Don Yule.

About this book

Indian Head Massage has been written to provide an invaluable learning resource specifically for those studying for a National Vocational Qualification Level 3 programme in Indian Head Massage or any comparable course of study, but it can also be used as an indispensable course companion for those taking shorter evening or part-time classes or pursuing home-study in Indian Head Massage.

The book covers all of the skills necessary to become qualified in this field. It is written to support you in your training, enabling you to gain the knowledge and skills required. Each and every chapter of *Indian Head Massage* has been devised to cover the current Habia beauty therapy occupational standards for Indian Head Massage and will take you through everything you need to know in order to be proficient in the following duties:

- maintaining employment standards in the workplace
- supporting a healthy, safe and secure work environment
- maintaining good working relations with clients and work colleagues
- providing practical services to the client.

The text is accompanied by certain extra features to help link theory and practice and to provide ongoing support and extension to your learning and progress:

- helpful learning objectives at the start of each chapter to highlight the essential knowledge and understanding to be covered in that chapter
- useful tip boxes and health and safety boxes in the margins to provide 'at a glance' expert advice

- practical equipment lists to refer back to when preparing for treatments
- end of chapter to question material to assess your learning
- an Independent Study section to record your progress and provide a handy revision aid.

Whatever Indian Head Massage unit, topic or course you are following, this new edition of *Indian Head Massage* will become your irreplaceable study guide.

Introduction to Indian Head Massage

Valued by the Indian people for generations, Indian Head Massage is perhaps the simplest, easiest and the most convenient effective therapy in the massage treatment range.

This massage gem, given from the East to the West, is not hard to learn, no expensive specialist equipment is needed and your treatment room can be any warm quiet place where you can create a calming ambience. With this book, and a little time, you can learn the techniques needed to give these highly effective treatments.

As a student of Indian Head Massage you will be in popular demand among your clients, friends and family of all ages. You will be able to use your skills to help calm hyperactive children, relax tired mums, help husbands and partners to sleep without snoring, encourage teenagers into better sleep patterns before exams and increase the concentration levels of your colleagues.

If you are new to massage therapies, this is your ideal starting point. If you are an experienced therapist, you will find Indian Head Massage an exciting and rewarding addition to your professional skills.

Remember, massage is old and at the same time new – ancient in its origin, but still finding and providing solutions and giving help to new health and well-being problems created by modern-day lifestyles.

Considering the relatively small movements, lack of deep pressure and length of treatment, the benefits gained through this treatment are quite remarkable, rendering this an exciting therapy, when correctly given, for any student of massage.

All holistic therapies require a degree of belief; the depth of this belief is personal to the individual. Students who have experienced convincing results through other therapies will find that Indian Head Massage ranks very highly as an effective treatment, creating an excellent two-way communication link between client and therapist. Those new to holistic therapies will find giving Indian Head Massage treatments a journey of discovery with many rewarding and unexpected outcomes. They can look forward to experiencing their first insight into the healing powers of shared energy, inner peace and sense of fulfilment through giving effective treatments. Even students whose approach is somewhat sceptical and scientific will gain great personal benefit from giving this unique treatment.

Indian Head Massage is a unique massage treatment. It has many advantages, including the following:

No need to undress In preparing for a treatment the client need not undress. This is encouraging for clients who are nervous or new to massage treatments.

Oils are optional There is no necessity to use oils, but they may be used if particularly requested by the client.

Versatile This is an ideal treatment for the less able-bodied client, and can easily be performed on a client in a wheelchair. The treatment is so versatile that it can be carried out almost anywhere where there is a comfortable upright chair that has a reasonably low back which allows the shoulder massage movements. (A 'Director's chair' is ideal for the independent therapist, as this folds easily and can be carried. The use of a cushion in addition allows for a little height adjustment.)

Cost-effective Indian Head Massage is very cost-effective – the full treatment takes approximately 30 minutes.

Suitable for all Indian Head Massage is suitable for all ages. It can be used effectively to calm small children with hyperactive tendencies; it can relieve exam stress in young adults; it is proven in alleviating stress in the busy executive, the office worker and the person at home, helping to calm and relax them and to promote good sleep patterns. Indian Head Massage is calming and soothing for the elderly and the disabled. Whereas many therapies cannot be used with pregnant women, Indian Head Massage can: it can safely be enjoyed throughout a healthy pregnancy.

Usable anywhere The treatment is invaluable as an introduction to massage, and can be carried out in varied environments, such as the home, the workplace, nursing or residential care homes, and even at the office. It makes good business sense to keep the workforce alert and stress-free, and therapists are beginning to be invited into workplaces to carry out treatments over the lunchtime period as this has already proved to be effective.

A brief history of Indian Head Massage

1

Learning objectives

Essential Knowledge and Understanding NVQ Level 3 areas covered in this chapter are:

- **The history of Indian Head Massage.**

- **Its origins and traditions.**

Massage has been a major part of medicine for at least 5000 years, and significant in Western medical traditions for at least 3000 years. It was primarily administered by physicians, and was the first and most important of the medical arts.

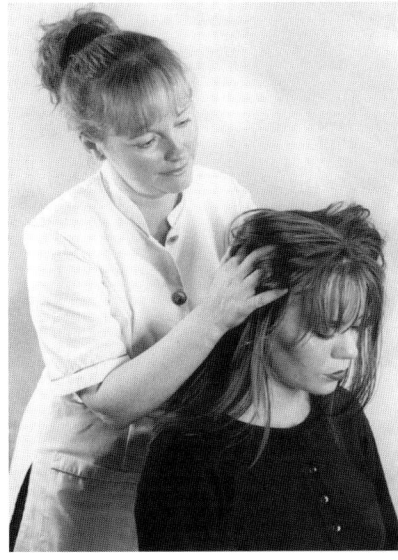

Ancient Greeks and Romans used massage as their principal means of pain relief and healing. In the 5th century BC Hippocrates wrote comprehensively about the benefits of massage and insisted that physicians should be experienced in rubbing, 'as rubbing can bind a joint that is too loose and can loosen a joint that is too rigid' – he recognised that massage can tone and stimulate weak, inactive muscles and can relieve tension in tense, knotted muscles. Julius Caesar was treated daily by being pinched all over to relieve neuralgia and headaches.

From the 5th century AD (after the fall of Rome), however, the development of medicine in Europe made little progress and it was left to the Arabs to study and develop the teachings of the classical world.

The historical record

Throughout history, massage has been written about extensively, from the writings of medical texts in 500 BC to the production of the first medical books after the development of the printing press by Gutenberg around 1450.

China

Records in the British Museum show that as early as 3000 BC the Chinese were practising massage systems. They developed their technique, **amma**, over many years. Chinese massage today is an integral part of China's medical clinics and hospitals. The modern term for Chinese massage is **tui-na** which literally means 'push–pull'.

Japan

In the 6th century AD the practice of *amma* entered Japan. It remained much the same as in China, but the points of stimulation were called **tsubo**. The Japanese believe that applying pressure to these points releases energy which balances the body's life force (**ki**). This finger-pressure technique the Japanese called **shiatsu**, and in recent years this has become a popular massage method in the West.

India

On the Indian sub-continent massage has been practised for over 3000 years. Knowledge of massage came to India from China, and was based on finding the various points on the body where pressure, rubbing and manipulations were most effective; in India the ayurvedic term for these is marma points. Records indicate that ancient Hindus, Persians and Egyptians used forms of massage for many ailments. The *Ayur-Veda* (*Art of Life*), a sacred book among Hindus, was written around 1800 BC. It included massage amongst its hygienic principles.

The family tradition of massage in India dates back to the beginnings of Hinduism, which has been the main religion of India for almost 2000 years and still claims the loyalty of 80 per cent of Indians. Today this centuries-old tradition is still as important a ritual as taking food, and plays a central role in the life of the family.

Newborn infants are massaged daily from birth to the age of three, which promotes bonding. The mother of the newly-born infant herself receives ceremonial massages daily for a minimum of 40 days after the birth. The child will continue to receive massage twice or three times a week until the age of about seven. At this age the child will begin to learn the massage techniques, partly from experiencing massage and partly from watching other family members carrying out massage. He or she will gradually be encouraged to take an active part in massaging other family members.

Massage is also given ceremonially prior to a wedding. The bride and groom receive massage from members of their respective families, as an essential part of the preparation ritual. Massage is carried out using oils and organic extracts. These produce a beautiful glaze on the skin, are aromatic and induce relaxation. The couple gain stamina and physic strength, which in turn increases their beauty. After the wedding, the wife gives her husband a massage every day of their life together.

For Indian housewives, massage forms part of their social activities. When the chores are finished in the afternoon they will meet for a gossip and to enjoy a head massage. In old age, grandparents can enjoy massage given by their grandchildren. The *stimulating* effects of massage are seen as a benefit to the elders of the family, whereas the *calming* effects are valued in dealing with fractious or hyperactive children.

Different oils are used at different times of year, according to the season, availability and cost. Warming oils are used in the winter and cooling ones in summer. Oils in general use are coconut oil, used traditionally in the spring, and sesame oil, used in the summer to help keep the head cool in the high temperatures experienced in the sub-continent. The most expensive oils, used by rich women, are herbal oils with sandalwood and henna; these may also have ingredients added to promote hair growth and discourage dandruff.

In India, weekly massage is a family matter: almost everyone gives and receives it. At holiday locations, on the beaches and in the markets, from Bombay and Calcutta to Goa, you will find head massages being offered. A visit to the barber in India will always include a head massage as part of the service. Indians believe that massage preserves the body energy and saves the organism from decay. It is the most powerful method of relaxing and, at the same time, rejuvenating the body.

In order to be safe practitioners, therapists must have a thorough knowledge of the anatomy and physiology of the surface and the underlying structure of the treatment areas. The following chapters therefore begin with the study of all related anatomy, physiology, and health and safety, before leading the student through all aspects of preparation towards step-by-step instructions for the treatment itself. Students will gain an insight into the relationship between ayurveda, marma points and chakras through these chapters, which focus on the holistic aspect of traditional Indian Head Massage.

Anatomy and physiology

2

Essential Knowledge and Understanding NVQ Level 3 areas covered in this chapter are:

- **The structure and function of the skin.**

- **The position, structure and function of the bones and muscles in the treatment areas of the body.**

- **The effects of massage on: the lymphatic system; the skin; muscles; blood flow; and pulse rate.**

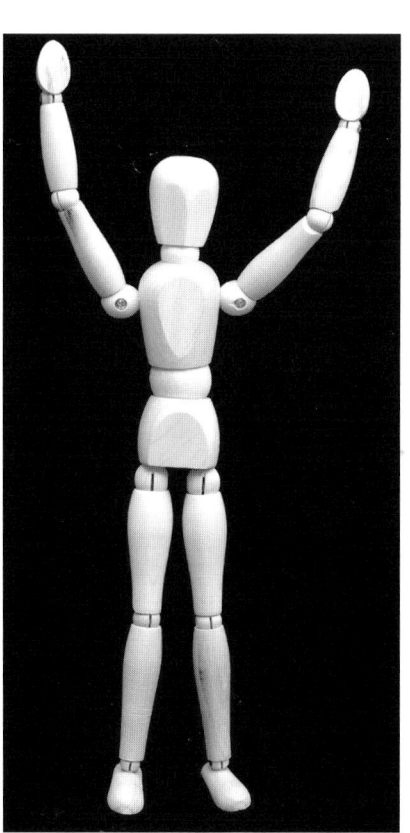

The skin

The **skin** is the largest organ of the body. It serves as an interface with the environment, and as a protection for the body; its efficient and effective functioning is essential to life.

The skin has three main layers: the **subcutaneous tissue**, the **dermis** and the **epidermis**, which are discussed below.

Roles of the skin

The skin has six main roles.

Protection

The skin protects the body from infection and from injury.

Heat regulator

The body seeks to maintain a steady temperature. The normal temperature of a healthy body is 37°C. If the body becomes cold, exercise or increased blood flow provide warmth. If it becomes too hot, sweat glands in the skin allow cooling to occur.

Secretion and excretion

Sudoriferous glands in the skin excrete perspiration. This cools the body.

Sebaceous glands in the skin secrete **sebum**. This coats the skin's surface and helps to waterproof it. It also slows down the evaporation of moisture from within the skin, and creates a barrier which inhibits the growth of harmful micro-organisms.

Absorption

The skin has very limited powers of absorption. Nevertheless, some chemicals, cosmetics and drugs *can* be absorbed in small amounts through the pores.

Respiration

The skin breathes through its pores in the same way as the body breathes through the lungs, though on a smaller scale. Oxygen is taken in and carbon dioxide is discharged.

Sensation

In the papillary layer of the dermis there are heat, cold, pain, pressure and touch receptors. Nerves within the skin register these basic sensations and carry messages to and from the brain.

Subcutaneous tissue

The *deepest* layer of the skin is the **subcutaneous tissue** or **sub-cutis**. (This layer is sometimes regarded as part of the dermis – see below.) The sub-cutis varies in thickness according to age, sex and the general health of the individual.

The layer contains fatty tissue (**adipose tissue**). It is this that give smoothness and shape to the body, and it also serves as a protective cushion. The subcutaneous tissue provides a reservoir for nutrients and energy, and it also acts as an insulator, reducing heat loss in the body. It contains small blood and lymphatic vessels.

Dermis

Above the subcutaneous tissue is the **dermis**. Also known as the **corium**, the **cutis** or **true skin**, it consists of two

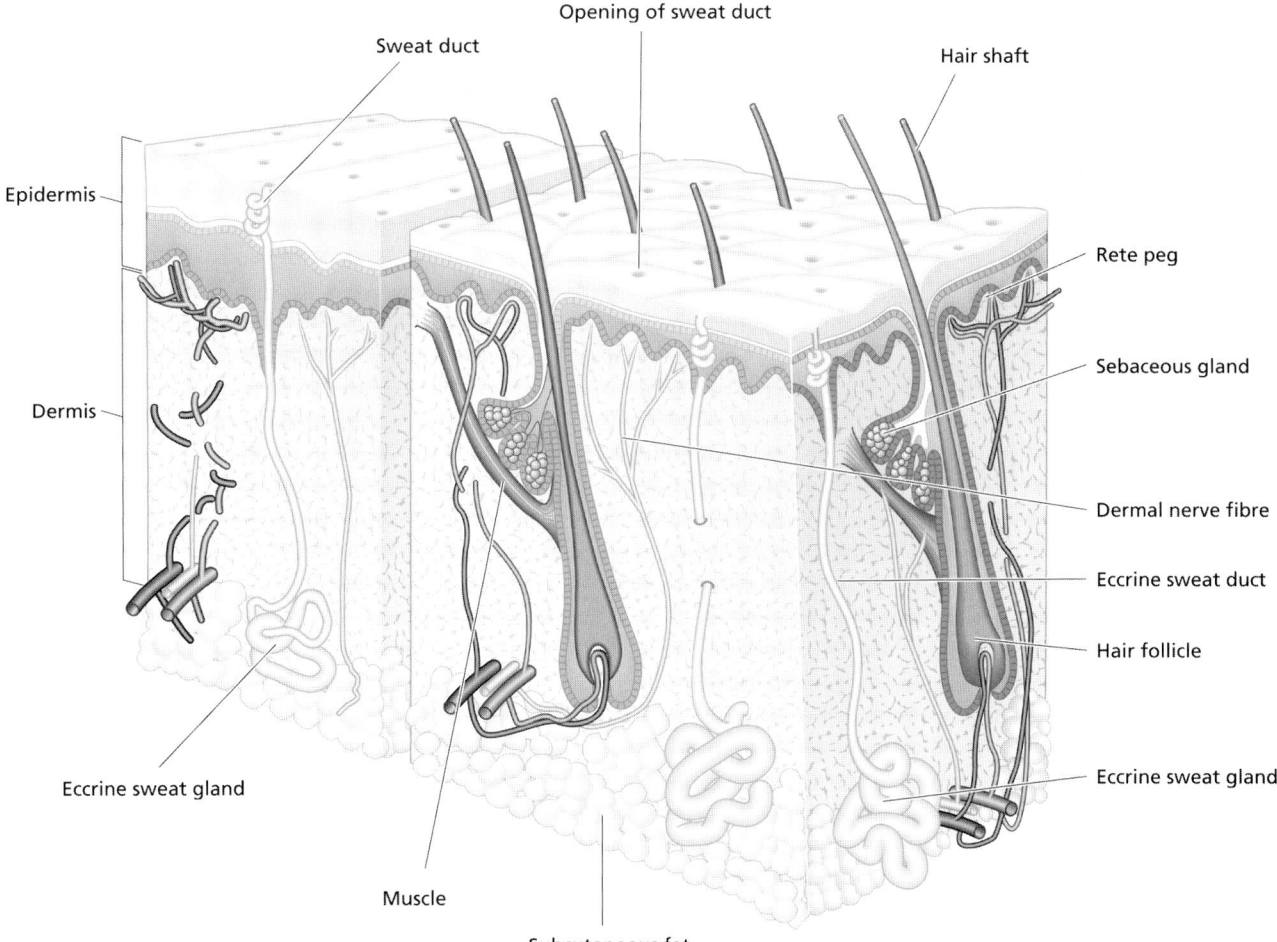

Structure of the skin: the thick, hairless skin of the palm of the hand (left), and the thin, hairy skin of the forearm (right)

main layers. (The subcutaneous tissue is continuous with the dermis, and is often classed as its third layer.)

- The **recticular layer** contains fat cells, blood and lymph vessels, sweat and oil glands, hair follicles and nerve endings.
- The **papillary layer**, directly underneath the epidermis, is made of fine strands of elastic tissue. It extends upwards into the epidermis in looped finger-like projections.

The dermis is thinnest on the eyelids, and thickest on the palms of the hands and the soles of the feet. It is thicker in men's skin than in women's.

Two kinds of fibres intermingle with the cells of the dermis.

- **Collagen fibres**: these make up almost 78 per cent of the dry weight of the skin. Collagen fibres contain **elastin**, a protein with elastic properties which helps to give the skin its resilience.
- **Reticulum fibres**: these form fine, branching patterns in connective tissue, helping to link the bundles of collagen fibres.

Epidermis

The **epidermis** is the outermost layer of the skin. It contains cells of different ages, from the inner basal cells, which have well-defined structure and nuclei, to flaky cell debris at the surface, from which the nuclei and all

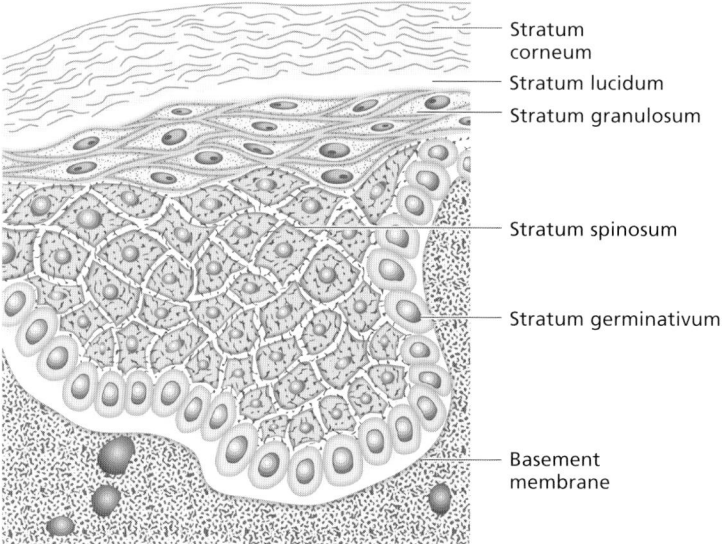

Layers of the epidermis

evidence of cell structure have disappeared. The epidermis is also termed the **cuticle** or **scarf skin**.

The epidermis rests on the dermis, a dense fibrous layer, and is interlocked with it by a series of finger-like projections called **papillae**.

Stratum germinativum or basal layer

The **stratum germinativum** is the deepest section of the epidermis. It is in contact with the dermis, from which it derives nutrients via the capillary blood vessels.

This layer is the site where new cells are formed. Cells grow and divide in a process called **mitosis**. As new cells form, older cells are displaced towards the surface. The stratum germinativum is at its most productive between midnight and four in the morning – perhaps this explains the term 'beauty sleep'!

In the stratum germinativum, one in every ten cells is a **melanocyte**. This is a cell that makes **melanin**, the pigment that protects the skin from ultra-violet radiation. Differences in skin colour are the result of differing amounts of melanin. When the skin is exposed to sunlight, more melanin is produced. In fair skins this increased melanin is apparent as a **suntan**.

Stratum spinosum or prickle-cell layer

The **stratum spinosum** is a very active layer, and consists of living, dividing cells. The layer is rich in **melanocytes**, cells that produce **melanin**. It is this layer that gives skin its colour. When the skin is exposed to the sun's rays, this layer produces additional melanin for protection. Light-skinned people then acquire a visible **tan**. Dark-skinned people also go darker if they sunbathe, but the tan is less noticeable.

The stratum spinosum is often coupled with the stratum germinativum as the **Malpighian layer**.

Stratum granulosum

The thickness of the **stratum granulosum** varies, from one cell to several cells. It is thickest on the palms of the hand and the soles of the feet.

As living cells grow and die, they gain **keratin**, the fibrous substance also found in hair and nails. The process of **keratinisation** begins in the stratum granulosum. As they are displaced towards the surface, cells lose fluid and become drier and flatter. At some point they also lose the nucleus.

Cells in the stratum granulosum reflect light and give the skin a light appearance.

Stratum lucidum

The **stratum lucidum** derives its name from the Latin words for 'layer' and 'light' – it is clear and almost transparent in appearance. This layer is only a few cells deep, and is thought to form a barrier zone which controls the movement of water through the skin.

Stratum corneum

The **stratum corneum** is the outside layer of the skin. Its cells contain fatty material that keeps them waterproof and helps to prevent the skin from cracking, which would leave it open to infection. In many parts of the body, this layer forms the thickest part of the epidermis.

Connective tissue

Connective tissue consists largely of a fluid matrix and collagen fibres that together support, connect and bind other body tissues. The main structural protein in connective tissue is **collagen**.

Connective tissue forms a continuous net-like framework throughout the body, binding and supporting the organs and muscles, and anchoring lymph and blood vessels.

Each bundle of muscle fibre has a connective tissue sheath. Connective tissue also forms **tendons**, or flat tendinous sheets (**aponeuroses**), which link the muscles to bones, or bones to other bones. One such sheet, the **epicranial aponeurosis**, lies between the cranium and the deep connective tissue of the scalp.

Connective tissue thus provides a complicated system of connecting sheets and linkages that allow the muscles to operate and to move the bones of the skeleton. Without it, motion and postural stability would not be possible.

The growth cycle of hair

Hair is grown and shed in a continuous cycle.

In each follicle, a period of hair growth is followed by a resting period. The growing phase is known as **anagen** and the resting period as **telogen**. Between them comes a breaking-down period known as **catagen**. At the end of telogen, the resting period, a new hair will normally begin to grow from the follicle, and the original hair will be shed.

As the follicle approaches the end of the growing phase, the hair root becomes brush-like. The bulb and the lower part of the follicle break down, except for a strand of cells, the **epithelial column**, which remains in direct contact with the **dermal papilla**.

The hair is now called a **club hair**, because of its shape. The follicle has shortened to about half its original length. The epithelial column has shortened and formed the **secondary germ**, and is still in contact with the dermal papilla.

The follicle remains in this condition throughout telogen. At the end of this resting phase, the secondary germ becomes active. It has two centres of growth. Its lower end, in contact with the dermal papilla, forms the new bulb that produces a new hair. The upper part forms the new cells which lengthen the follicle below the club hair.

The lengthening of the follicle keeps pace with the growth of the new hair, so that the hair tip remains just below the end of the club hair. Only when the follicle is fully grown does the tip of the new hair push past the base of the club hair and grow up to the surface. The old hair simply drops out of the follicle, or is dislodged by brushing or combing.

With the follicles of the scalp, the growing stage is long and the resting stage short. Although some hair follicles appear singly on the scalp, the great majority are found in clusters

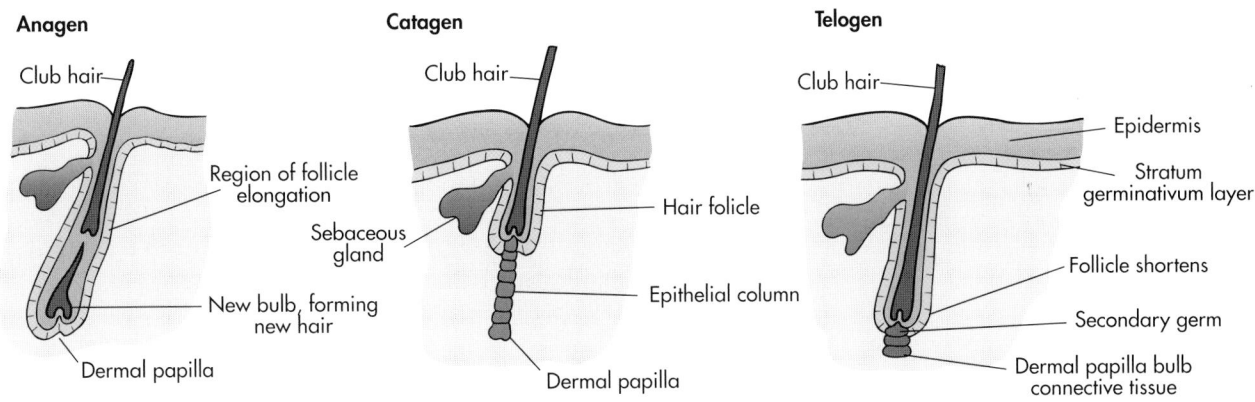

Anagen
- Club hair
- Region of follicle elongation
- New bulb, forming new hair
- Dermal papilla

Catagen
- Club hair
- Sebaceous gland
- Hair folicle
- Epithelial column
- Dermal papilla

Telogen
- Club hair
- Epidermis
- Stratum germinativum layer
- Follicle shortens
- Secondary germ
- Dermal papilla bulb connective tissue

of three or four – these form what are known as **pilosebaceous units**. These units frequently share a common opening at the surface of the scalp.

- Scalp hair: anagen, 1.25–7 years; catagen, 2 weeks; telogen, 3–4 months.
- Eyebrow and eyelash hairs: anagen, 1 month; catagen, 5–7 days; telogen, 3.5 months.
- Body (vellus) hairs: anagen, 3 months; catagen, 5–7 days; telogen, 2.5 months.

Bones

The skeletal system

The skeletal system is primarily made up of bones, the hardest structure in the body. Bones come in different shapes, depending on their function and are connected to each other at joints by less dense connective tissues, cartilage and ligament.

Supported by skeletal muscles, the skeleton makes the framework of the body. Functions of the skeletal system are to:

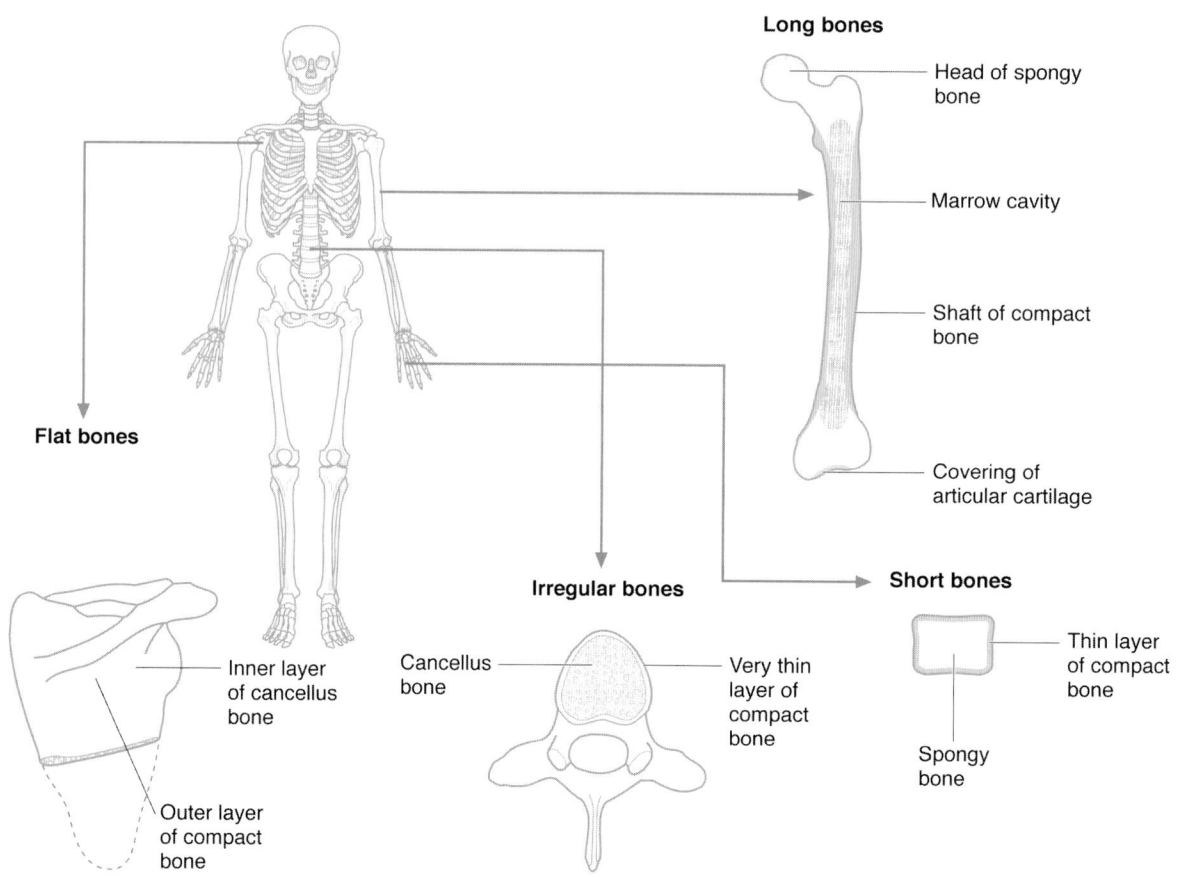

Long bones
- Head of spongy bone
- Marrow cavity
- Shaft of compact bone
- Covering of articular cartilage

Flat bones
- Inner layer of cancellus bone
- Outer layer of compact bone

Irregular bones
- Cancellus bone
- Very thin layer of compact bone

Short bones
- Thin layer of compact bone
- Spongy bone

The skeletal system

- protect the underlying structures such as the brain and lungs
- provide an attachment point for the muscles to allow movement
- support the softer tissues
- give shape to the body
- blood cells are made inside the bone known as the bone marrow
- the skeletal system provides a structure from which many internal organs are suspended and kept securely in place.

Structure

The human skeleton consists of 206 bones divided into two main groups: the **axial skeleton** which is made up of the bones around the centre of the body (i.e. the skull and vertebral column together with the ribs and sternum); and the **appendicular skeleton**, which consists of the bones of the upper and lower limbs together with the pelvic and pectoral girdle.

The shape of the face and head is largely determined by:

- the bone structure of the skull
- the muscles covering the bones of the face.

The skull, which protects the brain, consists of two parts; the **cranium** and the **face**. There are eight bones in the cranium and 14 in the face. The only movable bone in the skull is the lower jaw, or mandible.

Bones of the cranium

The bones that form the cranium are slightly curved and thin. They are held together by connective tissue. As we grow from childhood, the joints, called **sutures**, become immovable.

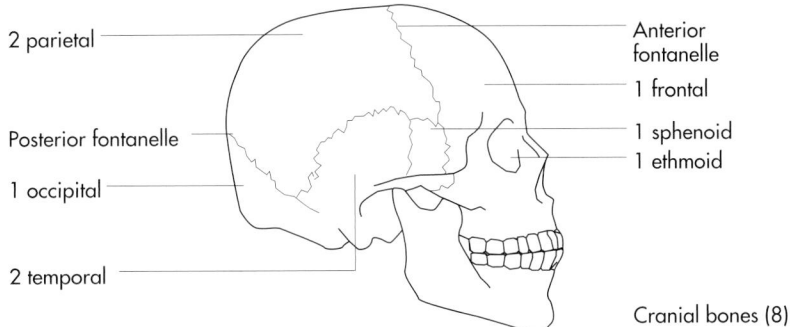

2 parietal • Posterior fontanelle • 1 occipital • 2 temporal • Anterior fontanelle • 1 frontal • 1 sphenoid • 1 ethmoid • Cranial bones (8)

- The **frontal bone** forms the front part of the roof of the skull – the forehead and the upper wall of the eye sockets.
- The two **parietal bones** form the sides and roof of the cranium – the crown.
- The two **temporal bones** form the sides of the head – the lower region and sides of the cranium, around the ears. They provide two attachment points for muscles, the zygomaticus process and the mastoid process.
- The **occipital bones** form the back and base of the cranium. They leave a large hole, the **foramen magnum**, through which pass the spinal cord, blood vessels and nerves.
- The **sphenoid** forms the anterior part of the cranium base, at the back of the eye sockets. It is bat-shaped, with wings on either side that form the temples. It joins all the bones of the cranium.
- The **ethmoid bone**, between the eye sockets, forms part of the nasal cavities.

Bones of the face

The facial bones form the facial features and support structures such as the teeth and eyes.

- The two **nasal bones** form the bridge of the nose.
- The two **maxillae** form the upper jaw.
- The two **palatine bones** form the floor and side walls of the nose and the roof of the mouth.
- The two **lacrimal bones** form the inner walls of the eye socket.
- The two **turbinate bones** form the outside of the nose.

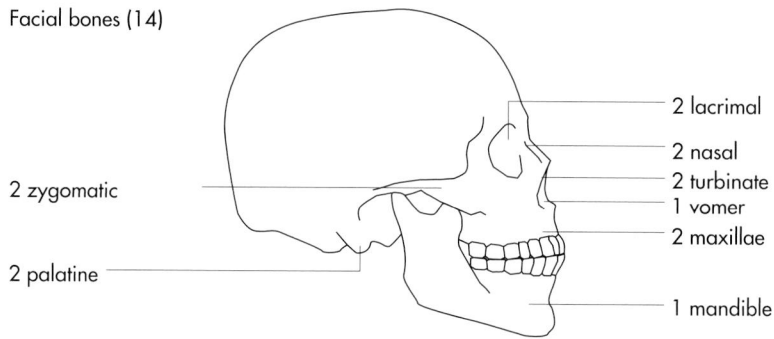

Facial bones (14)

2 zygomatic

2 palatine

2 lacrimal
2 nasal
2 turbinate
1 vomer
2 maxillae
1 mandible

Bones of the face

- The **vomer bone** forms part of the nasal septum, the dividing bony wall of the nose.
- The **mandible**, the only facial bone that moves, forms the lower jaw. This is the largest and the strongest facial bone.

Bones of the neck, chest and shoulders

- The **cervical vertebrae** are the vertebrae at the top of the spine. The **atlas** vertebra (first vertebra) supports the skull; the **axis** (second vertebra) allows the head to rotate.
- The **hyoid** bone supports the tongue. It is a U-shaped bone at the front of the neck.
- The two **clavicles** form the collar bone. These are long, slender bones which meet at the base of the neck. The collar bone allows movement of the shoulders, forming a joint with the scapulae and the sternum.
- The two **scapulae** are the shoulder blades in the upper back. They are triangular-shaped and provide attachment for muscles that move the arm. The shoulder girdle, composed of the scapulae and the clavicle, allows movement at the shoulder.
- The **sternum** is the breastbone. This provides a surface for muscle attachment, allowing muscle movements, and protects the internal organs.
- The **humerus** is the bone in each upper arm. The humerus meets the scapula in a ball-and-socket joint, allowing movement in any direction.

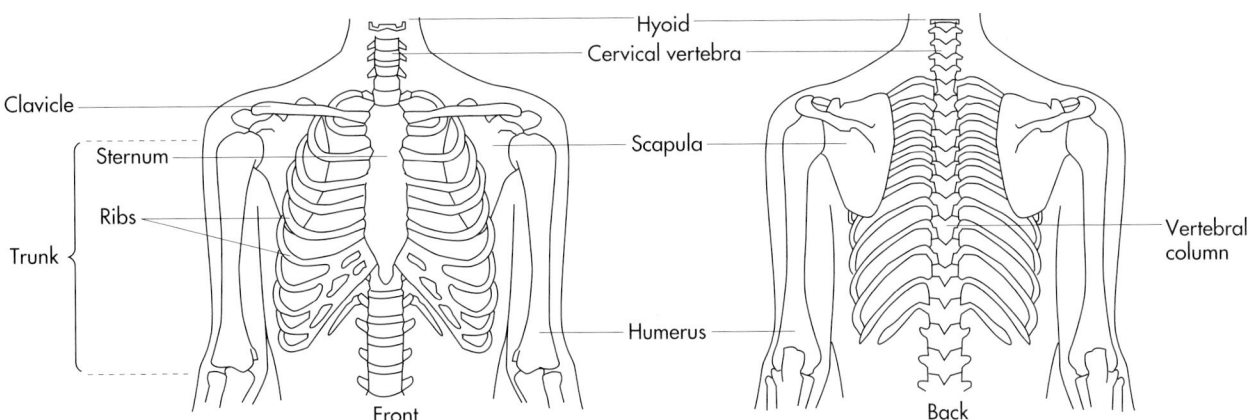

Bones of the neck, chest and shoulders

Bones of the arm and hand

Ulna and **radius** are the long bones of the forearm. They are tied together by a fibrous ring and allow a rotating movement. The radius is shorter than the ulna bone and is positioned on the thumb side of the forearm. The ulna is positioned on the little finger side. The joint between the two bones produces a movement called pronation. This is when the radius moves obliquely across the ulna resulting in the thumb side of the hand being closest to the body.

The wrist contains eight **carpals**. These are irregular-sized bones and are arranged in two rows of four, which are very close together and held in place by ligaments. The carpals comprise on the proximal row scaphoid (on the thumb side), lunate, triquetral and pisiform. The distal carpals comprise the trapezium (thumb side), trapezoid, capitate and hamate.

The hand is made up of five metacarpals which make up the palms and 14 phalanges which make up the fingers – two in each thumb and three in each finger.

Effects of massage on bones

When massage is applied to bones it does not have any direct effect. What does happen is that because of the

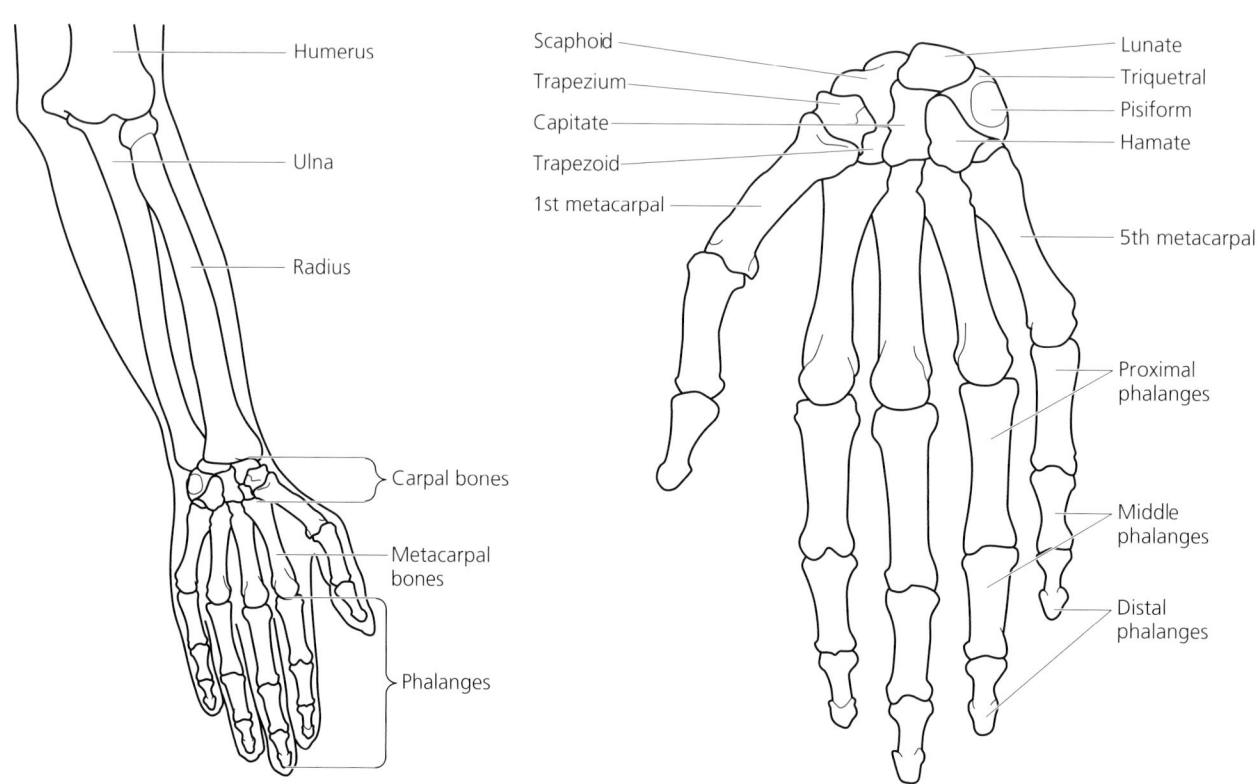

Bones of the arm

Bones of the hand

increased blood circulation the bones are fed fresh oxygen and waste products are absorbed more quickly.

Never massage over painful bones if you do not know the reason for the pain. Make sure that any fractures or breaks have healed completely prior to treatment and seek medical advice if the client has any metal pins or discs.

The blood system

The composition of blood

Blood is a liquid tissue. It consists of a *fluid* component, **blood plasma**, and a *solid* component, which includes **blood cells**. Plasma constitutes 50–60 per cent of the blood volume.

Red blood cells (erythrocytes) are formed in the bone marrow and account for as much as 98 per cent of the total blood cells. These cells carry oxygen from the lungs to the rest of the body. **White blood cells** (leucocytes) are produced in the spleen, the lymph nodes and the bone marrow. They protect the body against disease. Also in the blood are **platelets**. These too are formed in the bone marrow and play an important role in allowing blood to clot at a wound site.

Plasma provides the fluid in which the red blood cells, white blood cells and the platelets can be carried around the body. About 90 per cent of plasma is water. Of the remainder, 7 per cent is protein and 1.5 per cent other substances. Plasma regulates the fluid balance in the body and also the pH of the blood (how acidic or alkaline it is). The blood also carries fluids and dissolved gases.

The skin may hold as much as one half of all the blood in the body.

The blood supply

Blood provides the main transport system in the body, carrying oxygen from the lungs to the muscles and body tissues, and the waste product carbon dioxide from the tissues to the lungs. Blood leaving the lungs is **oxygenated**; that returning from the body is **deoxygenated**.

The blood flows around the body continually, pumped by the heart which has four chambers. Blood leaving the left side of the heart (from the ventricle) contains oxygen, held in the red blood cells, and nutrients in various states of biochemical breakdown. It enters the aorta, the main

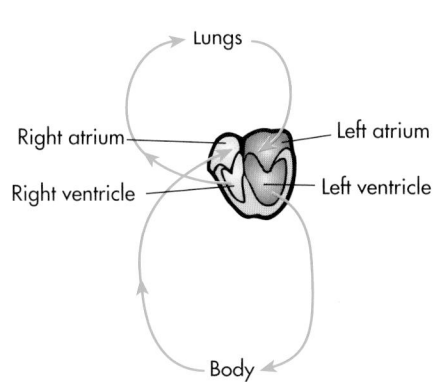

Circulation of the blood: overview

artery, and is then distributed through smaller and smaller blood vessels around the whole body. Blood passing through the liver collects wastes; these are transported to the kidneys and eliminated as urine. Blood passing through the pituitary gland, the adrenal glands and the sex glands collects hormones. These have their effect when they later reach the target organs, such as the heart or the brain.

Blood returns via the veins to the right side of the heart – first the top chamber, the atrium, and then through a valve to the lower chamber, the ventricle. The ventricle pumps the blood to the lungs, where carbon dioxide is expelled and fresh oxygen collected. Finally the blood returns to the atrium on the left side of the heart, and passes through a valve into the left ventricle, ready to start its next journey round the body.

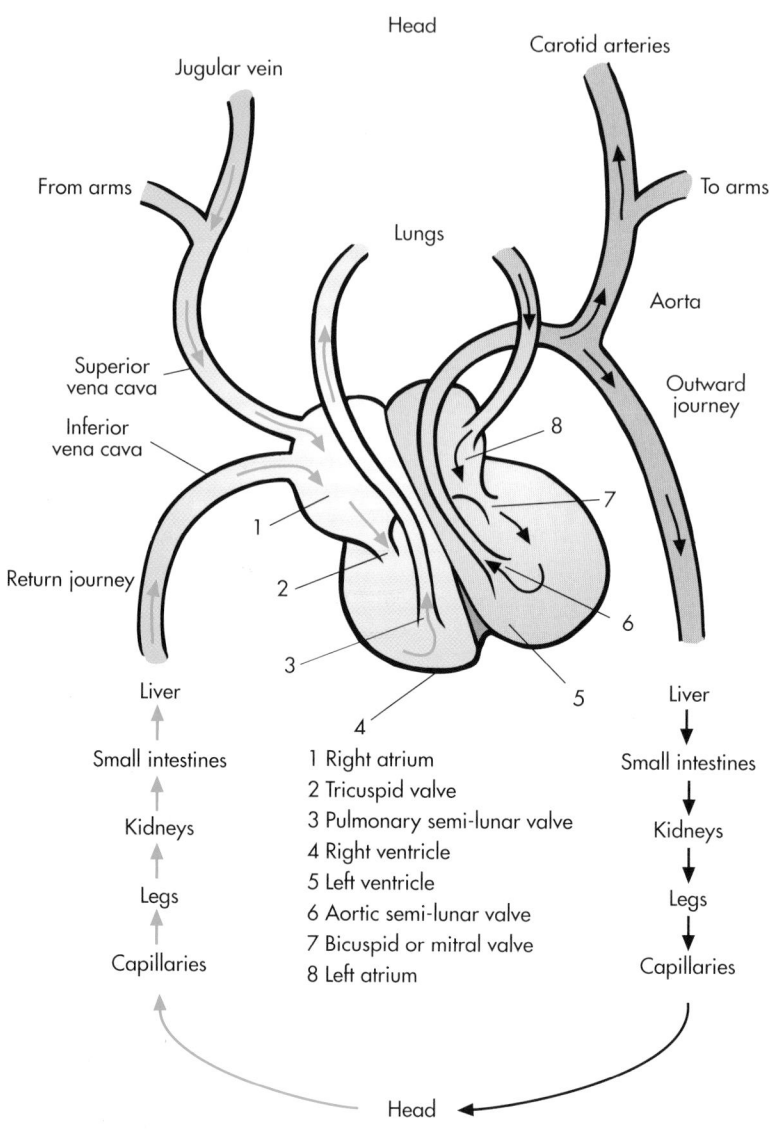

1 Right atrium
2 Tricuspid valve
3 Pulmonary semi-lunar valve
4 Right ventricle
5 Left ventricle
6 Aortic semi-lunar valve
7 Bicuspid or mitral valve
8 Left atrium

Circulation of the blood: details

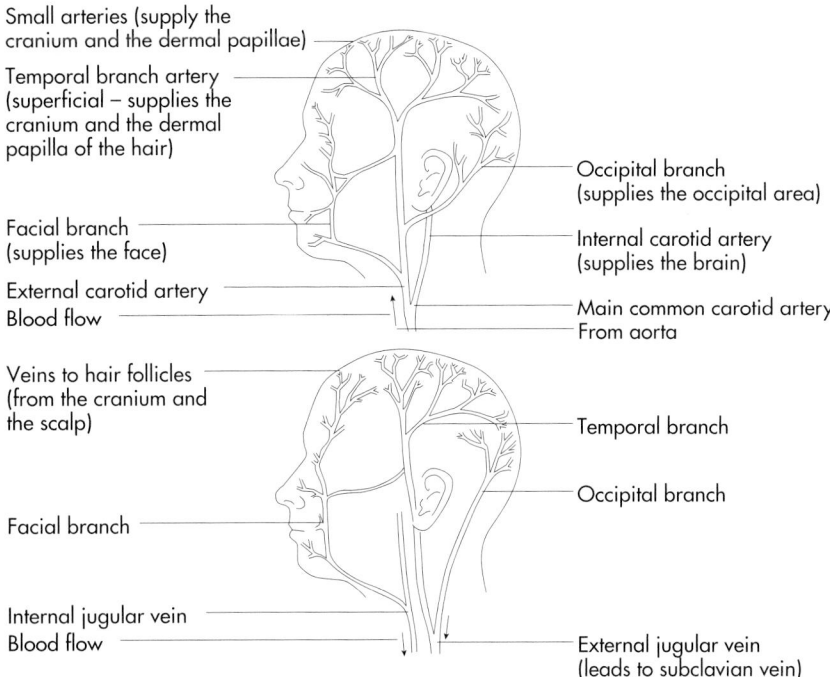

Small arteries (supply the cranium and the dermal papillae)

Temporal branch artery (superficial – supplies the cranium and the dermal papilla of the hair)

Facial branch (supplies the face)

External carotid artery
Blood flow

Occipital branch (supplies the occipital area)

Internal carotid artery (supplies the brain)

Main common carotid artery
From aorta

Veins to hair follicles (from the cranium and the scalp)

Facial branch

Temporal branch

Occipital branch

Internal jugular vein
Blood flow

External jugular vein (leads to subclavian vein)

Blood supply to and from the head

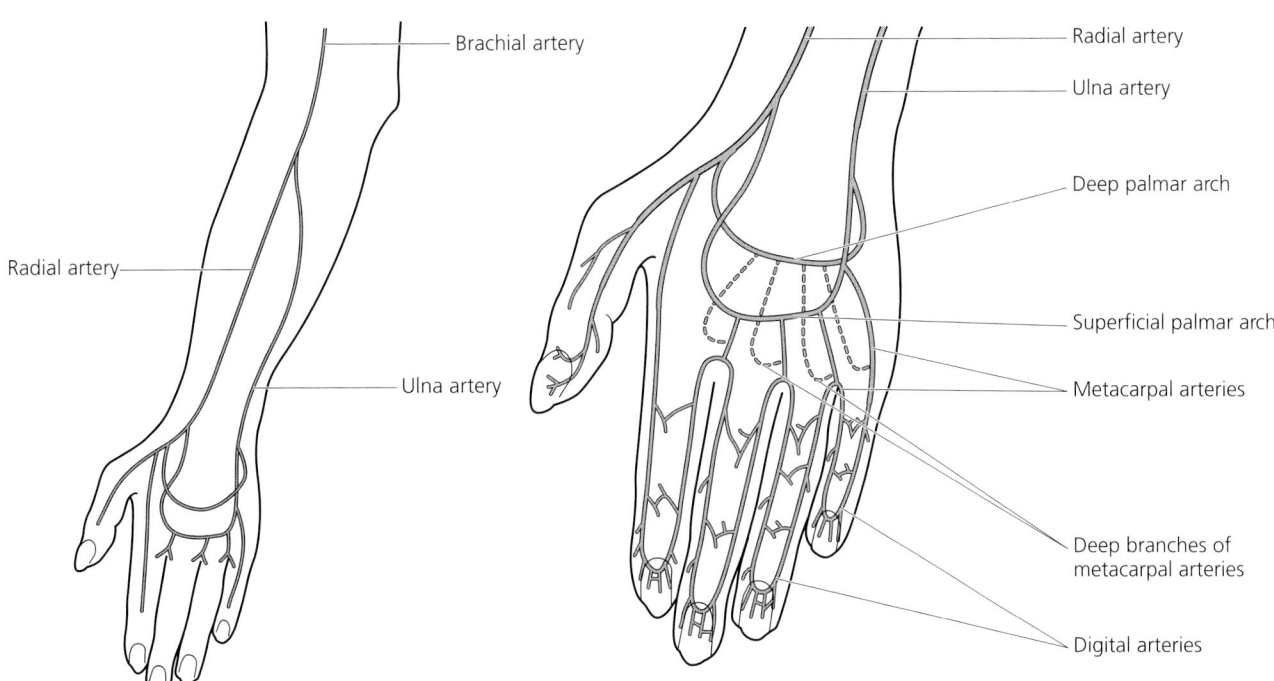

Brachial artery

Radial artery

Ulna artery

Radial artery

Ulna artery

Deep palmar arch

Superficial palmar arch

Metacarpal arteries

Deep branches of metacarpal arteries

Digital arteries

Arteries of the arm and hand

The blood supply consists of six major circular routes:

1   heart → *pulmonary artery* → lungs → *pulmonary vein* → heart

2   heart → *aorta* → *carotid artery* → head → *jugular vein* → *superior vena cava* → heart

3   heart → *aorta* → *subclavian artery* → arms → *subclavian vein* → heart

4   heart → *aorta* → *hepatic artery* → liver → *hepatic vein* → *inferior vena cava* → heart

5   heart → *aorta* → *renal artery* → kidneys → *renal vein* → *inferior vena cava* → heart

6   heart → *aorta* → *iliac artery* → legs → *iliac vein* → *inferior vena cava* → heart.

Blood pressure

Blood pressure in the circulatory system is closely related to the heartbeat; anything that makes the heart beat faster will raise blood pressure.

Factors that affect blood pressure include anger, stress, pain, smoking, drugs, exercise, excitement, anxiety, fright, age, weight and sex. Blood pressure is lower in veins than in arteries.

Normal blood pressure reading is between 100 and 140mm Hg systolic and between 60 and 90mm Hg diastolic.

The pulse

The pulse is a pressure wave that can be felt in the arteries which corresponds to the beating of the heart. The average pulse in an adult is between 60 and 80 beats per minute.

Factors that affect the pulse rate include exercise, heat, anger, stress, excitement, grief and fear.

Effects of massage on the circulatory system

Blood leaving the heart is under strong pressure. It travels through **arteries**, then the smaller **arterioles**, and eventually very small vessels called **capillaries**. By the time it leaves the capillaries, the pressure behind it is much reduced. In the **venules** and **veins**, therefore, there are **valves** to stop the blood flowing backwards. The valves prevent backflow, so the flow of venous blood is always *towards* the heart.

The smaller veins at the surface of the skin link up to the larger and larger ones, and eventually to the two main venous trunks, the **inferior vena cava** and the **superior vena cava**. These return the blood to the right side of the heart. Massage helps this process: effleurage movements help empty the small venules into the veins, carrying away the waste products, toxins and carbon dioxide from the body tissues. As 'stale' blood leaves the tissues, fresh blood brings oxygen and nutrients to the tissues. Massage can help lower blood pressure caused by stress and anxiety as it has a relaxing effect causing the pulse rate to slow. Gentle stroking causes the walls of the capillaries in the skin to contract. This has a cooling effect on the body.

Kneading massage movements can be used with similar benefits to the lymphatic system.

The lymphatic system

The main functions of the **lymphatic system** are:

- to remove bacteria and other foreign material
- to help prevent infection
- to drain away excess fluids, which are then eliminated from the body.

Lymph is clear and colourless, a watery fluid resembling blood plasma. It contains nutrients, including fatty acids, glucose, amino acids, mineral ions, dissolved oxygen and hormones, all of which are necessary to the health and growth of tissues. Lymph is filtered through the walls of the capillaries. In the spaces between cells where there are no blood capillaries, lymph provides nourishment. It also removes carbon dioxide and nitrogen waste, and carries a type of white blood cell, called **lymphocytes**.

The lymphatic system consists of the lymph fluid, lymph vessels and lymph glands (or nodes). When you are fighting an infection, the lymph glands may swell. The lymphatic system has no muscular pump like the heart for the blood: lymph moves through vessels and around the body when movements of large muscles squeeze the vessels. Lymph travels in one direction, from the body tissue towards the heart.

During massage of the face, neck and shoulders, the lymph flow is assisted and the removal of waste products hastened.

Lymph vessels

Lymph vessels, like veins, have valves along their length to prevent lymph from flowing backwards. The vessels run very close to the veins. The vessels join to form larger lymph vessels, and eventually flow into one of two large lymphatic vessels, the **thoracic duct** (or left lymphatic duct) and the **right lymphatic duct**. The right lymphatic duct receives lymph from the right side of the head and upper body; the thoracic duct receives lymph from the left side of the head, the neck, the chest, the abdomen and the lower body. These large lymph vessels empty their contents into a vein at the base of the neck, which in turn empties into the **vena cava**. The lymph is mixed into the venous blood as it returns to the heart.

Lymph nodes

Lymph nodes, usually called glands, are tiny oval structures which filter the lymph. They extract poisons and bacteria, defending the body against infection by destroying harmful organisms. **Lymphocytes**, cells found in the lymph glands, produce **antibodies** which fight any invading micro-organisms.

When massaging, the movements are chosen to direct the lymph towards the nearest lymph nodes, as this encourages the fast removal of waste products.

Lymph nodes of the head and face

- The **occipital nodes** drain the upper neck and the back of the scalp.
- The **submental nodes** drain the lower lip and the chin.
- The **mandibular nodes** drain the lips, the cheeks and the nose.
- The **mastoid nodes** drain the temple area and the ear skin.

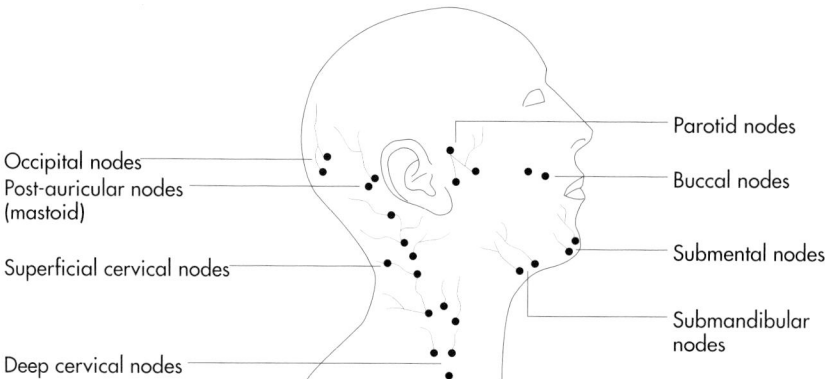

Lymph nodes of the head

- The **buccal nodes** drain the nose, the eyelids and the skin of the face.

Lymph nodes of the neck

- The **lower deep cervical nodes** drain the back of the scalp and the neck.
- The **upper deep cervical nodes** drain the back of the head and the neck.
- The **external cervical nodes** drain the neck below the ear.

Lymph nodes of the chest and arms

- The **deltopectorals node group** drain the upper arm.
- The **lateral nodes** drain the upper arm.
- The **pectoral nodes** drain the breast, the skin and the thoracic wall.
- The **subscapular nodes** drain the thoracic wall, the skin, and the posterior area of the neck.
- The **central nodes** drain the pectoral, subscapular nodes.
- The **subclavicular nodes** drain the deltopectoral nodes.

Effects of massage on the lymphatic system

Massage stimulates and increases lymphatic circulation. This leads to faster removal of waste products such as carbon dioxide and lactic acid which helps prevent fatigue.

Remember – never massage over-swollen lymphatic nodes and never massage a client if they have an infection.

The nervous system

The **nervous system** includes the **brain** and the **spinal cord**, and the many **nerves** throughout the body. It is the nerves that cause muscles to work, by stimulating them electrically.

When massage is applied to the face, neck and shoulders, the effect on the nerves is usually either to relax or to stimulate them.

Types of nerve

There are two types of nerves:

- **Sensory nerves** receive information and relay it to the brain. These respond to temperature, pain and touch. They are situated near to the surface of the skin.
- **Motor nerves** act on information received from the brain, triggering a muscle movement in response. They are situated in the muscle tissue.

Nerves of the face and neck

These nerves link the brain to the head, face and neck. There are 12 pairs of cranial nerves. The pairs that are particularly relevant to us when carrying out massage are the 5th, 7th and 11th.

The 5th cranial nerve (trigeminal nerve)

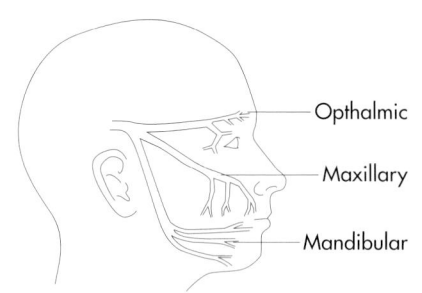

Opthalmic
Maxillary
Mandibular

5th cranial nerve

The **5th cranial nerve** takes messages to the brain from the sensory nerves of the teeth, the nose, the mouth and the skin. When eating, it stimulates the motor nerves to create the action of chewing.

It has three branches:

- the **maxillary nerve**, which serves the mouth and the upper jaw
- the **mandibular nerve**, which serves the lower jaw muscle, the muscle involved in chewing, and the teeth
- the **ophthalmic nerve**, which serves the skin on the forehead, the upper cheeks and the tear glands.

The 7th cranial nerve

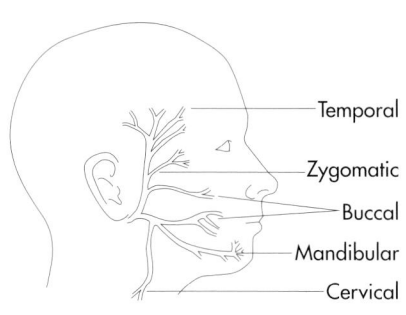

Temporal
Zygomatic
Buccal
Mandibular
Cervical

7th cranial nerve

The **7th cranial nerve** passes through the temporal bone and behind the ear. It serves the tongue, the palate, the muscles of the face and the ear muscle.

It has five branches:

- the **cervical nerve**, which serves the platysma muscle in the neck
- the **mandibular nerve**, which serves the muscle of the chin (mentalis) and the lower lip
- the **buccal nerve**, which serves the sides of the nose and the upper lip

- the **zygomaticus nerve**, which serves the muscle of the eye
- the **temporal nerve**, which serves the orbicularis oculi and the frontalis muscle.

The 11th cranial nerve

The **11th cranial nerve** serves the trapezius and the sternomastoid muscle.

Muscles

There are two types of muscles, voluntary and involuntary. **Voluntary muscles** are used for example in walking, talking or writing: they are muscles that are under our conscious control. Skeletal muscles are voluntary muscles. **Involuntary muscles** are muscles we *cannot* control: they keep the heart beating and allow food to be digested. Cardiac and smooth muscles are involuntary muscles. Muscles are well supplied with blood, to provide energy, and nerves, to deliver messages from the brain. Some muscles lie just below the skin: they are said to be *superficial*. Others lie underneath these superficial muscles, and are said to be *deep*.

A muscle consists of a number of elastic fibres, bound together in bundles. The bundles are usually spindle-shaped and held in a sheath. At the ends of the sheath are tendons, strong fibrous bands that attach the muscles to bones.

Most of the muscles in the face are extremely small. They are attached to facial skin or to other muscles. When they contract, they create facial expression.

Voluntary muscles

Structure and function

Voluntary muscle is composed of cylindrical cells, which then make up fibres. Each fibre contains nuclei on its outer membrane or sheath. All fibres run longitudinally and form bundles as described above.

Voluntary muscles appear stripy; this is because the fibres are made up of two different coloured protein filaments – myosin, the thicker of the two filaments, and actin. These play a major part in the mechanism or muscle contraction.

Each muscle has an origin and an insertion. The origin is usually the attachment or most fixed point – the proximal part. The insertion is usually the most movable point of attachment – the distil part. When muscles contract this is called an action.

The attachment of muscles can be by muscle fibrous bands, tendons and muscle fibres, to each other, skin, fascia, bones, ligaments and cartilage.

Muscles work in groups. There will be more than one muscle involved in generating any movement or action. Muscles usually work in pairs. One will be the agonist or protagonist, the function of which is to contract, and the opposing muscle is the antagonist, the function of which is to relax.

Agonists are the prime movers in all muscle action: while the agonists contract, antagonists have the controlling influence. Synergists help the protagonists to produce the best possible movement and prevent inefficiency. Fixators cut out any unnecessary movements that may hinder the prime movers. They are the stabilisers – they work to hold and fix.

When the muscles are stimulated to contract by the nervous system, a sliding movement occurs within the muscles' contractile fibres. The **actin** protein filaments move inwards towards the **myosin** and the two filaments merge. This causes the muscle fibres to shorten and thicken and pull on their attachment to achieve the movement required. When relaxing, the muscle fibres elongate and return to their normal shape.

Properties of a muscle

Muscle tissue has a number of properties that allow it to function. These properties are:

- the ability to contract and extend
- responsiveness – i.e. contracts in response to nerve impulses
- elasticity – i.e. ability to return to its original shape after contracting or extending.

Voluntary muscles work together with the nervous system and will only contract when stimulated. The muscles require energy in order to contract. This is produced by tissue respiration which is when glucose (delivered by blood and stored in the muscle in the form of glycogen) combines with oxygen (also supplied by the blood). Lactic acid is created as a result of energy production and must be removed from the muscle in order to prevent muscle fatigue.

In order to work effectively, muscles require a good blood supply to deliver oxygen and nutrients and take away lactic acid.

Muscle tone

When a muscle is relaxed, a few muscle fibres remain contracted to give the muscle a certain amount of firmness but not enough to produce movement. It is this muscle tension that is referred to as muscle tone, which we often describe as either firm or flabby.

Muscle tone is important in maintaining posture, as it assists the body in standing up and keeps the muscles prepared for action. **Extensors** are muscles that straighten out a limb, whereas **flexors** are muscles that bend a limb. Both the extensors and flexors need to be partially contracted to keep the body upright and the joints steady.

Firm muscle tone can be achieved by exercising. Flaccid muscle tone is usually a result of a lack of use but can be caused by damage to the nerve supply.

Voluntary muscles require regular exercise. When a muscle is not used it can become flaccid. In extreme circumstances and after a long period of disuse a muscle will eventually waste away (atrophy).

Muscles of the neck, shoulders and chest

The muscles of the neck, shoulders, upper arms and chest are shown in Table 2.1.

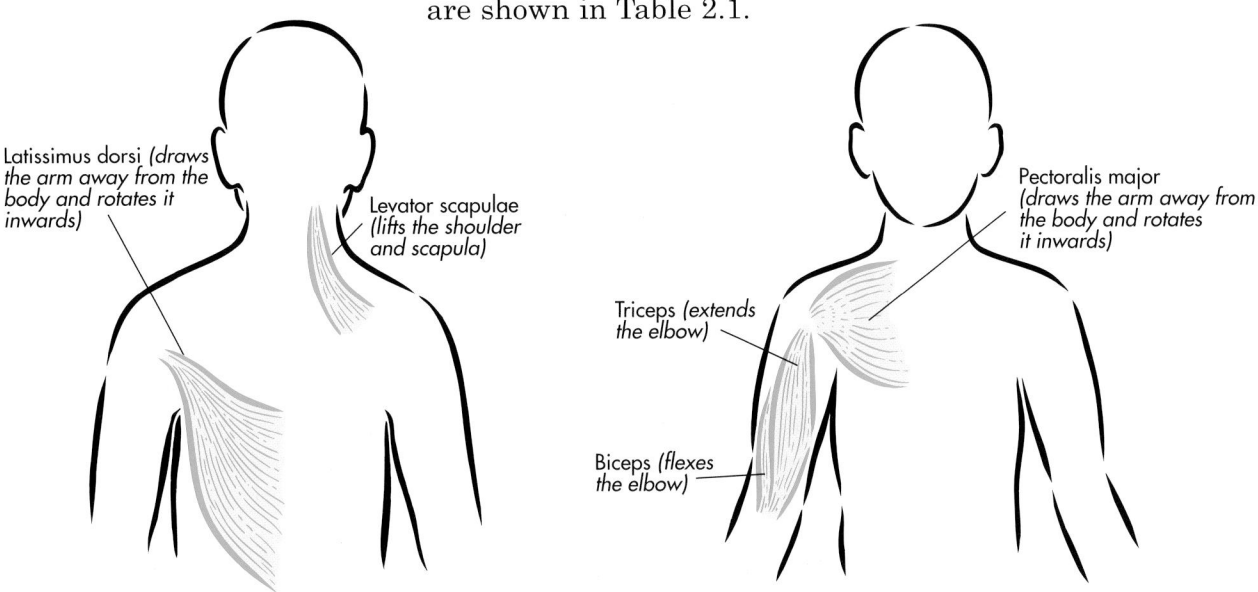

Muscles of the chest, back, neck and upper arms

Table 2.1: Muscles of the neck, shoulders and chest

Muscles	*Position*	*Action*
Levator scapulae	At the side of the neck and at the back on the shoulder	Lifts the shoulder and scapula
Pectoralis major	Beneath the breasts and across the front of the thorax (upper part)	Draws the arm away from the body and rotates it inwards
Latissimus dorsi	Down the back, in the lumbar and lower thoracic region	Rotates the arm; draws it away from the body and rotates it inwards (as when climbing with both arms in a fixed position, it helps to pull the body upwards)

Muscles of the neck

The muscles responsible for moving the head are shown in Table 2.2.

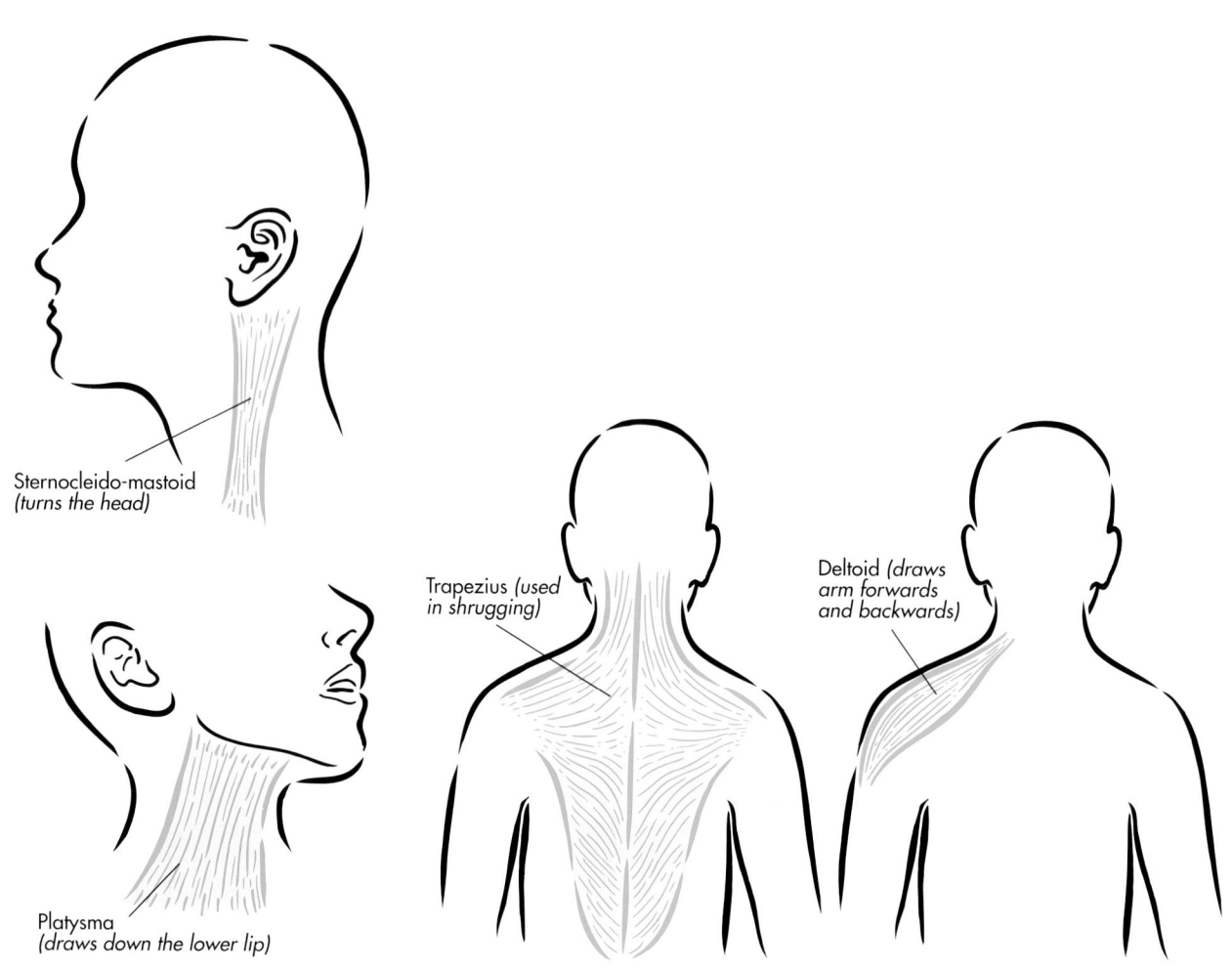

Sternocleido-mastoid
(turns the head)

Trapezius *(used in shrugging)*

Deltoid *(draws arm forwards and backwards)*

Platysma
(draws down the lower lip)

Muscles of the neck

Table 2.2: Muscles of the neck

Muscles	Position	Action
Sternocleido-mastoid	Down the side of the neck, from below the ear to the breastbone	Turns the head from side to side
Platysma	At the side of the neck and the chin	Helps to draw down the lower lip and jaw; used when yawning
Trapezius	Down the back of the neck, on to the shoulders	Lifts and raises the shoulders as in shrugging; extends the head
Deltoid	Capping the top of the shoulders and upper arm	Draws the arm forwards, backwards and away from the body

Muscles of the arm

The muscles responsible for moving the arm are shown in Table 2.3.

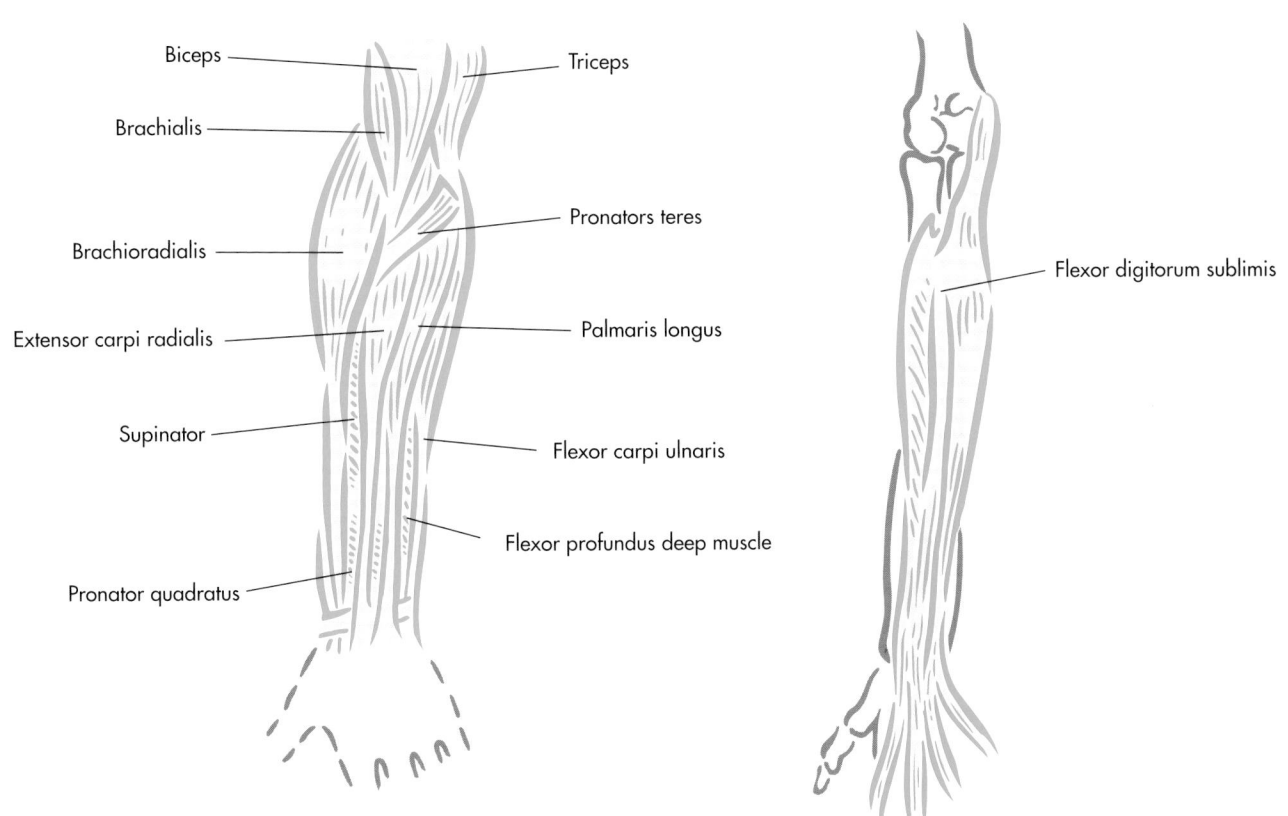

Muscles of the arm

Table 2.3: Muscles of the arm

Muscles	Position	Action
Biceps	Down the anterior surface of the humerus	Turns the palm upwards, flexes the elbow
Triceps	Along the posterior surface of the humerus	Extends the elbow
Brachialis	Under the biceps in front of the humerus from halfway down its shaft near the elbow joint to the ulna	Flexes the elbow
Brachioradialis	On the radial side of the forearm	Flexes the forearm
Supinator	Attached to the lateral aspect of the lower humerus and the radius	Supinates the hand and forearm
Pronators teres	Attached to the medial aspect of the radius and humerus	Pronates the forearm and hand
Pronator quadratus	Crosses at the lower part of the front of the forearm	Pronates forearm
Flexor digitorum profundus deep muscle	Situated along the ulna side of the forearm	Flexes distal phalanx of each finger

Muscles of the forearm, wrist and fingers

The muscles responsible for moving the forearm, wrist and fingers are shown in Tables 2.4 (anterior) and 2.5 (posterior).

Table 2.4: Muscles of the forearm, wrist and fingers (anterior)

Muscle	Position	Action
Flexor carpi radialis	Situated down the anterior side of the forearm from inside the elbow joint towards the thumb	Flexes and abducts the wrist
Flexor carpi ulnaris	Situated along the ulna side of the forearm	Flexes and adducts the wrist
Palmaris longus	Situated down the medial side of the forearm	Flexes the wrist
Flexor digitorum superficialis	Situated down the medial side of the forearm deep to palmaris longus	Flexes the middle phalanx of each finger

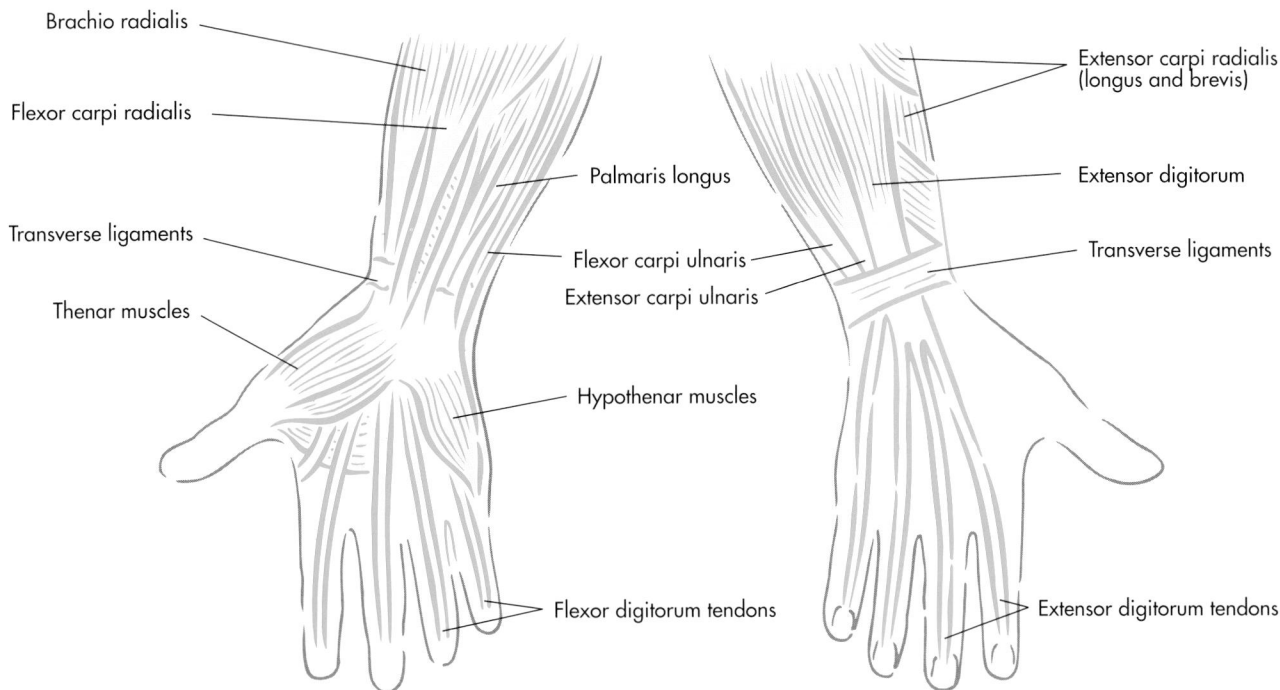

Muscles of the arm and hand

Table 2.5: Muscles of the forearm, wrist and fingers (posterior)

Muscle	Position	Action
Extensor carpi radialis logus	Situated along the radial side of forearm	Extends and abducts the wrist
Extensor carpi radialis brevis deep muscle	Situated along the side of forearm	Extends and abducts the wrist
Extensor carpi ulnaris	Along back of forearm on the ulna side	Extends and abducts the wrist
Extensor digitorium	Along back of forearm on the radial side	Extends the fingers

Muscles of the head and face

Two groups of muscles are important in Indian Head Massage. The first group is the **muscles of mastication**, which are used in chewing. These muscles make possible the movement of the lower jaw or mandible (see Table 2.6).

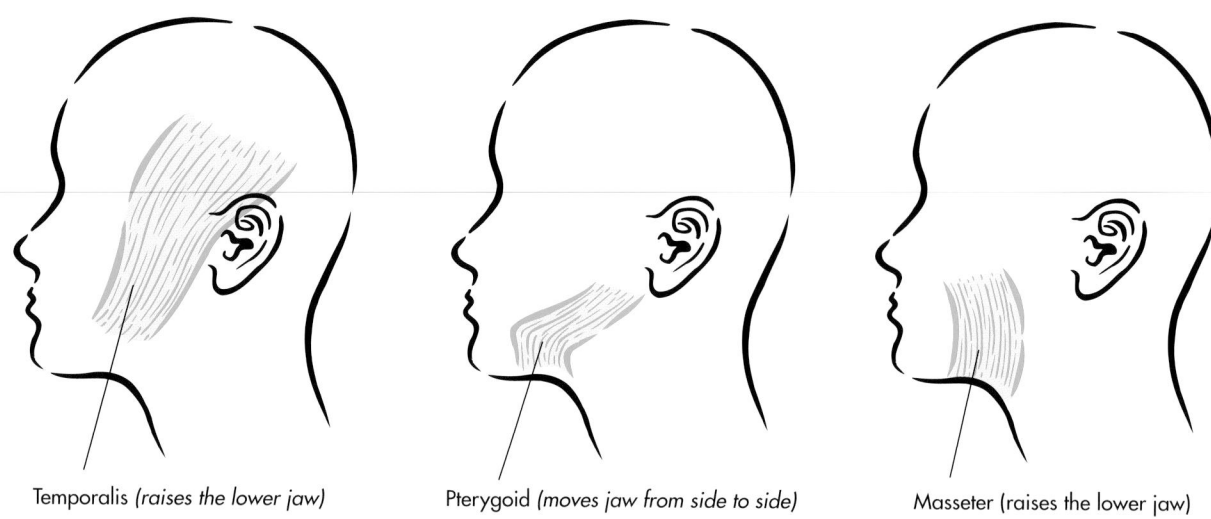

Temporalis *(raises the lower jaw)*   Pterygoid *(moves jaw from side to side)*   Masseter (raises the lower jaw)

Muscles of mastication

Table 2.6: Muscles of mastication

Muscle	*Position*	*Action*
Temporalis	At the side of the head, in front of and above the ear, down to the lower jaw	Raises the lower jaw
Pterygoid (lateral and medial)	In the lateral part of the cheek, underneath the masseter	Moves the jaw from side to side
Masseter	In the lateral region of the cheek, between the cheekbone and the angle of the jaw	Raises the lower jaw

The second group are the **muscles of facial expression**. These may be attached to skin or other muscles rather than bone (see Table 2.7).

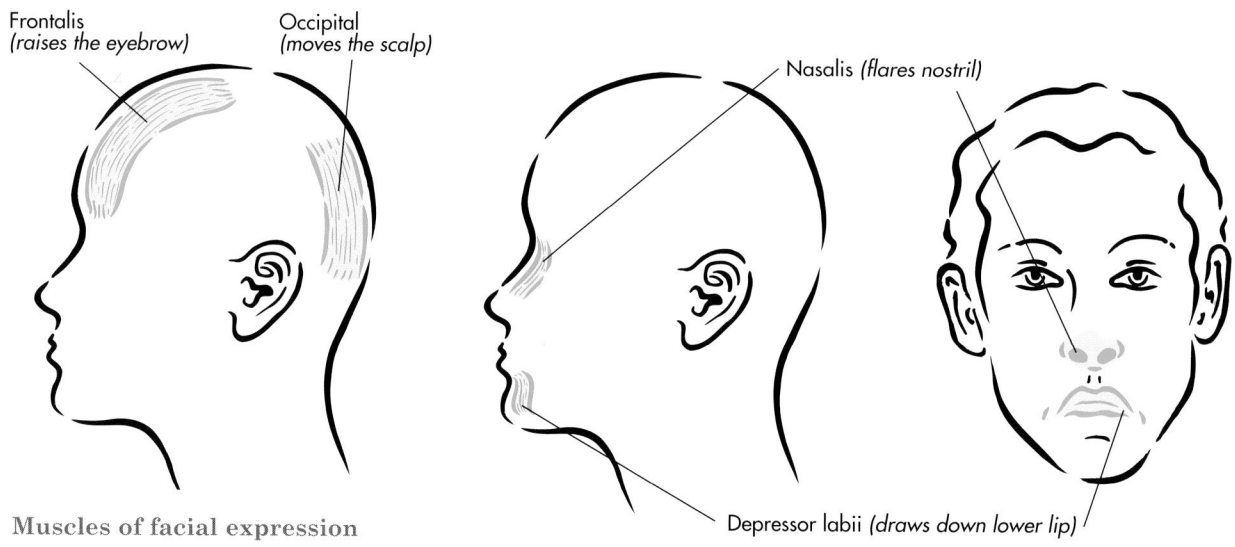

Frontalis *(raises the eyebrow)*   Occipital *(moves the scalp)*   Nasalis *(flares nostril)*

Muscles of facial expression   Depressor labii *(draws down lower lip)*

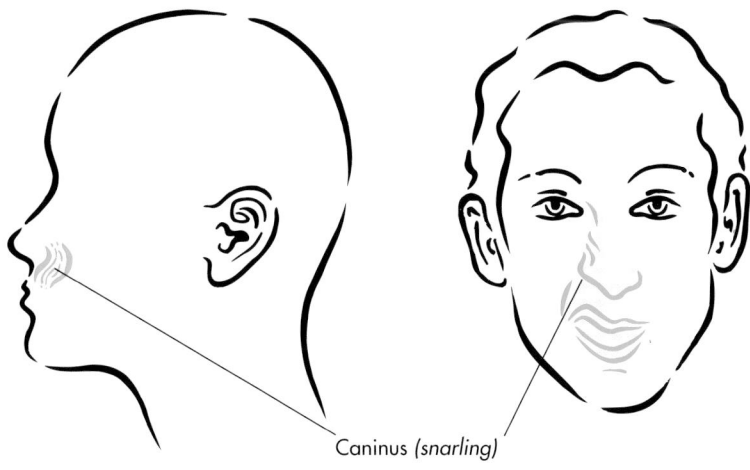

Caninus *(snarling)*

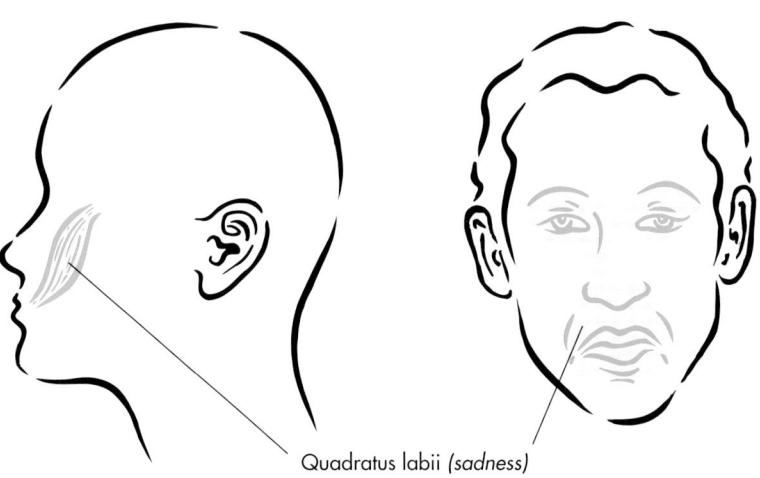

Quadratus labii *(sadness)*

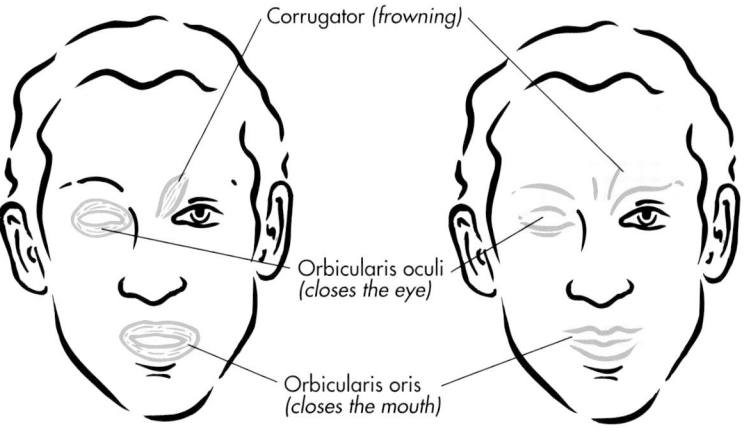

Corrugator *(frowning)*

Orbicularis oculi
(closes the eye)

Orbicularis oris
(closes the mouth)

Muscles of facial expression (cont.)

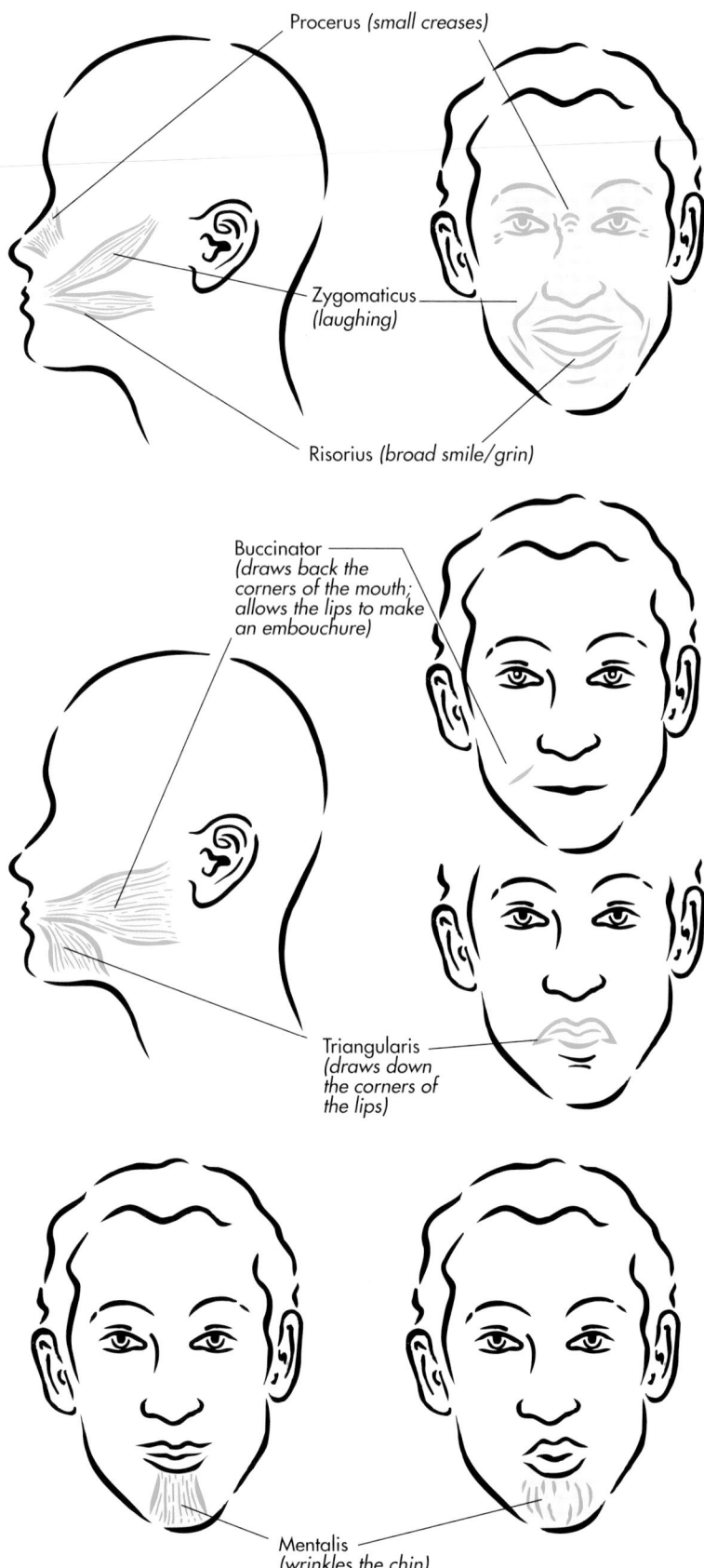

Procerus (small creases)

Zygomaticus (laughing)

Risorius (broad smile/grin)

Buccinator (draws back the corners of the mouth; allows the lips to make an embouchure)

Triangularis (draws down the corners of the lips)

Mentalis (wrinkles the chin)

Muscles of facial expression (cont.)

Table 2.7: Muscles of facial expression

Muscle	*Position*	*Action*
Frontalis	On the forehead	Raises the eyebrows, creases the forehead
Occipital	At the back of the head	Moves the scalp backwards
Corrugator	Below the eyebrow	Wrinkles between the eyebrows (vertically); frowns
Orbicularis oculi	Around the eye	Closes the eye; winks
Nasalis	At the side of the nose	Dilates the nostrils; expresses anger
Orbicularis oris	Surrounds the mouth	Closes the mouth; puckers the lips; shapes the lips during speech
Mentalis	Extends from the lower lip over the centre of the chin	Lifts the lower lip; protrudes the lip; wrinkles the chin
Triangularis	Radiates from the lower lip over the chin	Draws down the corners of lip
Procerus	On the nasal bone; in the skin between the eyebrows	Causes small horizontal creases at the root of the nose
Caninus	On the skin at the corner of the mouth	Creates an expression of snarling
Risorius	Radiates laterally from the corners of the mouth	Retracts the angle of the mouth; produces a broad (grin) smile
Buccinator	At the side of the face	Compresses the cheeks; draws the corners of the mouth out horizontally
Zygomaticus minor and major	Extends from the upper lip	Draws the mouth upwards, as when laughing
Depressor labii	Extends from the lower lip over the chin	Pulls down the bottom lip; creates a sulky expression
Quadratus labii	Radiates from the upper lip	Flares the nostrils; raises the lips, forms a furrow Nasolabial giving a sad expression

Effects of massage on muscles

Key points are as follows:

- Massage increases blood flow, which leads to an increase in oxygen and nutrients to the muscle tissues and speeds up the removal of waste. When muscles are working they need a greater supply of oxygen and produce more waste products.

- Massage relieves muscular fatigue by removing lactic acids that build up in the tissues. Muscles that are tense and contracted can become relaxed after a massage. Regular massage will help muscles function to their fullest capacity.

- Muscles work over joints. If the movements of the joints are impaired by adhesions – for example the shoulder joint – then the full range of movement will be prevented. Massaging the area can help to loosen and release these adhesions, gaining more mobility in the joints, more movement in the muscles and therefore increasing the range of movement.

The respiratory system

Ventilation, breathing or **respiration** are all terms used to describe the process whereby air is taken into the lungs (**inhaling**) and pushed out again (**exhaling**). At each intake of breath the **intercostal muscles**, between the ribs, contract: this raises the rib cage, creating a greater space in the thoracic cavity. At the same time the diaphragm contracts and is pulled down, causing air to be drawn into the lungs. As the diaphragm and intercostal muscles relax and return to their original positions, air is pushed out of the lungs.

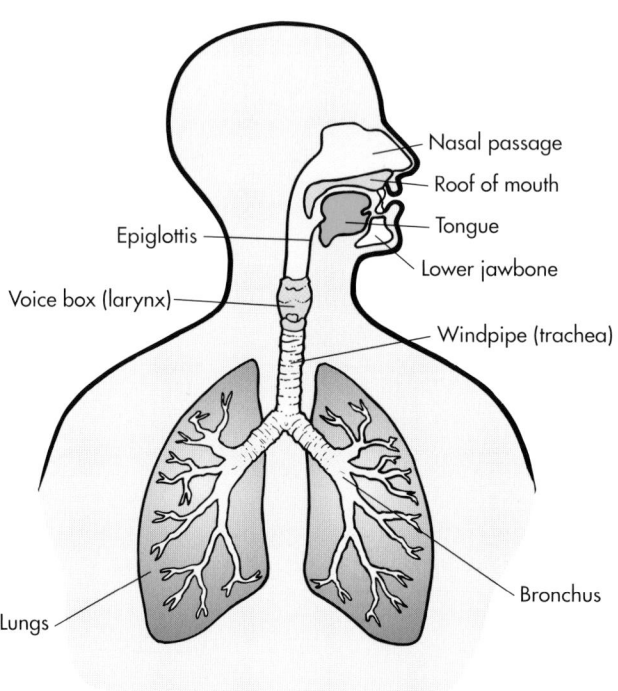

Respiratory system

The term 'respiration' is used more generally to signify the uptake of oxygen and the production and removal of carbon dioxide. This takes place in three contexts:

- An exchange between the air (from the external environment) and the blood. This exchange takes place in the lungs, and is referred to as **external respiration**.
- An exchange between the blood cells. This occurs throughout the body, and is referred to as **internal respiration**.
- An exchange within the cells of the body, where the oxygen is used to 'burn' foodstuffs, releasing energy or synthesising cell materials. This occurs throughout the body, and is referred to as **cellular respiration**.

During an Indian Head Massage treatment, the rate of *external respiration* slows to an even, easy rhythm. It involves mainly the thoracic region of the body, with only very small movements of the intercostal muscles. *Internal respiration* is increased slightly because the blood and lymph systems are being stimulated to rid the body of toxic waste. *Cellular respiration* occurs when the body's energies are not needed to carry out physical or mental activities. Some of this energy is used up by the normal functioning of the cell; the remainder is lost as heat. Most clients experience a feeling of warmth during and after an Indian Head Massage treatment.

Knowledge review – Anatomy and physiology

Skin

1 Name the three layers of the skin.

2 What is the normal temperature of the body?

3 Give two alterative names for the epidermis.

4 Papillae are _____, and they are a means of
   _____.

5 The thickest layer of the epidermis is _____.

6 The term used to describe the change in cells from round living
   cells to flat, dead, horny cells is _____.

7 The process of mitosis takes place in the
   _____ layer.

8 Skin colour is determined by _____.

9 The function of the reticulum fibres found in the dermis is
   to _____ ,
   _____

10 The deepest layer of the dermis is known as the sub-cutis.
   What other name is often used to describe this layer?

Bones

1 How many bones form (a) the cranium and (b) the face?

2 Which bone or bones form (a) the forehead and (b) the
   cheekbones?

3 Name the labelled parts of the skull.

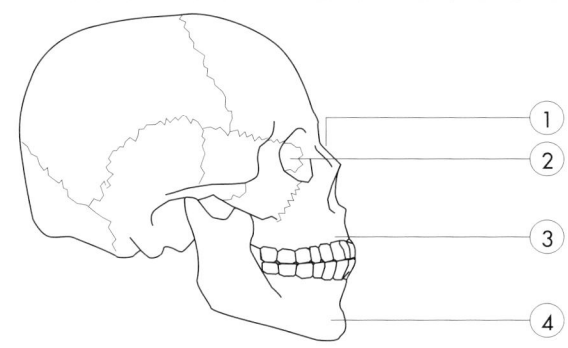

(1) _____

(2) _____

(3) _____

(4) _____

Blood

1 The main function of the blood is to _____

_____

2 The blood leaving the left ventricle is oxygenated/de-oxygenated.

3 The _____ is the main artery leaving the heart.

4 The external carotid artery supplies the _____

The lymphatic system

1 Name the lymph nodes in the head

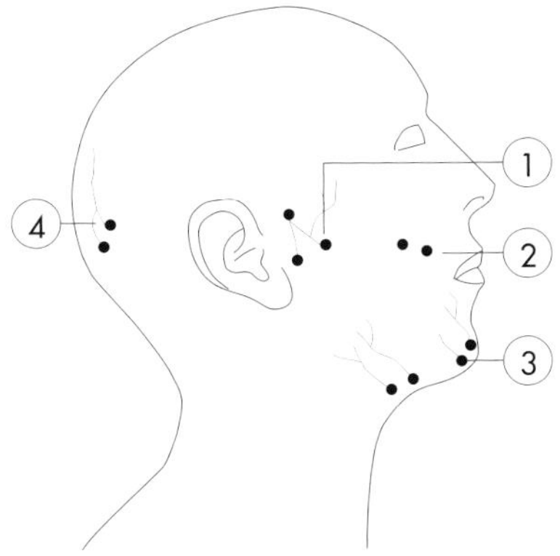

(a) _____

(b) _____

(c) _____

The nervous system

1 The difference between sensory and motor nerves is

_____

_____

2 The three branches of the 5th cranial nerve are

_____; _____ and

_____.

3 The 5th nerve carries messages to the brain from

which parts of the face? _____;

_____; and _____.

Muscles

1 Name the two types of muscle

(a) _____ (b) _____

2 The _____ muscle is responsible for raising the
eyebrows.

3 The function of the biceps muscle is to _____

Respiration

1 An alternative term for respiration is _____

2 The term used to describe the exchange between the

environment and the blood is _____

3 When oxygen is used to release energy within the cells

of the body, this is called _____

4 An Indian Head Massage affects the rate of external

respiration by _____

Health and safety

Essential Knowledge and Understanding NVQ Level 3 areas covered in this chapter are:

- **Effective communication and relationships.**

- **Health and safety legislation and responsibilities.**

- **Data Protection Act compliance.**

DANGER

This chapter covers the health and safety legislation relevant to students training to give Indian Head Massage. This legislation includes national **Acts of Parliament** and **regulations**, and you also need to be aware of any relevant local **byelaws**. Among those who charge for massage there will be a **code of ethics**, and lastly your place of work may also have its own **code of practice**. Good practice concerns not just the way in which you carry out massage but the way you relate to clients and colleagues.

Working relationships

It is important that clients enjoy their visit to the salon or clinic, and that they feel totally relaxed and comfortable.

For this to happen, staff must be sensitive to the fact that each client is an individual, with individual needs.

Non-verbal communication

Even before you speak to clients, in the way you approach them you begin to *communicate* with them. In the way you smile at a client and make eye contact, and in the way you act, move and look, you will be transmitting information to the client. For example, you will show something of how you feel, and your level of interest in the person to whom you are about to speak. This is called **non-verbal communication** and is central to any relationship.

Verbal communication

When talking with another person, remember to speak clearly without shouting. Be courteous in your tone and manner, and avoid slang. As well as talking you need to *listen*, so that you can identify what your client's needs are. You will then be able to guide the conversation appropriately.

Avoid interrupting clients while they are speaking. You will have to ask questions during the consultation, but try to ensure that the client does not feel interrogated. Try not to use jargon or technical terminology.

In general conversation, avoid subjects such as sex, religion and politics, about which you and your client may have different opinions. You may like to make a note, on clients' consultation or record cards, of topics of particular interest to them. You can bring up these topics during their subsequent visits, when they will appreciate the fact that you have remembered.

You need to gain clients' trust in your skill and in your personal integrity, and build up a good professional relationship with each person. When clients get to know you, they may share confidences with you. *Never* pass judgement on what they tell you, and always maintain their confidence – do not discuss with others what you have been told.

Liaising with colleagues

Each member of staff has a particular role and is a valued member of the team. Each will have a **job description**, outlining their job role, duties and responsibilities. This ensures that everyone knows what they are doing.

Remember that you are one member of a team. You need to have good working relationships with the other members of staff, so that you can work well together and support one another, and so that you present a professional image to clients.

Grievances

From time to time problems may arise. Often it will be possible to sort them out informally, but there will also be a **grievance procedure** for occasions when a formal approach is needed.

If a member of staff feels that she or he has been treated unfairly, the incident can be reported to the supervisor who will take the appropriate action.

Discipline

You will be expected to uphold the values in your workplace and to do your job in a professional manner. If there is a problem with your work, there will be a **disciplinary procedure** to deal with this. Typically this will first involve informal discussion. If that proves insufficient, you may be given a formal verbal warning. Finally, if your work or behaviour has not improved, you may receive a formal written warning.

Codes of conduct

At all times you should be polite and courteous. You are likely to find in any team that there are personality differences. Try to see your different approaches as an asset to the team as a whole. Treat your colleagues with respect, and never talk down to them.

Your public image is especially important: never lose your temper, or criticise or ridicule your colleagues, in front of clients. If you have a difference of opinion with a colleague, settle it as soon as possible so that it does not affect your work.

Code of ethics

Each profession has its own **code of ethics**. Although this is not a legal requirement, the code may be used in any criminal proceedings as evidence of improper practice or professional negligence.

A code of ethics imposes various obligations on professionals doing a particular kind of work, for the safety of members of the public. The code is usually a set of regulations and rules which:

- establish appropriate conduct
- establish good practices
- protect the public from dangerous or unprofessional practices
- maintain professional standards of behaviour – towards clients and other members of the public, and towards other therapists, members of the organisation, members of related organisations and colleagues within the industry.

As a professional therapist you must:

- comply with the local statutes and byelaws
- apply only those treatments in which you are qualified
- consult with a client's medical practitioner if necessary
- avoid treating any client when there are contra-indications
- maintain clients' confidentiality
- treat other colleagues with respect
- refrain from criticising other businesses or attracting their clients to your own.

Health and safety

The law is made up of many different types of **legislation**. In the way they are written **Acts of Parliament** tend to be more general, and **regulations** to be more specific.

Whatever type of business you may be working in – whether in a salon, a leisure centre or a clinic, or offering home visits – you are part of a **service industry**. You are legally obliged to provide a hygienic and safe environment, and it is essential that you follow health and safety guidelines.

If you put clients at risk or cause them any harm, you will be held responsible and may be fined, and in some instances prosecuted. For your own protection, as well as that of your clients, you need to be aware of the publications that highlight your responsibilities and your rights.

Principal legislation

The **Health and Safety at Work Act 1974** covers all aspects of health, safety and welfare at work. It identifies the responsibilities not only of employers but also of employees, who are responsible not just for themselves but also for anyone else who enters the premises.

The **Workplace (Health, Safety and Welfare) Regulations 1992** now incorporate the Health and Safety at Work Act 1974 and other, earlier legislation, including the **Offices, Shops and Railway Premises Act 1963** and the **Fire Precautions Act 1971**. The regulations state the minimum standard of health, safety and welfare required in each area of the workplace.

Health and safety policy

If an employer has more than five employees, the establishment must have a **health and safety policy**, and this must be available to all staff.

Areas covered must include details of:

- chemicals that are stored on the premises
- details of the stock cupboard or dispensary
- records of checks carried out by a qualified electrician on any specialist equipment
- escape routes and emergency evacuations
- names of key holders.

Regular checks must be made in the workplace to ensure that safety is being maintained at all times.

It is the employer's responsibility to implement the Act, and:

- to ensure the workplace is safe for employees and clients
- to ensure safety when storing and using substances and equipment
- to provide the training, information and instruction needed to ensure health and safety
- to maintain and provide access to the place of work and to keep all exits clear
- to provide a safe system of handling cash, and to ensure that employees are never exposed to any risk when handling cash or transferring money to the bank.

Failure to carry out these duties may result in criminal liability and a claim for damages.

Employees too have responsibilities. They must:

- provide a healthy and safe environment, by working closely with the employer
- be responsible for health and safety in relation to other employees, the general public and themselves
- report any hazard to the relevant person, usually a supervisor or the manager, so that it can be put right.

Management of Health and Safety at Work Regulations 1999

These regulations require employers to appoint a person to be responsible for assessing the risks to health and safety of employees, clients, visitors and anyone entering the premises and to take the appropriate action to eliminate or minimise the risks. The appointed person needs to be trained and fully aware of all the procedures involved, and they must also document the findings of their assessments.

If any risks have been identified, an action plan must be drawn up and all staff must be aware of the risks and the procedures that will be enforced to control the identified risks. Health and safety training for all staff must be ongoing.

Working environment

The **salon temperature** should be 16°C (minimum) within one hour of the employees arriving for work. The working environment must be well ventilated (see below) and the lighting (see below) must be adequate to ensure that all treatments can be carried out safely without risk of an accident. Adequate **toilets** and **hand-washing facilities** must be provided.

Food and drink

A suitable area should be provided for the staff to eat, drink and rest on the premises (and a supply of wholesome drinking water must be available).

Ventilation and humidity

Ventilation is the process of allowing **fresh air** to replace stale air. In many situations adequate **natural ventilation** can be achieved simply by opening doors and windows, but clients who are having treatment may be distracted by the noise from outside, and feel concerned that their situation is not sufficiently private. For these reasons, **artificial ventilation** may be more appropriate, and can be achieved in several ways:

- an exhaust system will propel air from inside the building to the outside
- a supply system will bring in fresh air from outside, filtering it to remove any dust
- an air-conditioning system will combine the exhaust and the supply systems.

Note that free-standing fans, which are usually portable, only provide air *movement* – they do not actually change the air, and are therefore not really suitable.

The air in the workplace also needs to contain the right amount of **moisture**. If the air is too humid or too dry, people may experience problems such as headaches, fatigue and irritability.

As well as providing fresh air and filtering out dust, **air-conditioning units** can correct both temperature and humidity.

Lighting

There must be sufficient lighting for the therapist to be able to work safely and efficiently. Lighting must be suitable in all work areas, and windows and skylights must be kept clean.

Clients will not be able to relax if the lights are too bright, so the best solution may be adjustable spotlights. These can be pointed in any direction, and dimmed as required.

Privacy

Although individual treatment rooms make it easy to provide **privacy**, in many clinics there is not enough space to allow this. Treatment areas with curtains around them provide a degree of privacy for the client, though conversation may be overheard.

Health & Safety

Waste or out-of-date oil should be returned to the supplier for safe disposal.

The Environmental Protection Act 1990

This Act states that all waste must be disposed of safely. It is important to exercise care when disposing of surplus/out-of-date stock and manufacturers' guidance should be sought. If in any doubt ask the manufacturer to dispose of the stock for you.

Hazards

Preventing accidents

Many accidents occur because working conditions are unsafe or employees are negligent. With care, therefore, most accidents can be avoided.

The employer must make a **risk assessment**. This may reveal potential **hazards**, and the employer must then remove these to minimise the risk of an accident.

The following general points will be helpful:

- all entrances and exists must be kept clear
- any glass doors, windows or partitions that are glazed must be made safe (toughened or laminated glass should be used) and marked correctly
- the premises must be well lit
- all staff should be adequately trained in the use of the equipment.

Handling stock

Posture

Many accidents result from incorrect lifting, carrying and handling techniques. Some sprains and strains are caused over a period of time, others result from a single incident.

These matters are covered by the **Manual Handling Operations Regulations 1992**. Employers are required to carry out an assessment of risks, and then to provide appropriate training for the employees. In some instances potential problems may be solved simply, such as by reorganising shelves and storage areas in the storeroom.

Many injuries are caused by incorrect lifting and working postures. Incorrect postures can result in:

- backache
- muscular spasms
- slipped discs
- muscle and ligament strain.

When lifting or working, it is important to keep your spine straight. Do not do work beyond your physical strength, such as unloading very heavy boxes of stock. If a load is heavy but manageable, it is best to keep the back straight and drag the load with one arm with the body sideways on.

Lifting a box   **Carrying several boxes**   **Carrying equal weights in both hands**

When lifting, always bend your *knees*, not your back. Hold heavy objects close to your body – never hold objects at arm's length, as this puts a strain on the back.

The standing position is a problem for therapists who have to stand for much of the time. When standing, it is best to keep the ears, shoulders, hips and ankles in a straight line at right angles to the floor. Try not to stick out your bottom or your head.

Protective equipment

By law, all employers must provide suitable protective equipment and clothing for their employees, if a hazard has been identified by a risk assessment. Such equipment must be properly maintained, and all staff must be trained to use it correctly.

Personal Protective Equipment (PPE) at Works Regulations 1992

All employers must provide suitable personal protective equipment to all employees who may be exposed to any risk while at work. It is the employees' responsibility to use this equipment.

Accidents

Reporting accidents

Any accidents that *do* occur in the workplace must be recorded in the **accident book** and on a **report form**. The report form requires more details than the accident book. The following points must be noted:

- the name of any person or persons injured
- the date
- details of the accident
- the injuries incurred
- the action that was taken.

Reporting injuries and diseases

The reporting of accidents and illnesses at work is a legal requirement of the **Reporting of Injuries, Diseases and Dangerous Occurrences Regulations (RIDDOR) 1995**. The information is needed by the local **environmental health officer (EHO)**. With this information, the EHO can identify how and where risks arise, and can investigate serious accidents so that future ones may be prevented.

- If an accident at work results in someone dying or being taken to hospital, the employer must telephone the EHO as soon as possible, and within ten days send in a completed **accident form**.
- If an accident at work involves a member of staff being absent from work for more than three days, the employer must send a completed accident form to the EHO.
- If the employee suffers from a work-related illness notified by her or his doctor, the employee must send a completed **disease report form** to the EHO.

Clearing up after accidents

Accidents may result in **spillages, breakage** of containers and **damaged stock**. Breakages and spillages should be dealt with straight away, to ensure that no one slips or falls. When clearing broken glass, always wear suitable gloves, and put the broken glass in a secure container before disposing of it in the waste bin.

First aid

The **Health and Safety (First Aid) Regulations 1982** state that the place of work must have an adequately stocked first aid box. This must contain:

- basic guidance leaflet
- 20 assorted sterile adhesive dressings
- 6 individually wrapped triangular bandages
- 2 sterile eyepads
- 6 safety pins
- 6 medium-sized (10 cm × 8 cm) individually wrapped sterile unmedicated wound dressings
- 2 large (13 cm × 9 cm) individually wrapped wound dressings
- 3 extra-large (28 cm × 17.5 cm) sterile individually wrapped medicated wound dressings
- individually wrapped moist cleaning wipes.

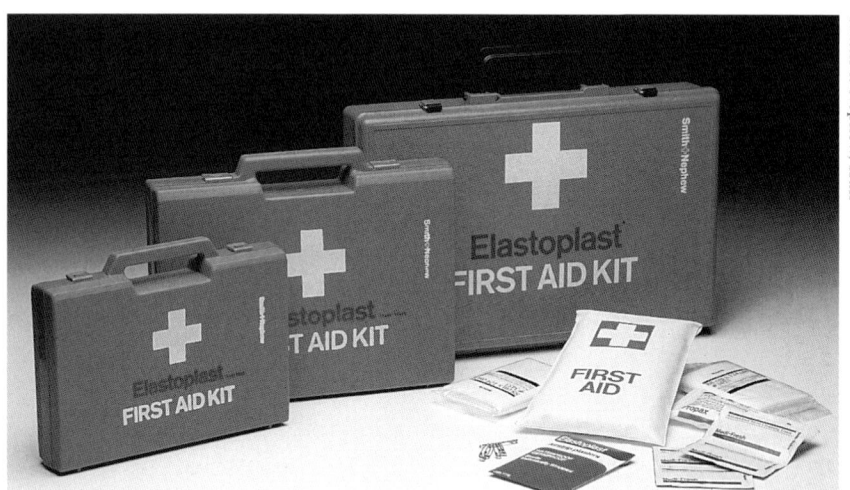

Smith & Nephew, Hull

First aid kit

Telephone numbers for the emergency services and perhaps a local doctor should be listed and displayed in the first aid box.

At least one member of staff must have been trained in first aid. All staff should know the location of the first aid box and who the first-aider is. When an accident occurs the first-aider must:

- assess the situation
- try to identify the problem
- provide appropriate treatment
- if necessary, arrange transport to the hospital or a doctor.

Burns, falls and insect bites – to name but a few – can happen to anyone, anywhere, at any time. It is therefore in everyone's interest to have a basic knowledge of first aid so that assistance can be given promptly when required.

If a person becomes unconscious for no apparent reason, you must call for an ambulance straight away. You can then check to see whether the person has any medical identification giving details which would allow ambulance personnel to administer the correct treatment immediately. For example, people may carry medical cards, bracelets, necklaces or keyrings to tell others of unusual medical conditions such as diabetes, epilepsy, a steroid regime or a condition treated with anti-coagulants.

Other items that may indicate the problem are:

- an insulin syringe (carried by diabetics)
- an inhaler (carried by asthmatics)
- medicines or tablets.

Equipment and materials

Electrical equipment

All electrical equipment should be well maintained and correctly wired.

- Power points should never be overloaded.
- Equipment should be checked regularly for cracked plugs, frayed wires and the like.
- Equipment should always be switched off before being cleaned.
- Equipment should never be touched with wet hands.

The **Electricity at Work Act 1990** states that every piece of electrical equipment in the workplace must be tested every 12 months by a qualified electrician. All checks must be recorded in a book, along with the results, any recommendations and any action taken. This must be signed by the person who has carried out the checks. This book can be used as evidence if any legal action is taken.

Gas equipment

The **Gas Safety Regulations 1994** state that the gas equipment – such as gas boilers, water heaters, central heating systems, and the flues and pipework – must be adequately maintained and checked once a year by a Corgi-registered gas engineer. A written record of these checks must be kept.

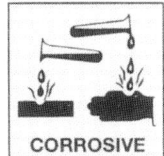

Hazard symbols

Chemicals

Many substances that seem quite harmless can in fact be hazardous if incorrectly used or incorrectly stored. The **Control of Substances Hazardous to Health (COSHH) Regulations 1988** (consolidated in 2002) require each employer to consider which substances are harmful and assess the possible risks to health. For example, hazardous substances may enter the body via the nose (inhalation), the mouth (ingestion), the skin or the eyes.

All containers that contain chemicals must be clearly marked. Hazardous substances must be identified by the use of standard symbols, and these symbols must be shown on the packaging. Hazardous substances must be stored and handled correctly. Suppliers of such substances are legally required to provide guidelines on how their materials should be stored and used.

The employer has to carry out a risk assessment to assess which materials could be a risk to health from exposure and to ensure that these are recorded; this must be carried out regularly. Whenever possible, high-risk products should be replaced by low-risk products.

Premises

Chubb Fire Ltd

Fire extinguishers

Fire regulations

The local fire service will provide advice on firefighting equipment and the correct procedures for evacuation. If any structural alterations are made, these must comply with fire regulations.

The **Fire Precautions Act 1971** states that all staff must be aware of, and be trained in, emergency evacuation and fire procedures for their workplace. A smoke alarm should be fitted to warn if there is a fire, and fire doors should be fitted within the premises to help prevent fire from spreading.

Firefighting equipment must be located in specified areas. Such equipment includes fire extinguishers, blankets, buckets and water hoses. Different **fire extinguishers** are designed to deal with different kinds of fire. If you are tackling a fire, it is important that you first identify the *cause* of fire. Using the wrong extinguishers might actually make the fire worse.

- A fire caused by *solid material*, for example paper or wood, must be extinguished by a water extinguisher (red).

- An *electrical* fire could be extinguished by a dry-powder extinguisher (blue), a carbon-dioxide extinguisher (black) or a halon-gas extinguisher (blue).
- A fire caused by *flammable liquids* should be extinguished by a foam extinguisher (cream).

Fire blankets are used on small, localised fires – they act by smothering the fire. **Sand** is used on burning liquids – this too smothers the fire and also soaks up the liquid. **Water hoses** are used on large fires, which are often caused by paper materials. **Buckets of water** are used to put out small fires. Remember to *turn off the electricity first!*

Building regulations

Building regulations must be strictly followed. They are administered by building control officers working for the local council, who ensure good health and safety for the public.

Registration and licensing

If the business provides treatments such as ear-piercing, epilation, tattooing or any form of body-piercing, the person who is carrying out these treatments must have a **certification of registration** from the local council.

Some local councils require that businesses which offer certain treatments, such as body massage, have a **licence** to do so. Such licences are usually valid for one year and are granted, with a set of standards and conditions, for a fee. If the standards are not met, the licence is revoked.

Inspection and registration of premises

The local authority environmental health department enforces the Health and Safety at Work Act, and the environmental health officer visits and inspects the premises. If the inspector identifies any area of danger, the employer must remove this danger within a stated period of time. Failure to do so can lead to prosecution. If necessary, the inspector has the authority also to close the business until satisfied that all dangers to the public and employees have been removed.

Insurance

Public liability insurance

Public liability insurance provides insurance for employers and employees in the event of any death, injury or damage to personal property sustained by a third party while on the business's premises. Although this is not a legal requirement, it should be taken out to cover any claims made by the public.

Employer's liability insurance

Every employer must comply with the **Employer's Liability (Compulsory Insurance) Act 1969**. This insurance provides financial compensation to an employee if she or he is injured while in the workplace.

Professional indemnity insurance

If an employee gives damaging treatment or advice, an injured client may sue. **Professional indemnity insurance** provides insurance cover to protect the employee from heavy financial penalties.

General consumer-protection legislation now enables damages to be awarded against employees who have caused damage by advice, treatment or inaction. Employees who are not covered by their employer's policy must therefore have their own insurance cover.

Other legislation

Describing goods

The **Trade Descriptions Act 1968** (amended in 1987) prohibits false trade descriptions. It also says that if a manufacturer has made a false claim, anyone who repeats this claim to another person is equally liable.

Selling goods

The **Sale of Goods Act 1968** (amended 1987) covers the consumer's rights in respect of purchased goods, which must be of satisfactory quality and fit for their purpose. It also defines the conditions under which goods may be returned after purchase.

Product safety

The **Consumer Protection Act 1987** protects the consumer against unsafe products. It covers general safe-handling requirements, product liability and misleading prices.

Cosmetics

The **Cosmetic Products (Safety) Regulations 1996** implement EU regulations regarding the description of cosmetic products, their labelling, their composition and their marketing. The regulations were made under the Consumer Protection Act 1987.

Data protection

The **Data Protection Act 1984** requires all businesses that store details of clients on the computer to register with the Data Protection Register and comply with a code of practice.

The **Data Protection Act 1998** covers manual records and filing systems, and stipulates the following additional points:

- Salons and workplaces must have a secure method of storing all records.
- Information kept on records or files must be relevant to the treatments given.
- All information must be accurate and, in the case of handwritten records, legible.
- Salons must gain written consent for personal details to be kept.
- Clients must be allowed access to their own records – failure to do this contravenes the Act.

All salons should check whether registration with the Information Commissioner is necessary. Non-registration could lead to prosecution.

Be aware of the Data Protection Act when storing and filing records

Performing rights

If you wish to play recorded music to the public in your workplace, you will probably need a licence from

Phonographic Performance Ltd (PPL). This organisation collects licence payments and distributes them, as royalties, to record companies and copyright performers. If you fail to pay such licence fees, PPL can take legal action against you.

Some music, though, comes from composers who are not members of PPL, and in that case no fee is payable. Before playing music, therefore, it is advisable to seek advice from the supplier of the music.

Equal opportunities

The United Kingdom has equality legislation specific to protecting employees, and covers the provision of goods and services.

Equal opportunities policy

The Equal Opportunities Commission (EOC) states that it is best practice for all workplaces to have a written equal opportunities policy. This will include an equal opportunity commitment by the employer and details of how the policy will be implemented. All employees should know and understand this policy, and it should be monitored regularly to review effectiveness.

Race Relations Act 1976

This Act makes it unlawful to discriminate on the grounds of colour, race, nationality, ethnic or national origin.

Disability Discrimination Act 1995 (DDA)

This Act makes it unlawful to discriminate on the grounds of disability.

Under the DDA, as a provider of services, goods and facilities, your workplace has a duty to ensure that no clients are discriminated against on the grounds of disability. It is unlawful because of a disability to:

- Provide a service to a lesser standard or on worse terms.
- Fail to make adjustments that are reasonable to the way that services are provided.
- From 2004 to fail to make reasonable adjustments to the service premises' physical features, in order to overcome physical barriers to access.

Services can only be denied to a person who is disabled if it is justified and other clients would be treated in the same way.

It is the employer's responsibility to ensure adequate training is provided to employees to prevent discrimination practices taking place and that reasonable adjustments are made to the workplace to facilitate access for people who are disabled.

Sex Discrimination Acts 1975 and 1985 and the Equal Pay Act 1970

These Acts were implemented to prevent less favourable treatment of a man or woman on the basis of gender, and to promote equal opportunities, as well as covering pay and conditions.

Byelaws

Byelaws are laws made by the local council, and may affect the running of your business. For example, if you wished to make some major changes to the premises, or even just to change the shop window, you would need to apply to the planning department and the public highways department for planning permission. These departments would decide whether the proposed changes would cause any problems to local residents. They would consider, for instance, whether parking facilities were adequate, or whether the volume of traffic would increase.

Knowledge review – Health and safety

1 What does the abbreviation COSHH stand for?

2 Which legislation requires the business premises and equipment to be safe and in good order?

3 The correct working temperature for clinics and salons is

_____.

4 The correct technique for lifting heavy objects is

_____.

5 You would extinguish a fire caused by:

(a) electricity by using _____.

(b) paper by using _____.

6 Give two main differences between the Data Protection Acts 1984 and 1998.

4

Stress

Learning objectives

Essential Knowledge and Understanding NVQ Level 3 areas covered in this chapter are:

- **The principle of wellness with reference to the body, mind and spirit.**

- **The benefits of continuous treatments.**

One of the primary outcomes of experiencing an Indian Head Massage treatment is its calming, relaxing and de-stressing effects. Therapists can increase the effectiveness of their treatments by developing their skills in recognising undue stress levels in themselves, their clients and, particularly for those in a supervisory role, stress symptoms in their colleagues.

Definition of stress

In its simplest terms stress is the body's interaction to its immediate environment and emotions, via the senses. The body has a sophisticated, involuntary mechanism for dealing with any changes in these – for example a sense of danger will produce an adrenaline rush giving us the necessary energy to either stay and fight or run away (the well-known 'fight or flight' situation). In some instances you can actually feel the adrenaline rush: for example, drivers who have experienced narrowly avoiding a collision often feel the 'tide' of adrenaline sweep up the body and then recede.

The large region of the brain called the hypothalamus could be termed the sorting office for the messages from the senses and the direction centre as it decides on the action to be taken and the amount of 'fuelling hormones' necessary for remedial actions. It orders the slowing down of some systems and the stepping up of others by organising nerve impulses to organs through the sympathetic and parasympathetic systems, and controls the hormonal delivery via the blood stream to the necessary action sites.

Understanding stress and the nervous system

To appreciate what causes stress levels to fluctuate we need to have an overview of what actually happens.

The nervous system comprises two main parts: the **autonomic system** where functions take place automatically without conscious thought – heart, lungs and stomach; and the **voluntary system** where we have control over the actions of the limbs and so forth.

The brain communication system uses electrical impulses, sending its messages via a complex network made up of billions of interconnected nerve cells called neurons. The neuron endings do not quite touch the organs and it is the job of a chemical called a **neurotransmitter** to carry the message across this gap.

The neurotransmitter is contained in a tiny sac at the end of the neurons, and the electrical impulse from the brain causes the sacs to burst open allowing the chemical to spread over the surface of the organ, deliver its message and bring about the required change in activity.

The autonomic system is the system responsible for the changes in activity produced to deal with stress demands; it encompasses the parasympathetic and the sympathetic systems. The sympathetic system controls the stress response to increase activity; the parasympathetic system plays the role of bringing the increased activity back to a balanced state.

The main function of the parasympathetic system is to conserve energy; it is also responsible for the defence of the body against bacteria and foreign matter, and assisting the digestive process. Conversely, the role of the sympathetic nervous system is to make available enough energy to prepare the body for emergency action. It does this by deepening the breathing, quickening the heart rate, and sending more blood and oxygen to the muscles, resulting in increased strength and stamina.

Hormones

The organs also receive messages from the brain via hormones in the blood stream. Each hormone has a specific message responsible for altering activity. The pituitary gland lies close to the base of the brain, and the release of hormones from this gland is influenced by messages from the hypothalamus.

Stress response glands

The two adrenal glands lie one on top of each kidney, and they consist of a **medulla** (middle) and a **cortex** (outer). The medulla is responsible for the production of two hormones – adrenaline and nor-adrenaline, which are very similar. The adrenal cortex produces the hormone **cortisol**, which prepares the body to deal with long-term energy demands. The body's response to stress demands involves the action of these main hormones, with major immediate demands met by adrenaline and nor-adrenaline, and prolonged stress demands by cortisol.

The whole system of dealing with stress is a balancing act. When stress levels are at their highest breathing deepens, heart rate increases, output of red blood cells from the spleen is increased, blood flow increases in the muscles of the arms and legs, digestion systems slow down, pupils dilate to increase visual perception, decision making is heightened, the kidneys reduce their activities, blood clots more easily to assist in possible injury repair, skin sweats more and looks pale due to redirection of blood to the muscles, and there is suppression of allergic reaction reducing the risk of breathlessness from dust and irritants during flight or fight.

Positive versus negative stress

Stress can be quite healthy in the right circumstances. Up to a point, stress helps us to live more fully, facing new challenges with the feeling of adrenaline flowing through the body; without challenges life would be rather boring.

Happiness in everyday life in terms of excitement due to, for example, holiday expectations, falling in love, sex or anticipation of a special event/celebration, are all ways of experiencing positive stress. Yet we each have our own stress threshold – the point beyond which the challenges of everyday living become too much to cope with. Combined with other factors, such as poor diet and lack of sleep, the stress level can become too high and result in exhaustion.

Stress is psychophysiological – it can result in mental or physical disorders.

Negative stress

When a person becomes anxious the body responds by preparing for action, and to maintain this state of preparedness the body calls on its reserves of energy. If the anxiety/tension is not relieved within a comparatively short time he or she enters the stress stage and it is not long before the reserves of energy are depleted. This is followed by feelings of emptiness and lethargy, with everything becoming too much effort, bringing on feelings of depression.

The same thing happens to insomniacs; because their bodies are unable to recharge their energy systems during sleep, they find that by mid-morning they have hardly any energy left and have to force themselves to complete the rest of the day's work.

Negative stress results in feelings of panic, low self-esteem, inadequacy, depression and sleeplessness. Negative stress, suffered constantly, can result in **physical or psychological disorders** as the body is constantly in a state of prepared action. Table 4.1 lists ailments recognised to have a stress background.

Table 4.1: Stress-related ailments

Physical disorders	*Psychological disorders*
Hypertension – high blood pressure	Tiredness
Coronary thrombosis	Anxiety
Migraine	Anger
Hay fever and allergies	Phobias
Asthma	Poor concentration
Pruritus – intense itching	Depression
Peptic ulcers	Low self-esteem
Constipation	Feelings of hopelessness
Colitis	Irritability and/or excessive tearfulness

Table 4.1: Stress-related ailments continued

Physical disorders	*Psychological disorders*
Menstrual difficulties	
Skin disorders	
Tuberculosis	
Indigestion	
Neck or backache	
Muscle tension	
Addiction to medication or drugs	
Impotence	
Irritable bowel	

Stress can also trigger and aggravate forms of eczema and psoriasis. One in three of the UK population is affected with psoriasis, with symptoms most common in the 15–40 age range.

Observing stress in your clients

The intention of this chapter is not to provide therapists with diagnostic skills, but rather to give them an insight into some of the reasons for, and bodily activities involved in, stress management. The cause of many problems is rooted in the pace and demands of modern living. An ability to relax and securing uninterrupted, regular sleep are the prime antidotes for almost all of the problems created by undue stress. The main benefits of Indian Head Massage are to provide relaxation and promote sound sleep patterns. In a short space of time, and without any medication, this treatment will give some instant relief to all who suffer from stress-related conditions, creating from the outset a feeling of wellness and confidence, which can be maintained indefinitely with regular treatments.

Common stress-induced ailments, which may be combated by Indian Head Massage therapy are:

- *Headache.* Therapists should give a good, balanced treatment and allow extra recovery time.
- *Sinusitis.* Therapists should increase the repetitions of the facial movements 29–32 (as described in Chapter 11).
- *Neck ache due to prolonged use of a PC.* Therapists should increase the repetitions of movements 14–19.
- *Muscle tension in the upper back and shoulders.* Therapists should increase the pressure and repetitions of movements 3–9.

Therapists who recognise any of the symptoms of stress in their clients should have no hesitation in recommending that they have an Indian Head Massage, as massage offers one of the best ways to deal with stress. It can help to re-educate the body, reminding us of how to rest and relax. When the body has been rebalanced and the immune system boosted, the body is better able to fight off infection and begin recovery.

A good massage may occasionally induce the client to fall asleep; most clients at least fall into deep relaxation. Often clients feel more refreshed after a massage than after a full night's sleep. It is quite common following an Indian Head Massage for clients to sleep better than they have done for a long time previously. Massage is soothing. Clients suffering from the effects of undue stress may experience the following benefits:

- The mind can take a break, and, with increased oxygen to the brain, concentration and alertness afterwards often improve.
- Tension often brings with it emotional disturbances, which can be lessened by applying massage. As the client feels more relaxed and secure, barriers may break down and emotion may be released. Clients may talk about their problems, and quite often they are tearful. Later, though, and as a result, clients' depression, low esteem and feelings of hopelessness may be alleviated.
- The physical touch and the uplifting effect of the massage can help clients feel more confident.
- Energy levels are usually increased, as energy that has become blocked is released and allowed to flow freely.

Although therapists must never offer a diagnosis of any kind to a client, he or she can offer help to those clients who feel they are suffering from stress.

Relaxation or meditation

Encourage clients to build a little relaxation time into their lives, even if it is only a few minutes a day. Some people lead such a busy life that they actually need to be told to reserve some time to do nothing! Even if you can only persuade them to 'book' the bathroom for a specific time each week to indulge in a warm relaxing bath with no interruptions, this can be a wonderful 'de-stresser'.

Relaxation and mind-stilling techniques

Adopt a comfortable position, close your eyes and let your imagination take you to a seashore where you can relax and watch and hear the sea; to a country lane where you can walk and enjoy each season; to look at a favourite painting or flower – relax as you notice every detail of shape and colour; or to relive a happy childhood experience, focusing on every detail of the day.

Practise a simple meditation technique – imagine a pinpoint of your favourite colour, watch as it slowly comes towards you, gradually getting bigger until it totally enfolds you. Hold this image for a few moments, take the ball of colour back to the size of a football and hold this image for as long as possible. Try to keep everything except the colour out of your mind. If thoughts intrude acknowledge them and dismiss them, and return to your relaxation experience.

Recognising stress in your colleagues

Managers who are alert to the signs of stress around them can help to reduce staff relationship problems and promote a good, cohesive working team. Factors that may be caused by stress include:

- short temper
- impatience
- argumentativeness – a modern-day 'fight' response resulting in heated arguments
- over-emotional – being a modern-day 'flight' response, running away to shed tears
- fainting
- indigestion – no time to eat, or eating in a hurry
- lack of appetite – energies redirected to coping with the stress situation.

Beware of adding to the workload of staff members who are constantly dashing about trying to be everywhere at once. Find time to talk to staff who appear withdrawn and lacking in energy and enthusiasm.

Self-massage

For the busy therapist the following routine may be useful in inducing relaxation and providing relief from some of the symptoms of stress, such as tension headaches, tense neck muscles, etc. All it takes is just a few minutes, leaving you feeling totally re-energised and refreshed.

As regards preparation, try to find a place where you won't be disturbed for about ten minutes, sit comfortably with both feet firmly on the ground ensuring body weight is evenly distributed, and close your eyes. Practise slow, deep breathing, and imagine taking the breath in up from your feet and it travelling up through the chest and out through the crown of your head. Repeat this three to five times then reverse the direction, taking the breath in through the crown and out through the feet. Just concentrate on your breathing until you have cleared your mind and feel relaxed. Now follow these simple steps:

1   Start with shoulder rotations. Lift up your right shoulder and slowly rotate backwards, repeat with your left, now repeat rotations forwards, then rotate both together in each direction.

2   Place your left hand on your right shoulder near to the neck, gently squeeze the flesh between the fingers, hold then release. Work along the shoulder towards the arm, then repeat on the left shoulder.

Preparation – step 1

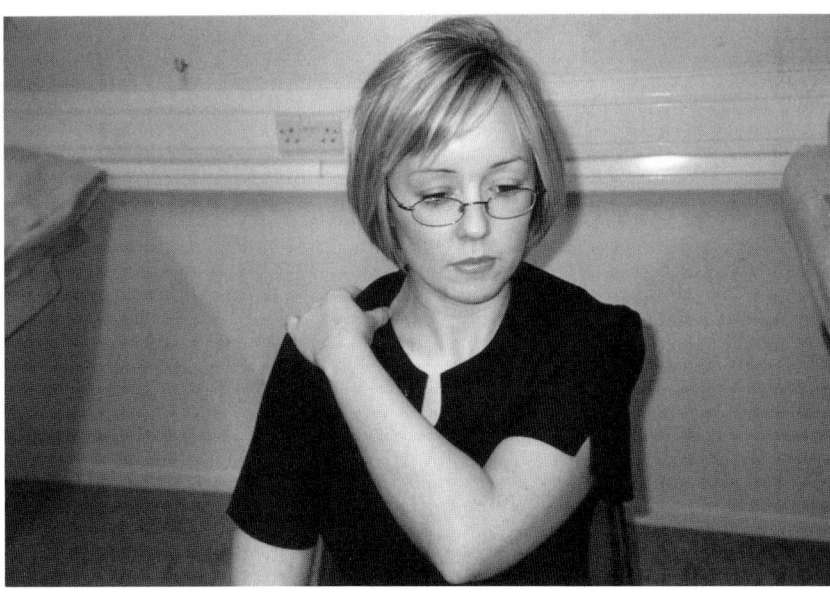

Step 2

3   Start with the head facing forward in an upright position. Turn the head slowly to the right looking along the shoulder, and then return to face forward. Repeat three times. Now repeat these movements turning to the left.

Step 3

4   Massage the back of the scalp with the thumbs and the fingertips using circular movements as though you were shampooing your hair. Move slowly to the front covering all the scalp area.

Step 4

5 Using the fingers against the scalp, take large handfuls of hair and firmly tug and release, working all over the scalp.

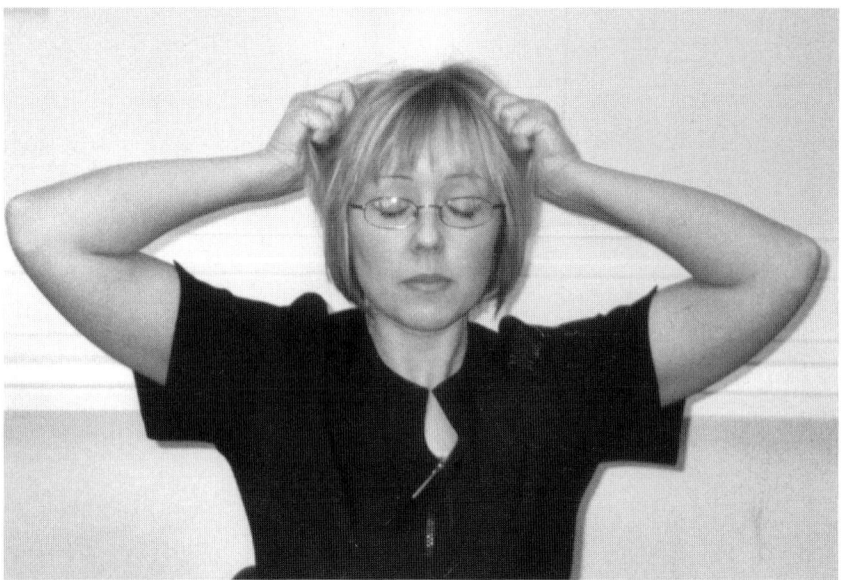

Step 5

6 Rest the fingertips on the centre of the forehead over the bridge of the nose, press firmly, and then pull the hands apart across the forehead.

Step 6

7   Gently massage the temples using the pads of the fingers and very light movements.

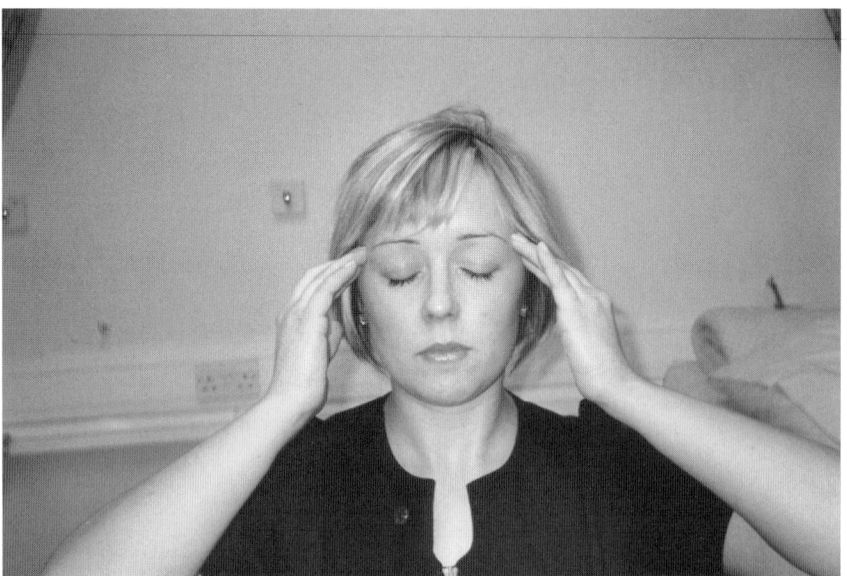

Step 7

8   Finish by stroking the scalp and face lightly with the fingertips.

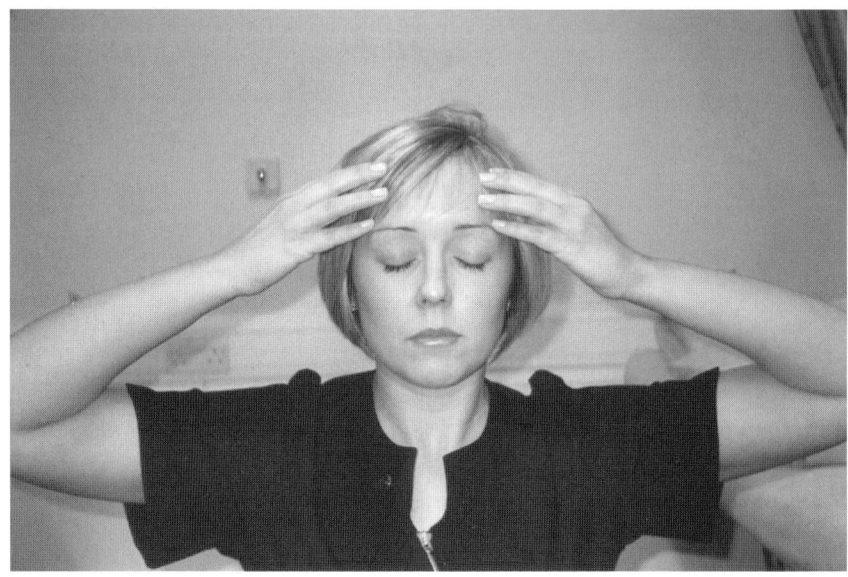

Step 8

Finally, allow yourself a few quiet moments before continuing your day.

Knowledge review – Stress

1   The nervous system comprises two parts. What are they?

The _____ and the _____ system.

2   The job of the neurotransmitter is to

_____

3   The _____ is the system responsible for the changes in activity produced to deal with stress.

4   The pituitary gland lies _____.

5   All stress is harmful. True or False?

5

Preparation

Learning objectives

Essential Knowledge and Understanding NVQ Level 3 areas covered in this chapter are:

- The importance of maintaining standards of hygiene, including sanitising your hands and the principles for avoiding cross-infection.

- Creating the most effective ambience in the treatment room – music, lighting, heating and décor.

- Accessory checks for the client and therapists and why they should be removed/minimal.

- Recognition of contra-indications; those that restrict treatment and those requiring medical referral.

- The importance of effective breathing prior to the commencement of treatments.

- Efficient appointment systems and why treatments should be completed in the given time.

Personal hygiene and appearance

Your own appearance and that of your workplace are a reflection of your professionalism. They will enable prospective clients to make a judgement about you, so remember: first impressions count.

Dream Workwear

If you always look clean, well-groomed and smart, clients are more likely to have confidence in you.

Personal hygiene

As you will be working in close proximity to your clients, it is essential that you maintain bodily cleanliness by daily bathing or showering. This removes the sweat, dead cells and bacteria that would otherwise cause body odour.

Anti-perspirants are astringent – they have a tightening effect on the pores. Applied under the arms daily, an anti-perspirant will help to reduce perspiration and thus the smell of sweat. Perfume, if used, should be light and applied sparingly.

Underwear should be clean and changed daily.

Oral hygiene

Teeth should be cleaned every morning and evening, and after every meal. Dental floss should be used to remove the build-up that causes plaque. **Breath fresheners** and **mouthwashes** may be required to freshen the breath.

To maintain healthy teeth, remember to visit the dentist regularly.

Hands

It is essential that you wash your hands regularly. Your hands will come into contact with many germs. Most of

Health & Safety

Using strong perfume could cause an allergic reaction, headache or feelings of sickness in the client.

If you need to blow your nose, or cough or sneeze during treatment you must sanitise your hands before continuing.

them will not be harmful, but some can cause ill health or disease. It is especially important that you wash your hands after you have been to the toilet, and before eating.

When washing your hands it is more hygienic to use liquid soap, with a detergent containing **chlorhexidine**, from a sealed disposable dispenser. Disposable paper towels or warm-air hand dryers should be used to dry the hands.

If you have any cuts or abrasions on your hands, cover them with a clean dressing to prevent the risk of secondary infection.

Wash your hands before and after treating each client, and if necessary *during* the treatment as well. This will minimise the risk of cross-infection, and also conveys a hygienic and professional image.

Do not wear nail enamel when treating a client, as the client may be allergic to it and develop an unpleasant rash. Enamel would also hide any dirt underneath your nails. It is much better to present a clean, enamel-free nail: this will inspire confidence in your clients.

Feet

To ensure fresh and healthy feet, wash them daily. Always ensure that they are dried thoroughly. **Foot sprays** and **medicated powders** can be used to keep the feet dry and cool.

Make sure that your shoes are comfortable, correctly fitted and have heels. You will be on your feet continually, all day long.

Hair

If your hair is long, tie it securely back so that it cannot fall forwards over either your own face or your client's face as you work. Hair should always be clean as well as tidy.

Posture

Your **posture** is the way in which you hold yourself when walking, sitting and standing. Correct posture will enable you to work much longer without becoming tired, and will prevent stiff joints and muscle fatigue.

When you stand, keep your head up and balanced centrally. In addition, keep:

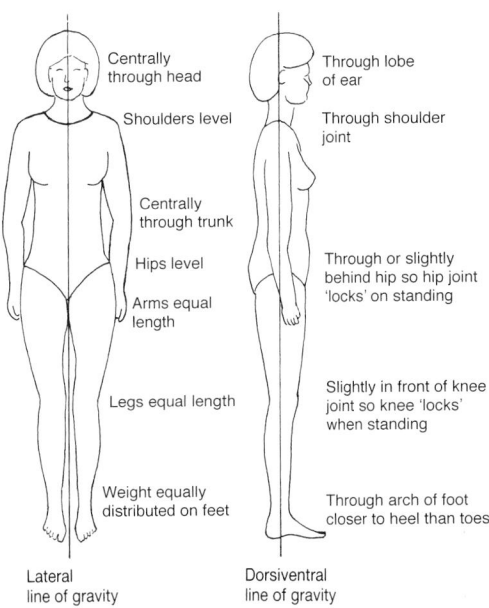

Good posture – standing

- your shoulders relaxed but slightly back
- your abdomen pulled in
- your hips level
- your bottom tucked in
- your knees level
- your weight evenly distributed and your feet slightly apart.

Overall

You will need to wear a protective overall, clean and pressed each day. An overall may consist of a dress or a tunic top with corresponding trousers.

The fabrics are normally lightweight and comfortable to work in. Cotton is ideal as air can circulate, allowing perspiration to evaporate, which discourages body odour. The overall should be fairly loosely fitted, and not too short. White is a good colour for an overall: it shows the client that the overall is clean.

Jewellery

Keep jewellery to a minimum. A flat wedding ring is acceptable, but avoid wearing a watch strap or bracelets which may catch the client's skin during treatment.

Health & Safety

Never eat or drink in the treatment area.

Every salon or clinic has its own rules on dress, jewellery and the like, to create a particular professional image. You will need to follow the rules at your workplace.

Hand exercises

The suppleness of your hands and their joints is very important if you are to perform massage effectively. Practise hand exercises daily until all the joints are free and mobile. Both hands should work equally well. Your hands should be well-manicured, smooth and warm.

Try these simple exercises to help your flexibility:

1　Rotate wrists clockwise then anti-clockwise to loosen the wrists.

2　Clench the fingers together with backs of hands facing. Pull fingers apart but maintain contact.

3　Rotate fists in a circular motion.

4　Finger-pad resistance – press the fingers against each other one by one.

5　Place alternate fingers down on a hard surface as if playing a piano.

6　Place palms together and apply slight pressure, maintaining the contact.

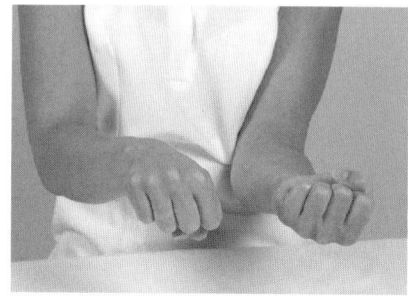

Hand exercises: Step 1

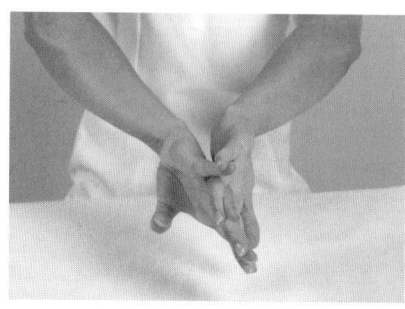

Step 2

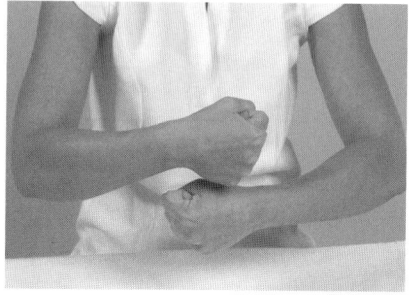

Step 3

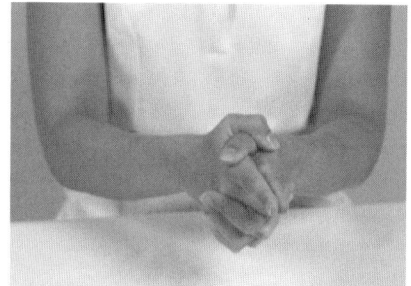

Step 4

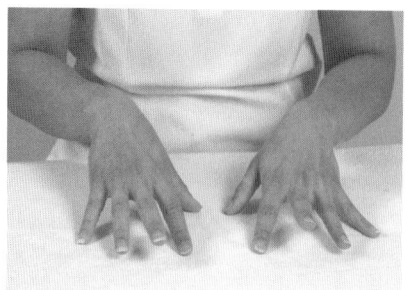

Step 5

Step 6

All photos © Ellisons

Breathing

Personal preparation

The effectiveness of an Indian Head Massage treatment can be enhanced or diminished by the mental state of the therapist. The therapist should be aware that the quality and success of the treatment depends to a large degree on a calm and relaxed state of mind and should try to develop a routine of relaxation prior to giving each treatment.

Effective breathing exercises are a useful and time efficient way to achieve this.

A simple but effective breathing exercise is to adopt a relaxed standing position, commence by focusing your attention on your normal breathing pattern, then gradually increase the depth of each breath. Maintain these deep breaths for a few moments and gradually reverse the pattern until you are breathing normally again. Repeat the exercise until you feel relaxed and able to focus your whole attention on the treatment to be given.

Consciously taking relaxing breaths at key points throughout the treatment will help the therapist to maintain stamina and concentration levels. Key points to consider are:

- Shoulder massage ('smoothing down'; routine point 9 in Chapter 11).
- Neck massage ('grasp and pull back'; routine point 14).
- Scalp massage ('petrissage to the scalp'; routine point 28).
- Face massage ('palmar pressure placing'; routine point 37).

Clients who are very stressed and tense on arrival at the salon will benefit from a few moments of breathing exercises after the consultation process and immediately before the commencement of the treatment.

The therapist could suggest that the client undertakes regular breathing exercises as part of their aftercare advice.

Aftercare breathing exercises to promote and maintain relaxation

The complete breath

The yoga complete breath is easy to do and very effective, especially when carried out first thing in the morning, as it

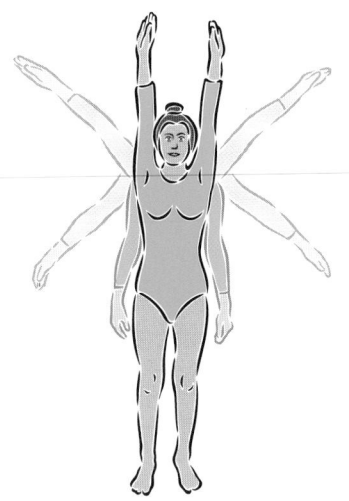

The yoga complete breath

allows the spine to experience a gentle stretch and ensures a supply of fresh oxygen to all the major organs of the body.

Begin by standing with the feet a hip width apart, hands at your sides. Breathe in slowly lifting your arms out to the sides and up above your head – stretch upwards with your fingers as high as you can, and if possible raise up on your toes as you do this. Relax as you exhale, lowering the heels and arms. Try to keep a steady rhythm.

Repeat this for approximately ten continuous breaths. As you become more confident you will be able to move your arms more slowly and maintain your balance as you increase the depth of your breath.

Exercise for mental well-being and balance

Begin in a relaxed position, either sitting or standing. Take your client through the imagery of being strongly rooted to the ground. Invite them to breathe in, and as they inhale ask them to visualise the breath entering their body through the feet (as a tree takes up its energy through its roots), travelling up their bodies and being exhaled through the crown of the head. Step two is to reverse the pattern, inhaling through the crown and exhaling through the feet. Repeat these alternate steps until you feel calm and refreshed, always ending on an out breath through the crown.

This breathing exercise is a simple adaptation based on the ideology of the balancing of chakras.

Preparing to treat a client

Being well prepared means that you promote your salon or business as professional and efficient. Correct implementation of timings of your treatments, as stated in leaflets and price lists, which have been calculated carefully on a cost-effective basis, should be worked to all at times. Although this is a very relaxing treatment, and at no time should you make the client feel hurried, it is part of the professional therapist's job to keep to the times set for each treatment so that an efficient appointment system can be managed.

Health & Safety

Keep naked flames away from drapes and furnishings. Don't leave candles unattended. Place candles in a dish of water.

The treatment room or salon area

If possible, use a quiet room where interruptions will be minimal. Check the heating and lighting levels. Light candles or oil burners. Choose a relaxing music tape or CD. Set the music level – it should be audible but not intrusive.

Before the client arrives, make sure that the treatment area is fully prepared. Check that everything you will require is to hand. It is very bad practice to stop the massage, once you have started. To do so would disrupt the treatment, disturbing the client and breaking the relaxation: the client would thus not achieve the full benefit of the treatment.

Equipment and materials

Before you start, make sure you have the following materials and equipment (see Tables 5.1 and 5.2).

Table 5.1: Materials

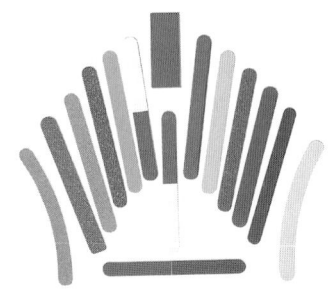

●	An emery board	Before beginning, check your hands and nails for any rough or sharp areas. Remove any rings, bracelets, and your watch: put these away securely.

●	A large hair clip	Use this to secure long hair on top of the client's head during the first part of the treatment. Busy therapists should have enough hair clips to provide a clean one for each client.

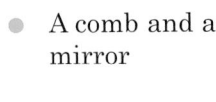
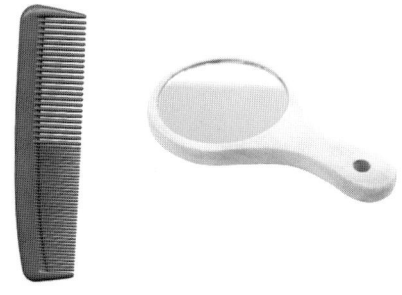

●	A comb and a mirror	Offer these to your client after the massage.

●	A barbicide jar	Use this to sterilise hair clips and combs.

Table 5.1: Materials Continued

● Mineral water — In a covered glass or bottle. Many clients will feel thirsty immediately after treatment. Always remember to offer your client a drink of water or herbal tea at the end of the massage.

● A selection of oils — Use as required.

● Talc — Necessary to have to hand in the summertime as clients may be wearing sun or vest tops. A light dusting of the client's shoulder and/or neck area will help the therapist's hands to glide over the skin without dragging. Talc may also be used by the therapist to help to keep their hands cool and comfortable in unusually warm conditions.

● Hand wipes — It is useful to have hand wipes to hand when using oils during the massage as they enable the therapist to quickly remove any residue oil before commencing the facial movements, avoiding creating a break in the general continuity and flow of the massage.

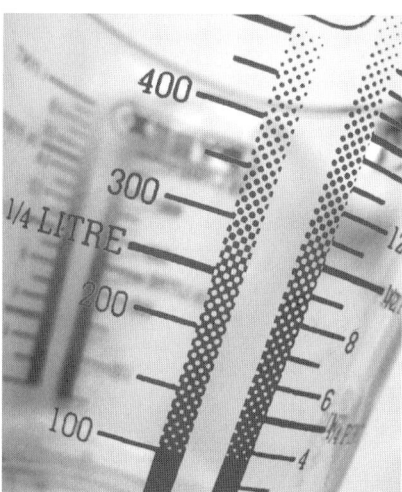

● Small lipped container — Capable of allowing the therapist to pour a fine stream of oil. Using excessive oil is wasteful, will tend to clog the pores and will render the massage ineffective as the therapist's hands will not be able to maintain the necessary firmness of movement.

Table 5.1: Materials Continued

• Small hand towel — This is used folded into a small pad and placed between the back of the client's head and the therapist's chest. When carrying out the facial movements this maintains the head in an upright position and protects the hygienic state of the therapist's overall.

Table 5.2: Equipment

• Chair — A suitable, upright, low-backed chair.

• Cushion — A firm cushion to allow for height adjustment.

• A towelling wrap — For those clients who prefer oils to be used for the whole of the treatment.

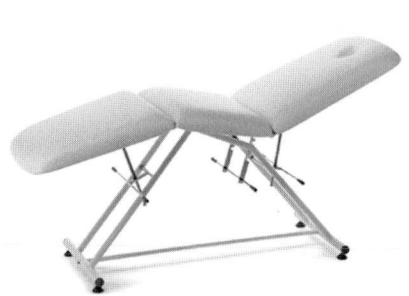

• Couch — Equipment and materials for giving treatments in a beauty salon would also include the provision of a massage couch for those clients having an Indian Head Massage as an addition to other massage therapies performed in a prone position.

The treatment

1 Begin by carrying out your consultation. Look for contra-indications (see below).

2 Ask your client to remove any necklaces, chains or earrings, placing them securely in her or his own keeping.

3 Check that your client is sitting correctly and is comfortable.

4 When you are ready, sanitise your hands then take a few seconds to clear your mind and prepare yourself mentally. Massage movements should be appropriate and adapted to suit the client's needs – for example, if the area you are working on is bony, you must use very little pressure, to avoid discomfort. Your massage movements should be rhythmical and flowing. Mental preparation will help with this.

Hygiene

Hygiene is vital: it prevents both cross-infection and secondary infection. These occur through poor practice, such as failing to recognise skin diseases, or not carrying out the correct hygiene procedures, such as washing one's hands.

Cross-infection

Cross-infection occurs when micro-organisms are transferred from one person to another, usually through personal touch. Cross-infection can happen if sterilisation procedures are not carried out properly.

Infection and secondary infection

Infection can occur as a result of injury to the client during treatment. **Secondary infection** can occur if the client already has an infected wound, and additional micro-organisms penetrate this wound during treatment.

Infectious diseases contra-indicate body treatments and require medical attention. Certain skin disorders, even though they are not contagious, also contra-indicate treatment: this is because treatment might lead to secondary infection.

Certain skin diseases and disorders contra-indicate massage treatments – both you and your other clients must be protected from the risk of cross-infection. It is therefore extremely important that you can distinguish a healthy skin from one with a skin disorder or a disease. You need to be able to recognise such conditions, and if necessary to refer clients tactfully to their physicians.

Contra-indications to treatment

Contra-indications are injuries, diseases, disorders or any other factors which indicate that you should not carry out the Indian Head Massage treatment. It is essential that you check thoroughly for these at the consultation, as inappropriate treatment would incur risk to the client, the therapist and other clients. The most common risk is of **cross-infection** (transferring infection from the client to yourself or another client).

It is vital that you are familiar with contra-indications and can recognise them. You may identify certain contra-indications whilst examining the client, of which the client is unaware.

The following contra-indications are relevant to Indian Head Massage. *If any of these conditions is present, you must not carry out the massage.*

1 Any recent head or neck injury, including whiplash. This would be painful and could exacerbate the injury and seriously delay recovery.

2 Severe bruising in the treatment area. This would be painful and could delay normal recovery time.

3 Epilepsy. Treatment might bring on an attack due to possible sensory disturbance.

4 Recent haemorrhage. Treatment could create a recurrence.

5 High or low blood pressure. The client may feel faint or lose consciousness.

6 Migraine – see 'Notes on particular conditions' on page 85.

7 A history of thrombosis or embolism. These blood clots or blockages could be moved by the increase in blood flow induced by the massage, with serious or fatal results.

8 Diabetes. As a disorder of the metabolism this condition would be adversely affected by a treatment that stimulates the metabolic system.

9 A spastic condition. Generally this is a contra-indication but as there are several degrees to this condition a full

consultation with the carer and the consent of the GP of the client would be essential before any form of treatment could be given.

10　Any dysfunction of the nervous system. Client feedback during treatment, checking pressure and comfort, would be impeded, therefore presenting a danger.

11　Skin disorders. Infectious disorders will always be classed as a contra-indication, whereas many non-infectious skin disorders benefit from treatments. See the section on 'Skin diseases and disorders' on page 86.

12　Scalp infections. All scalp infections are contra-indicated. See the section on 'Skin diseases and disorders' on page 86.

13　Cuts or abrasions in the treatment area. Small cuts and abrasions in the treatment area may be classed as a localised contra-indication – i.e. treatment to be avoided in the location of the injury whilst being carried out in other areas. However, severe cuts and abrasions should be classed as a full contra-indication to treatment as treatment may adversely affect the wounds.

14　Recent operations. Clients should wait until full recovery has taken place and their GP has given his or her consent before they attend for an Indian Head Massage treatment.

15　Chronic ME (myalgic encephalomyelitis). See 'Notes on particular conditions' on page 85.

16　High temperature, illness and fever. An increase in the blood flow will increase the severity of these conditions.

17　Any infectious disease. Always contra-indicated due to the high risk of infection to the therapist and subsequent clients with litigious leanings.

18　Intoxication. This is not conducive to an effective therapy.

19　Aneurosa (localised dilation of blood vessels such as a blood vessel in the temple or forehead area in the elderly). Increased blood flow could result in this condition being extremely dangerous.

Watch out also for any other condition that may affect massage.

Localised contra-indications

Occasionally small areas of skin in the treatment area may be affected by some of the conditions listed as contra-indications

– for example, small cuts or bruises in the treatment area, facial pustules, or evidence of herpes simplex. These are classed as localised contra-indications – i.e. treatment is to be avoided in the location of the injury whilst being carried out in the other areas. Care must be taken to avoid *any* contact with the affected area, which should be covered if possible. If in any doubt treat as a general contra-indication and defer treatment until a later date.

Tip

Remember to enter details of discussions and outcomes in consultation records.

Notes on particular conditions

Below are some notes on particular conditions. If you are in any doubt about whether or not to carry out massage, do *not* give it without first getting medical approval from the client's doctor.

Migraine

If a client suffers from migraine but only occasionally, and provided that there is no sign of the onset of an attack and none has been very recently experienced, massage may be given. Some people have noticed an improvement in their migraine following massage, with longer periods between attacks. However, clients should be aware that treatment *may* provoke an attack.

Skin disorders

Improved circulation to the skin can have a positive effect on psoriasis. Provided that there are no breaks in the skin, massage treatment may be carried out using gentle movements over the affected area.

Myalgic encephalomyelitis (ME)

This debilitating condition is generally a contra-indication, as the treatment leaves sufferers with almost no energy. It has been found to be beneficial to those who are already beginning to show signs of recovery, however. Reports state that although treatment is followed by a feeling of tiredness, energy levels the following day have shown a marked improvement. Further research is needed; meanwhile, therapists are advised to discuss these possibilities thoroughly with any client who has ME.

The client's general practitioner should also be consulted. If approval is given, the therapist should proceed with caution initially.

Osteoporosis

Although osteoporosis (brittle bones) is not a complete contra-indication, only soothing and relaxing techniques should be used.

Chronic fatigue

For clients with chronic fatigue, use only relaxing movements.

Spondylitis or spondylosis

If the client has inflammation of the vertebrae in the neck, only gentle massage should be used, and this must avoid working the neck.

Painful cysts

Work around painful cysts, and use only relaxing movements.

Frailty

If the client is frail, use a light, gentle touch and adapt or omit stimulating movements.

Skin diseases and disorders

As a therapist offering head massage, you should be fully aware of the most common skin diseases and disorders which you may encounter on the client's head or neck. You must be able to make an informed judgement about whether or not the treatment is contra-indicated.

On the skin are many **micro-organisms** such as bacteria and fungi. These are of differing sizes, but none can be seen without a microscope. Some micro-organisms are harmful because they can cause disease: these are said to be **pathogenic**.

An **infectious disease** is usually passed from one person to another by airborne droplets caused by coughs and sneezes. A **contagious disease** is passed by direct or indirect contact – for example touching the infected area or using materials such as towels used by the infected person.

A **non-pathogenic organism** is one that is *not* harmful. Many micro-organisms are in fact beneficial to us, and contribute to our general health.

Terminology

- *Lesion.* A visible sign on the skin's surface of injury, disease or disorder.
- *Disease.* An infectious, transferable, pathogenic condition.
- *Disorder.* A non-infectious, non-pathogenic condition of the hair, scalp or skin. Examples are formations such as skin tags, unusual colorations, such as strawberry marks, and hereditary conditions such as male-pattern baldness.
- *Parasite.* A living plant or animal that survives by feeding off its host, another plant, animal or human.
- *Infestation.* An invasion of small animal parasites, which live in the folds of the skin or any of the hairy areas of the body.
- *Naevus.* Abnormal skin pigmentation, such as a birthmark.

There are three main types of micro-organisms:

- *Bacteria.* When present in an infectious condition, bacteria are involved in the production of yellow pus.
- *Viruses.* Classed as parasites, viruses must have living tissue to grow and reproduce. They multiply within a tissue cell until they burst the cell wall, then invade other cells. This process continues, spreading the infection.
- *Fungi.* Fungi such as moulds and yeasts are also parasites. Fungal diseases may be spread by direct or indirect contact.

Bacterial infections

Impetigo

Indicated by blisters filled with clear fluid, usually in groups. These burst, and yellow crusts are formed. Impetigo is most often found on the face near the mouth, the nose and the ears, but it can also appear on the scalp. *Highly infectious and contagious.*

Conjunctivitis

Inflammation of the lining of the eyelid and the mucous membrane that covers the eye. The eyes become red and itchy, and may exude pus. *Infectious and contagious.*

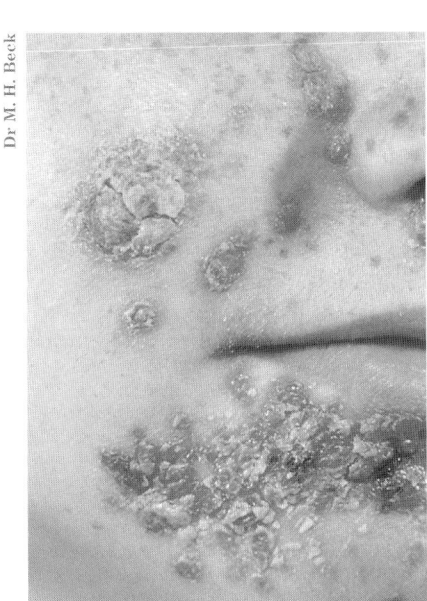

Dr M. H. Beck

Impetigo

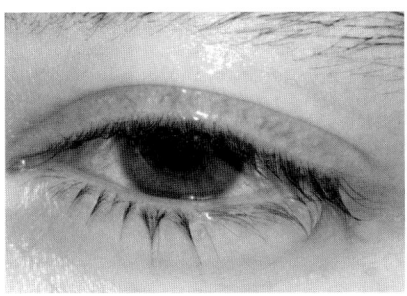

Conjunctivitis

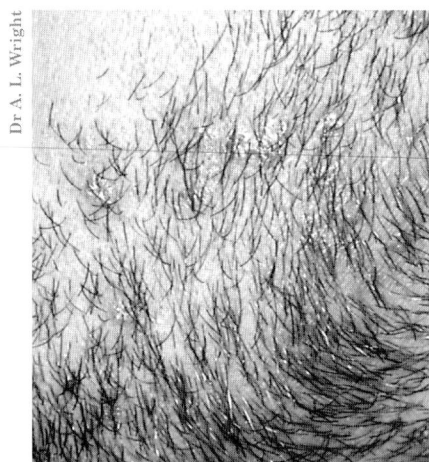

Sycosis barbae

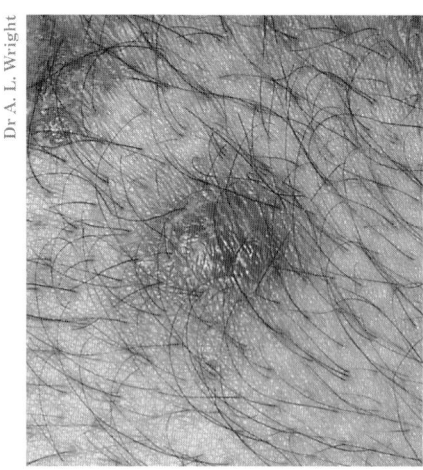

Boil

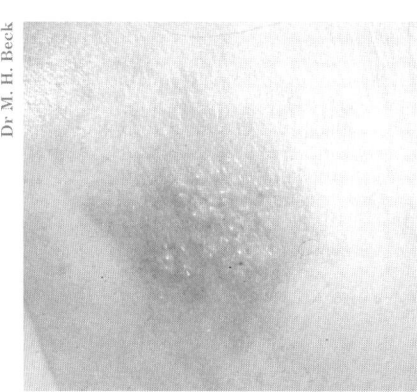

Herpes simplex

Stye

A small adhesion on the lashline of the eye, which is filled with pus. Styes result from infected hair follicles. *Infectious.*

Sycosis barbae (barbers' itch)

Inflammation of the follicles in the beard area, with visible pustules. The condition causes intense itching, with the possibility of secondary infection. *Infectious.*

Furuncle (boil)

A large red raised area of skin, often with hairs growing through it and a head of pus at the centre. Boils are very painful. A common site is the back of the neck, but boils can also be found on the face. Medical advice should be sought immediately, particularly if the site is near to the eyes or in the temple area. *Infectious.*

Carbuncle

An abscess which has the appearance of several boils grouped together. It has more than one head of pus. Carbuncles are usually found at the back of the neck. *Infectious.*

Viral infections

Herpes zoster (shingles)

This virus attacks the nerve pathways and is *very* painful. On the surface of the skin near the nerve endings, small blister-like spots appear; these itch and are also painful. Shingles can be found anywhere on the body, but is most painful when the nerves of the head and neck are affected. *Infectious.*

Herpes simplex (cold sores)

Blisters form around the mouth, and later burst, forming an oozing crust. The virus is present in approximately 90 per cent of the population and can be triggered into activity by changes in temperature, by ultra-violet light, by ill-health or by stress-related illnesses. *Infectious and contagious.* The most common means of transmission is kissing. People with active herpes simplex should not kiss babies.

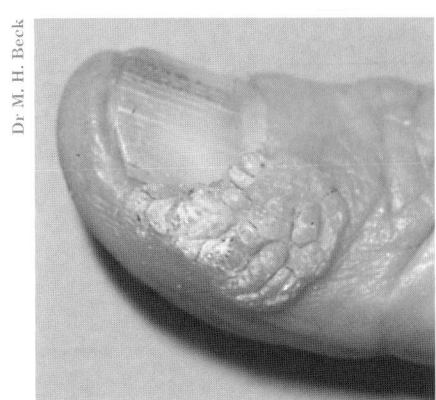

Dr M. H. Beck

Wart

Warts

Common warts appear on the hands and face, as a result of areas of abnormal reproduction of the cells in the germinativum layer of the epidermis. All warts should be treated as infectious and the client referred to the doctor for treatment. *Infectious and contagious.*

Animal infestation

Pediculosis capitis (head lice)

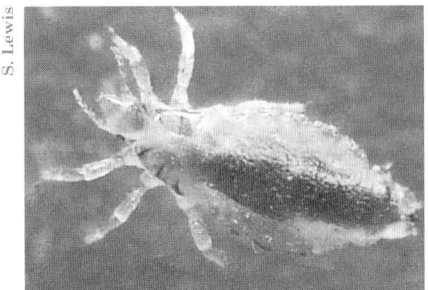

S. Lewis

Head louse

The head louse is a small animal parasite that lives for approximately 30 days, sucking blood from the scalp. It first injects the site with an anti-coagulant. This causes irritation, and the resultant scratching can cause secondary infection. Lice lay up to 300 eggs in their lifetime, but only a few survive: a typical infestation has approximately 20 lice. *Contagious, by direct and indirect contact.* Contrary to common belief, head lice *cannot* jump – they crawl from head to head or hitch a lift on hats, scarves, combs or brushes.

Fungal infection

Tinea corporis (ringworm of the body)

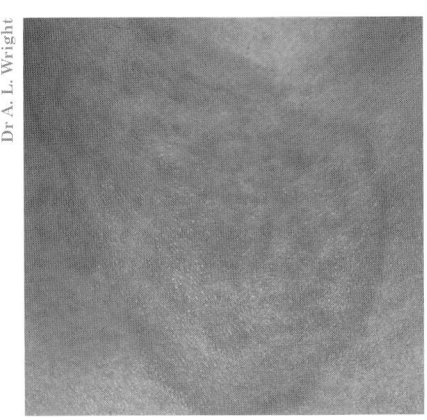

Dr A. L. Wright

Tinea corporis

Starting as small red circular patches, ringworm spreads outwards. Healing takes place from the centre, resulting in a visible ring. The condition is often found on the face. *Highly infectious and contagious.*

Non-infectious disorders

Milia

Sebum-blocked pores with a thin covering of epidermal cells. They appear as white raised beads or pimples.

Comedones (blackheads)

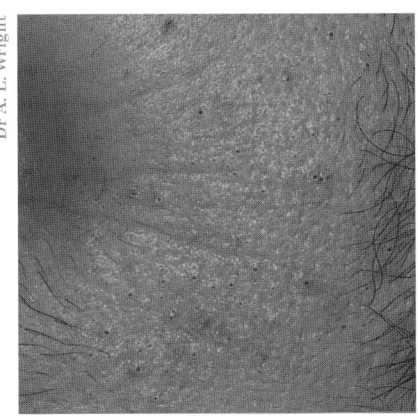

Dr A. L. Wright

Comedones (blackheads)

Sebum-blocked pores open to the oxidising effects of the air, which gives it a black appearance.

Acne vulgaris

Blocked sebaceous openings with infection, forming pus-filled spots. Acne is due to hormonal imbalances or excessively greasy skin, or both, combined with a poor cleansing routine. *Non-infectious.*

Acne rosacea

Visible as large red or purplish areas, acne rosacea is due to dilated blood capillaries and the over-production of sebum from the sebaceous glands. Clients should be referred to a doctor for medical treatment. *Non-infectious.*

Acne vulgaris

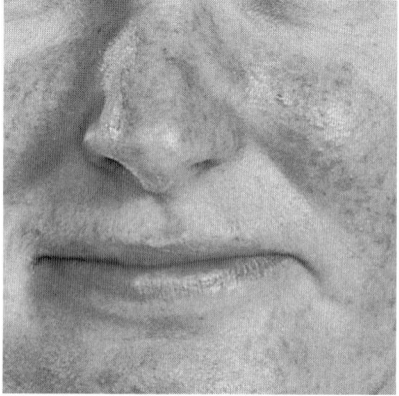

Acne rosacea

Pigmentation disorders

Chloasmata (liver spots)

Large pigmented areas of skin, often found on the face, the backs of the hands and the upper body. They may be caused by hormonal changes, for example in pregnancy or when taking the contraceptive pill. In young people they usually fade, but in the older person they are part of ageing, and remain as a permanent discoloration. *Non-infectious.*

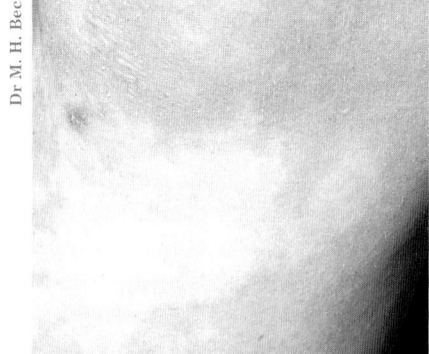

Vitiligo

Vitiligo

Areas of skin with no pigment, found on the hands, face, neck and lower abdomen. *Non-infectious.*

Vascular and cellular naevi

Conditions resulting in visible changes in pigmentation and the cellular structure of skin. They do not contra-indicate head massage.

Spider naevi (stellate haemangiomas)

Dilated blood vessels, forming a star shape or spider-like pattern.

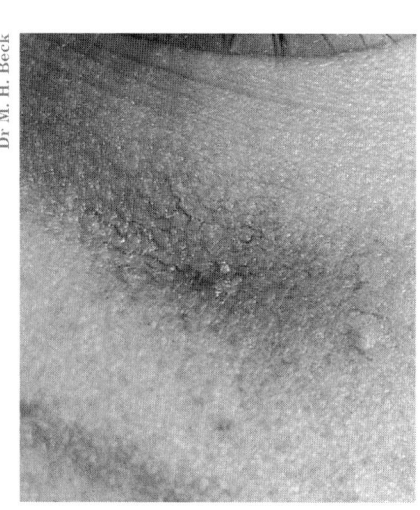

Spider naevus

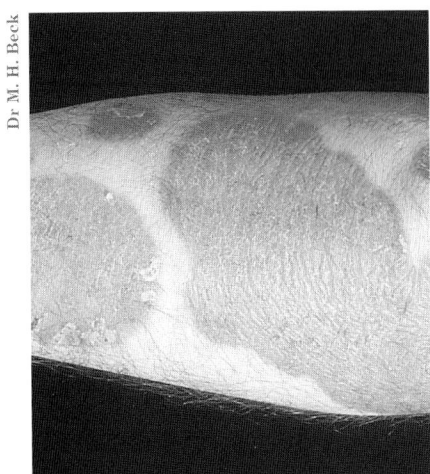

Psoriasis

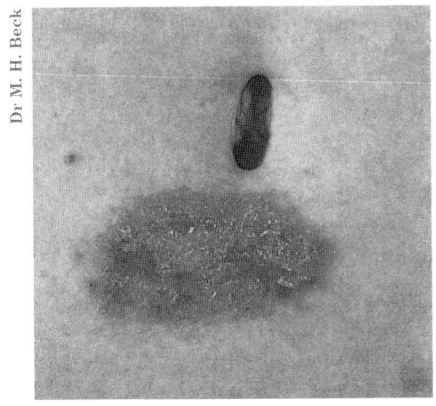

Allergic contact dermatitis

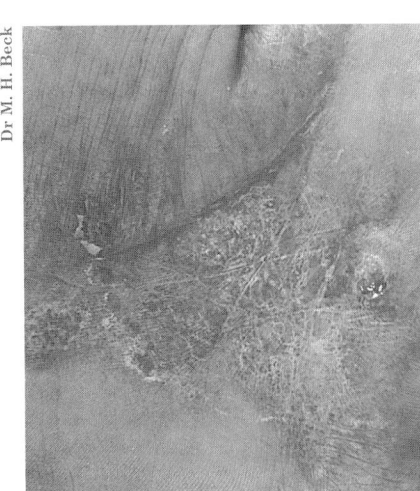

Eczema

Port-wine stains

Dilated capillaries appearing in large areas, found on the head, the face and the neck.

Moles

Cellular malformations on the skin's surface. Moles appear in many different sizes and colours, and should not be confused with warts. Moles are common, and usually do not change their appearance over long periods of time. However, moles should be checked regularly: if there is any change in size or colour, the client must be referred immediately to a doctor.

Xanthomas

Usually found on the eyelids, xanthomas are small, yellow, flat or raised growths of skin. Clients should be advised to consult their doctor.

Non-infectious, non-contagious skin conditions

Psoriasis

Dry raised areas of thickened stratum corneum. Psoriasis has the appearance of silvery scales, with the underlying skin being red and tender. Bleeding can occur if this sensitive area is handled roughly. Psoriasis is thought to be either hereditary or the result of stress-related illness. It is treated with products based on coal tar. Normally skin is replaced in up to 28 days; in psoriasis the turnover is as little as 7 days. Psoriasis does not contra-indicate treatment.

Dermatitis

This term is applied to the visible sign of an allergic reaction to substances which have been taken into the body or which have come into contact with the skin. The skin is usually red and itchy, and there may also be tiny raised vesicles (blisters). When the vesicles burst, a dry crust usually forms: this can crack and cause bleeding, risking secondary infection. Clients should be advised to seek medical attention.

Eczema

Eczema differs from dermatitis only in that it can have an hereditary link. It is most likely to be a result of contact with an irritant, either internally or externally. If this irritant can be identified and avoided, then the condition can be improved. Clients should be referred to a doctor.

Dandruff (pityriasis simplex)

In its simple form, dandruff is the normal shedding of the stratum corneum, the uppermost layer of the epidermis. Use of a specialist shampoo will usually help to control it. However, if scales are allowed to build up, there is a risk of trapping bacteria on the scalp. Yeasts may also grow, resulting in a musty smell from the scalp. Medical treatment should be advised if this condition is suspected.

Indian Head Massage treatments will greatly improve pityriasis simplex, but bacterial infections should be cleared first.

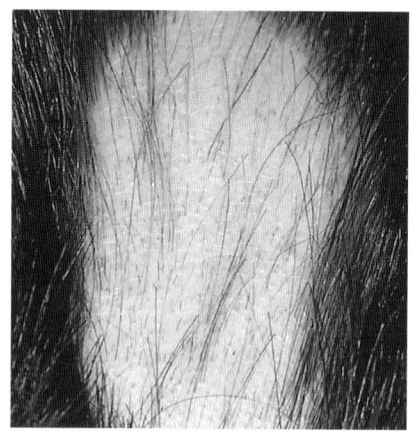

Alopecia

Alopecia (hair loss)

There are many different categories of **alopecia**, or baldness, ranging from **alopecia universalis**, a completely hairless body, to **alopecia totalis**, loss of hair from the face and head, to **alopecia areata**, small areas of hair loss on the scalp. This last category is often due to shock or stress-related illness, but can also be an after-effect following major surgery or illness. The hair almost always grows again as the patient recovers, but it may have lost all colour pigment and now appear white.

Indian Head Massage has been found to promote healthy hair growth and so may greatly improve these conditions.

Sebaceous cysts (wens)

Raised, dome-shaped areas of the skin, caused by a blockage of the sebaceous glands and resulting in a build-up of sebum in the area. These cysts are harmless, but care should be taken not to catch them with your fingernails during the massage routine.

This section has listed only the conditions *most* likely to be found in the treatment area. The list is not exhaustive.

Knowledge review – Preparation

1 Why is it advisable to keep an emery board with your other items of equipment?

To _____ or _____ on the nails prior to treatment.

2 Name five items you should always include in your preparation.

(a) _____ (b) _____ (c) _____

(d) _____ (e) _____

3 The purpose of carrying out hand exercises prior to

treatment is _____.

Contra-indications

1 What is a contra-indication? Any _____.

2 How would you proceed if you encountered a condition not listed in this chapter?

I would _____.

3 How would you treat a client suffering from osteoporosis?

I would _____.

Diseases and disorders

1 A pathogenic organism is harmful/harmless?

2 What is a disease ? A disease is _____.

3 An example of naevus is an _____.

4 The three main types of micro-organisms are

(a) _____ (b) _____ (c) _____

5 What causes a stye adhesion to form?

_____

6 The most common viral infection found on the face

is _____.

7 Would the presence of psoriasis contra-indicate an Indian Head Massage treatment?

Yes/No.

8 Pityriasis simplex is a scalp condition commonly

termed _____.

6

Oils

Learning objectives

Essential Knowledge and Understanding NVQ Level 3 areas covered in this chapter are:

- **Benefits and properties of carrier oils used in Indian Head Massage.**

Using oils

The general term for head massage in India is *champissage*. In the West this term has been adopted to denote a form of 'hacking' used in Indian Head Massage: this uses a cage-like hand position, explained in detail in the massage routine, stage 7 (Chapter 11). This form of hacking is peculiar to the Indian Head Massage treatment.

In India champissage **oil** is used for both men and women to keep the hair lustrous and well-conditioned. The oil is applied to the head and is absorbed into the roots of the hair. It strengthens the hair, in part by removing dryness which is responsible for brittle hair and for some scalp disorders. It also softens the skin of the scalp, which promotes hair growth, slows down hair loss, and encourages vibrant, shiny hair.

Applying oil

If you wish to use oil in the traditional way, follow the following simple steps. After consultation, including an allergy check, prepare your chosen oil or blend of oils. Place the oil in a small bowl within easy reach of your client, so that you can reach it easily without interrupting your massage contact and flow.

Apply the oil at the beginning of the scalp massage (massage routine, stage 20 in Chapter 11). Have to hand a clean towel or tissues so that you can quickly wipe your hands before carrying out the facial massage section.

Traditionally oil is applied in three places, as below.

First point of application

Measure eight finger-widths back from the eyebrows: this will bring you inside the natural hairline. Pour a little oil here, while making small circular movements on the scalp with the fingertips of your other hand. (This is the Tenth Gate mentioned in yoga scriptures.)

Second point of application

Move to the crown of the head and look for the crown whorl, a circular pattern of hair growth. Carefully pour more oil onto this spot from about 10 cm above, massaging in a circle in the direction of the hair-growth pattern.

Hindus call these crown-whorl hairs by a special name, *shikha*. They twist these hairs and knot them together, a technique essential for those who practise *pranayama*.

Third point of application

With the client's head down, feel for the occipital bone and apply the oil at the uppermost part of the spine as it meets the occipital bone. Use small circular movements again to distribute the oil in this area.

Tip

Oil spreads easily when warm and you will not need much to cover the whole scalp and hair. Ideally, oils should be left on the hair for at least 12 hours. If this is not possible, however, even a relatively short time will be beneficial to the client's hair and scalp condition.

To remove the oil, apply shampoo directly to the oiled hair, massage, rinse and repeat.

Choosing the oil

Organic vegetable oils are the best oils to use as they are partially absorbed through the pores of the skin and can work their effect internally as well as externally.

Sesame

Mustard

Examples of traditional oils are sesame, mustard, almond, coconut, olive oil and jasmine oil.

Allergies

An allergen is a substance that provokes an allergic reaction in hypersensitive people, and to which other people do not react. Allergens are usually proteins, which are taken into the body in food or drink, or chemicals that come into contact with the skin's surface.

Before using *any* nut oil, you must check with your client that there will be no allergic reaction. If you have any doubt about using it, choose an alternative oil.

Traditional oils

Sesame oil

Sesame oil is highly recommended as a good general oil for use in Indian champissage. It is said to be the most popular choice among Indian families practising traditional massage routines. It is claimed that, due to its high lecithin content, sesame oil helps to relieve swelling and muscular pains, and also to strengthen and moisturise the skin.

Sesame oil is said to be effective in preventing hair from turning grey. There are also claims that it can restore hair to its natural colour. This would be very difficult to prove scientifically. However, hair goes grey when it loses its natural colour pigment, **melanin**, and it is conceivable that regular massage encourages a steady supply of nutrients to the skin and hair roots and thereby delays the ageing process.

Sesame oil is a good balancing oil and is used particularly in the summer in India. It has rather a strong smell, however, which does not appeal to many Westerners. If, as does happen in some cases, sesame oil irritates the skin, olive oil can be used instead.

Mustard oil

Mustard oil is also a very popular oil, especially in the north-west of India. It opens the pores and has a strengthening and moisturising effect on the skin. Mustard oil is hot and sharp, and is effective in increasing body heat, relieving pains and swellings, and helping to relax stiff muscles. As heat is created, this oil is particularly recommended for use during the winter, but the warmth created by using this oil is also beneficial to clients with arthritis. Mustard oil is a particularly invigorating oil and used extensively for men.

Almond

Coconut

Care should be taken in using mustard oil, as its effects are very intense, stimulating and warming. Always consult with your client *before* using this oil, to check her or his medical background and that this oil will be tolerated.

Almond oil (check for allergies!)

Almond oil is a light oil, suitable for normal hair and scalp conditions, and for clients who have dry hair following chemical treatments. It is a good alternative to the heavier olive oil.

Coconut oil (check for allergies!)

Coconut oil has a beautiful aroma and is a pleasure to work with. Traditionally used in the spring, because it helps to keep the head cool and is therefore valued in the sub-continent, coconut oil is particularly recommended for women. It is a medium-to-light oil which helps to moisturise the skin, helping hair to become vibrant and alive.

Olive oil

Olive oil is rather a heavy, strong-smelling oil, but can be used on excessively dry hair and scalps. The purity of this oil also makes it highly suitable for children. Care should be taken to remove all the oil afterwards.

Jasmine oil

Jasmine oil is preferred by many Indian women, both for its beautiful perfume and for the shine and lustre it gives their hair.

Olive   Jasmine

Use of oils in the West

In addition to the oils listed above, almost any vegetable oil can be used – soya, sunflower or grapeseed oil, or peach kernel, apricot kernel or avocado oil, all of which are rich and nourishing and can be used to treat general dry-scalp and skin conditions.

The oils generally recommended for clients in the West are coconut and almond. However, many different blends are available to suit the individual client. Select an oil according to the condition of the hair and scalp. The use of oil is not recommended for *greasy* hair types.

Other oils

Evening primrose oil

Evening primrose oil can be used on any skin type, but is particularly good to use on dry hair, scalp and skin. Certain skin disorders and conditions, such as eczema and dermatitis, benefit from this oil as it is very nourishing and soothing and promotes healing.

Avocado oil

Avocado oil can be used on all skin, hair and scalp types. It is particularly beneficial for sensitive, dehydrated and dry conditions, as it is highly penetrative and soothing, and will relieve any conditions that itch.

Apricot kernel oil

Apricot kernel oil is effective with dry, sensitive and mature hair, and dry scalp and skin conditions: it is very nourishing, easily absorbed and soothing.

Calendula oil

Calendula oil is excellent for babies and children, as it has soothing and healing properties as well as being gentle. It is a good oil to use with very dry and sensitive conditions.

Grapeseed oil

Grapeseed oil is very light and a gentle emollient, and can be used on all types of hair, and with all skin and scalp conditions.

Hazelnut oil (check for allergies!)

Hazelnut oil absorbs into the skin very well. As well as being an extremely good oil for stimulating the circulation, it has a slightly astringent effect on the skin. This oil is usually used on oily hair, scalp and skin types.

Wheatgerm oil

Wheatgerm oil can be used on all types of skin, but is particularly beneficial for inflamed and ageing skin conditions, as it is very nourishing and soothing and helps to promote healing.

Peach kernel oil

Peach kernel oil is particularly good to use with dry and mature skin conditions, as it is an effective emollient that helps increase the skin's elasticity.

Jojoba oil

Jojoba oil is very light and fine in texture, and tends to be used as a natural moisturiser. It is readily absorbed, and has anti-inflammatory properties. Jojoba oil can be used on all conditions, but is particularly effective with acne and inflamed skin conditions.

Macadamia nut oil (check for allergies!)

Macadamia nut oil contains fatty acids that are found in sebum. It is a rich, nutritive and highly emollient oil. It may be used on all skin, scalp and hair types, but is most effective for dry and ageing conditions.

St John's wort oil

St John's wort oil is especially good for use on sensitive conditions. It is effective in soothing inflamed skin and wounds that are healing.

Tip

When carrying out an Indian Head Massage, it is not essential to use any lubricant. If the client has a specific problem or condition, an essential oil blended with a base oil could be incorporated into the treatment. Blends can be made to meet the client's individual requirements.

Health & Safety

Essential oils should never be used undiluted on the skin or scalp. They should only ever be blended by a qualified aromatherapist.

Knowledge review – Oils

1   Is the use of oils essential when carrying out an Indian Head Massage?

Yes/No

2   The first traditional point of application is located

_____

3   You would pour the oil on the _____ for the second application point.

4   It is necessary for the client's head to be well down for the third

point of application because the location is _____

5   Organic vegetable oils are preferred for treatment

because_____

6   Some oils may cause an allergic reaction on certain clients. Name these oils, and state why they may have this effect.

(a) _____

(b) _____

(c) _____

(d) _____

(e) _____

(f) _____

These oils may have this effect because

_____

Massage benefits and manipulations

7

Learning objectives

Essential Knowledge and Understanding NVQ Level 3 areas covered in this chapter are:

- **Correct positioning with regard to avoiding injury to clients and therapists.**

- **Massage technique classifications and their effects on the client.**

- **Application of massage techniques to meet individual client needs.**

The experience and effects of massage

Massage is one of the most enjoyable and relaxing activities one can experience. It is both physically and mentally relaxing. The therapeutic touch relieves stress and the tension of everyday living, leaving a good feeling of well-being and increased energy levels.

Indian Head Massage, which has been practised for thousands of years, benefits the client both physically and psychologically. The treatment manipulates the soft tissue and muscles of the body, and stimulates the blood, the lymph system, the muscles and the nerves. The massage manipulations can have either a stimulating or relaxing effect, depending on the technique carried out.

Physical benefits

Indian Head Massage involves the treatment of the upper back, shoulders, arms, hands, neck, scalp and face. This type of massage can help produce the following effects:

- *General relaxation.*
- *Improved blood circulation* – by warming the tissues massage increases the oxygen supply to the brain.
- *Improved lymphatic flow*, which aids removal of waste products and toxins and thereby helps the immune system.
- *Reduced muscular tension* – massage breaks down nodules and adhesions in the muscles, and releases toxins from tense muscles.
- *Regenerated skin* – layers of the skin are stimulated, which improves their cellular function.
- *Softer skin* – sebaceous secretions are stimulated and the removal of dead skin cells (**desquamation**) is accelerated.
- *Reduced stiffness in the neck and shoulder region*, which relieves pain.
- *Stimulated nerve endings* which relieves muscular pain and fatigue.

When applied to the scalp Indian Head Massage encourages hair growth, and the facial massage helps to relieve sinus problems, eyestrain, headache and insomnia.

Muscles and the joints

- When muscles are working they need a greater supply of oxygen and they produce more waste products, including lactic acid. The waste products may accumulate, particularly after strenuous exercise, and muscle stiffness may occur. Massage increases circulation, bringing oxygen to the muscle tissues, which helps to remove waste products more quickly. By removing the lactic acid that has built up in the tissues, massage relieves muscular fatigue.

- Muscles that are tense and contracted can relax fully when massage is carried out. Regular massage helps muscles to function to their fullest capacity.
- Muscles work over joints. If the movement of joints is impaired by adhesions, for example in the shoulder joint, then the full range of movement will be prevented. Massaging the area can help loosen the adhesions, giving greater mobility in the joints and more movement in the muscles, thereby increasing the range of movement.

Circulation

Massage improves the circulation.

- As the blood supply to the muscles is increased, the temperature rises and the area feels warmer. Redness (**erythema**) appears at the skin's surface. Blood in the veins carries waste, toxins and carbon dioxide away from the tissues; blood in the arteries brings oxygen and nutrients to the cells. Massage therefore helps to promote healthy cells.
- Flow is increased in the lymphatic circulation also, taking other waste products to the lymph glands and helping to combat infection.

Nerves

When massage is performed, it affects the particular area.

- If the movements are gentle, peripheral nerve endings are soothed and the area is calmed and revitalised.
- If the massage movements are brisk, they will stimulate the area.
- Any painful areas, especially around the neck and shoulder region, will be relieved for a time. The pressure applied to these areas will create a numbing effect.

Skin

The skin too benefits from massage. Any massage movement or manipulation affects the skin. As the circulation is improved the sebaceous glands are stimulated to produce more sebum (oil) and the sebum makes the skin soft and supple, and increases its resistance to infection. The skin is 50–70 per cent moisture: sebum coats the surface of the skin, and helps to maintain its moisture content. The sebum slows down evaporation of moisture from the skin, and keeps external water from penetrating into the skin.

During massage, the sudoriferous glands secrete more sweat, which helps to remove waste products from the skin. Massage also rubs away dead skin cells in the outer layer of the epidermis, the stratum corneum. This enables the skin to breathe more easily: tissue respiration improves, and the skin acquires a healthy glow. The sensory nerve endings in the skin can be either soothed to promote relaxation and a sedative effect or stimulated to increase alertness and prevent lethargy.

Lungs

Certain movements (tapotement and percussion) have a beneficial effect on the lung tissue. Improved circulation nourishes the tissues of the bronchioles, increasing their elasticity. This in turn improves the exchange of gases within the lungs, as carbon dioxide is breathed out and oxygen is breathed in.

Massage movements

The movements performed in Indian Head Massage are classified in five groups:

- effleurage, which includes stroking movements
- petrissage, or compressions
- tapotement, or percussions
- frictions
- vibrations.

Effleurage (stroking)

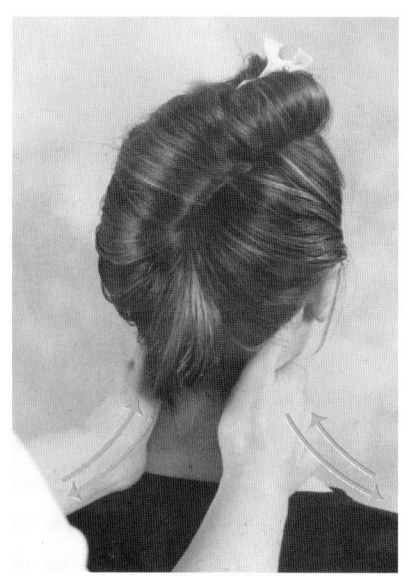

Effleurage

Effleurage is a sweeping, stroking, introductory movement. Its main uses are at the beginning and the end of the massage sequence, and as a connecting or link movement that can be used at any point during the massage procedure. Effleurage introduces clients to massage, allowing them to get used to the therapist's touch, and to become sensitised to the underlying muscles and tissues while the medium is applied to the area so that the whole area is lubricated. Effleurage has a soothing and relaxing effect.

Effleurage can be either superficial or a deep massage movement. It is performed with the palm of the hand and pads of the fingers, depending on the size of the area to be massaged and the amount of pressure to be applied. Relaxed hands mould to the body's contours: the fingers are relaxed and held closely together, and the thumbs are also relaxed and held closely to the first finger.

Effleurage follows the direction of the return of blood through the veins to the heart. Pressure is applied in that direction. On the return movement, less pressure is applied.

Health & Safety

If the client has any medical oedema, this will have a medical cause such as kidney malfunction. In these circumstances, **you must not carry out the massage**.

Benefits

Effleurage:

- has a soothing effect on the nerves (it induces relaxation)
- increases blood and lymphatic circulation
- relieves tension (contracted tense muscles relax)
- aids the removal of dead cells (desquamation)
- helps to reduce non-medical oedema, which is usually due to poor circulation and tiredness.

Petrissage

Petrissage movements are deeper strokes, usually applied with the thumbs, the fingers, or the heels of the hands. Manipulations include *kneading*, *picking up*, *wringing* and *rolling*.

In petrissage the tissue is firmly picked up and lifted from the underlying structures, and then released. The pressure is often intermittent.

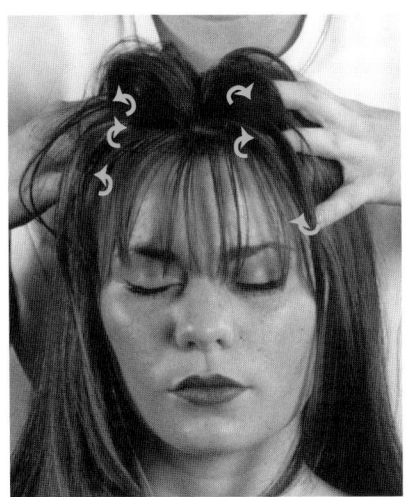

Petrissage

Kneading

Kneading movements may be performed in many ways. The effect can be achieved using both hands, one hand, or just part of the hand (the palms, the thumb or the fingers). The pressure is applied firmly, then released; and the movement is then repeated in an adjacent area. The pressure must always be applied *towards* the heart. Care must be taken to avoid pinching the skin at the end of the strokes.

Picking up

The movement of **picking up** can be performed with one or both hands, depending on the area to be massaged. For example, if movement is to be carried out on the deltoid muscle, then one hand is used and the muscle can be massaged on either side.

The technique is to grasp the muscle with the whole hand, with the thumb abducted. The muscle is lifted away from the underlying structure, squeezed and then released. On relaxation the other hand, without breaking contact, picks up a different part and the movement is repeated along the length of the muscle.

Wringing

In **wringing**, the muscle is lifted from the underlying structures and then moved from side to side across the muscle length, using the fingers of one hand and the thumb of the opposite hand. The tissue is grasped and stretched.

Rolling

In **rolling**, the hands are placed firmly on the area, the superficial tissues are grasped between the fingers and thumbs, and the tissues are gently rolled backwards and forwards against the thumbs and fingers.

Reinforced movements

If one hand or one or more fingers are placed over the other hand or corresponding fingers, this will give a deeper pressure. Any technique done in this way is said to use **reinforced movements**.

Benefits

All of the movements described above relieve muscular tension, fatigue and stiffness. Massage:

- increases blood and lymph circulation
- increases venous return
- breaks down tension nodules in the muscles (thereby helping to prevent the formation of fibrositis in the muscle, especially in the trapezius muscle of the upper back)
- speeds up removal of waste products that have accumulated in the tissues (aids the absorption of fluid, particularly around the joints)
- aids relaxation.

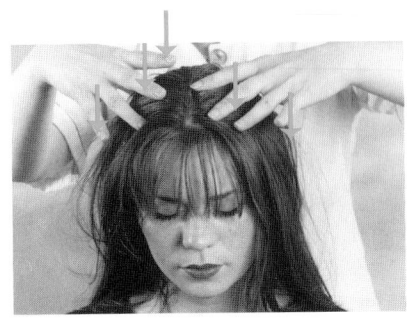

Tapotement

Tapotement (percussion)

Tapotement or **percussion** movements are used to stimulate and tone the area.

Tapotement includes *tapping*, *cupping* (*clapping*) and *hacking* or *champissage*. The client must have the necessary muscle mass if this movement is to be performed: without this, tapotement could be very painful and could lead to bruising, especially in thin or elderly people. These types of movement should be light and springy, and should not cause any discomfort to the client – your wrists need to be loose and flexible.

Tapping

Tapping is performed with the fingertips, which are relaxed. Only *light* tapping should be used. Rhythm is important as the fingers continually break contact with the skin. The movement is very similar to that used when playing a piano.

Cupping

Cupping is performed with the hands forming loose cups: these strike the area being massaged, making a very distinctive clapping sound. Erythema (reddening) is quickly produced, due to the vacuum formed under the palms as they contact the tissues.

Hacking

Hacking is a very fast, light movement. The hands face each other but do not touch, and are usually at right angles to the wrists. The fingers flick against the skin very quickly – normally the outer three fingers do all of the striking – in rapid succession.

Champissage is performed in the same way, but the hands are held together loosely, with the fingers and thumb pads gently touching.

Benefits

These types of movement:

- aid sluggish circulation
- when performed over the thoracic region, can help loosen mucus in chest conditions
- tone and strengthen muscles

Health & Safety

Tapotement movements should not be performed directly over the spine.

- produce a local rise in temperature
- stimulate sensory-nerve endings.

Frictions

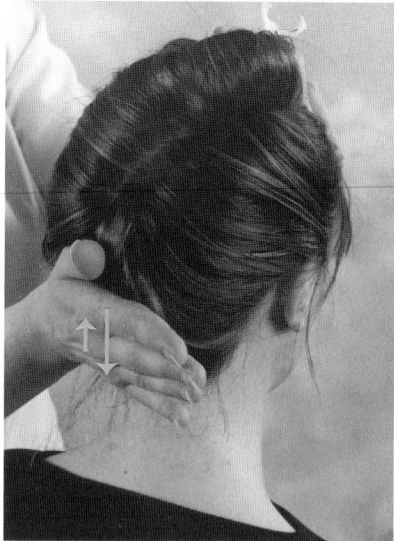

Frictions

Frictions are movements that cause the skin to rub against deeper underlying structures. They are applied in concentrated areas, usually on small areas of the surface tissue.

Benefits

Frictions:

- help to break down thickenings caused by fibrous, fatty deposits
- help to remove tight nodules – in areas of tension, frictions free adhesions, preventing the formation of fibrositis in the muscular tissue (especially in the trapezius muscle)
- aid in the removal of any *non-medical* oedema
- aid relaxation
- increase lymph and blood circulation.

Vibrations

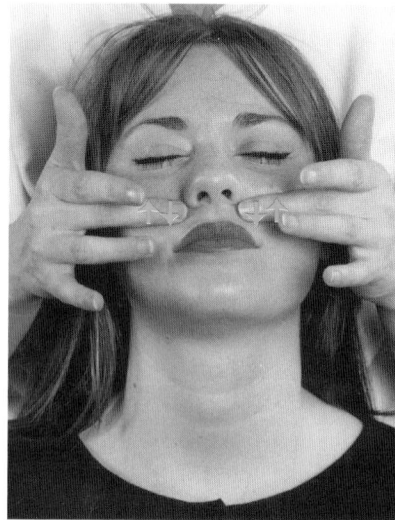

Vibrations – static

Vibrations are used to relieve fatigue and pain, by stimulating the nerves and thereby producing a sedative effect on the area. If performed in one place, they are known as **static vibrations**; if moving up or down, they are known as **running vibrations**.

Vibrations involve fine, trembling movements, which can be performed either with one hand or with both hands. Using the palmar surface of the hand or the pads of the fingers or thumbs, the muscles of the forearm are contracted continually and then relaxed, producing the vibration movements.

Tip

If the client is especially tense around the shoulders and neck region, the therapist should spend more time concentrating on this area and less time on other parts, adapting the massage to suit the client's needs.

Benefits

Vibrations:

- clear and stimulate the nerve pathways
- relieve tension in the neck and back, bringing about relaxation.

Knowledge review – Massage benefits and manipulations

1 The physical benefits of an Indian Head Massage are:

(a) _____

(b) _____

(c) _____

(d) _____

(e) _____

(f) _____

(g) _____

(h) _____

2 The gland, which produces sebum, is called the

_____ gland.

3 The main function of this gland is to:

(a) _____   (b) _____

(c) _____   (d) _____

4 The benefits of effleurage are _____

5 List the types of manipulations included in petrissage.

(a) _____

(b) _____

(c) _____

(d) _____

8

Ayurveda and ayurvedic principles

Learning objectives

Essential Knowledge and Understanding NVQ Level 3 areas covered in this chapter are:

- **The basics of ayurveda and ayurvedic body work.**

The traditional system of medicine in the Hindu religion is based on the balancing of the physical bodily systems and the mental state. This is sought through herbal remedies, yogic breathing, massage, diet and meditation.

Ayurveda, meaning the art of life, is one of the sacred books of Hinduism, and ayurvedic principles stem from its source. The central belief is that all activities in the universe are centred on three basic functions of existence:

- the beginning – creation
- the order of life – organisation
- the end of being – destruction.

These three main centres or energies (also referred to as 'humours') have specific names, locations and associations with the elements. They are called:

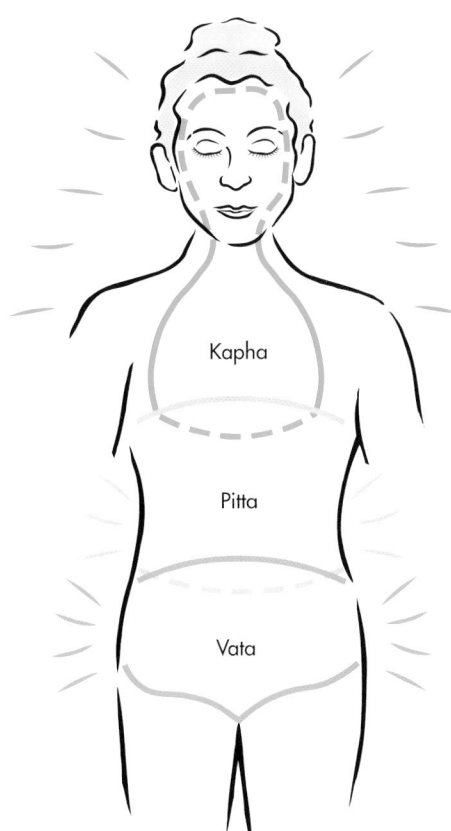

The three main centres of energy

- kapha, situated in the chest, but also covering the neck and head
- pitta, situated in the area of the solar plexus
- vata, situated in the abdomen.

Ayurvedic practitioners believe it is the balancing of these three energies that holds the key to physical, mental and spiritual well-being and health.

Kapha, pitta and vata all have sub-catorgories branching out and overlapping each other. They often share the same site, covering different aspects in order to promote balance and harmony, such as the stomach sharing pitta-pachaka and kapha-kledaka.

Kapha

Representing water and earth, kapha is concerned with maintaining and protecting the whole body. Kapha sub-divisions are:

1   *Kledaka.* Sited in the stomach, to protect and balance the hot fiery effects of pachaka.

Kapha – water and earth

2   *Avalambaka.* Protects against the wear and tear of the major organs – i.e. the heart, lungs, and also the spinal column.

3   *Bodaka.* Sited in the mouth and concerned with protecting the sensitive lining and taste receptors, to ensure the full and proper taste of food.

4   *Tarpaka.* Found in the spinal cord protecting the central nervous system and ensuring mental peace.

5   *Shleshaka.* Housed in the joints to protect them from the wear and tear of everyday movements.

Pitta

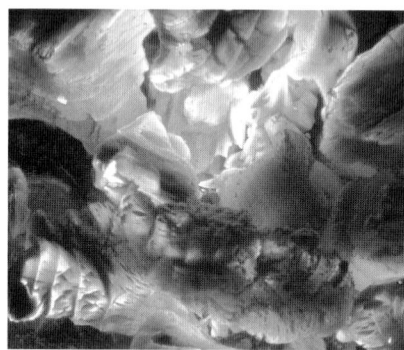

Pitta – fire

Representing fire, pitta is concerned with digestion and metabolism. Pitta sub-divisions are:

1   *Pachaka.* Found at the site of the stomach, it helps the digestive process.

2   *Ranjaka.* Found at the site of the liver, it is responsible for efficient liver function – i.e. digesting and processing waste products.

3   *Sadhaka.* Extends from the heart to the brain and is responsible for subsuming (digesting) knowledge and for sustaining cognitive memory.

4   *Alocchaka.* Sited in the eye, it helps towards clear vision, as we absorb (digest) the world around us.

5   *Bharahaka.* Present in the organ of the skin, the digestion of bharahaka is interpreted as the absorption of beneficial oils through the skin.

Vata

Vata – air and ether

Representing air and ether, vata is concerned with controlling destruction. Vata is shown as occupying the abdomen area in diagrammatical form, but vata's five sub-divisions cover a much wider field:

1   *Prana.* Life energy, mainly concerned with all the sense organs and respiration.

2   *Undana.* Relates to upward movements, and this energy is concerned mainly with memory and speech.

3   *Vyana.* Circulatory system, concerned with the distribution of nutrients throughout the body.

4 *Samana.* Digestion and metabolism, concerned with maintaining a balance within these two bodily systems.

5 *Apana.* The lowest sub-division of destruction, and concerned with the actions of the intestines and other organs in the pelvic region.

The basis of ayurvedic thought is that all life comes from, is part of and belongs to the universe, and at the end of its existence it is returned there. Seeking a true balance both within the individual's mental and physical state, and with the common environment, is the living goal of ayurvedic students.

The study of ayurvedic principles is a very wide field with many diverse opinions and dedicated students can access these using the internet.

Knowledge review – Ayurveda and ayurvedic principles

1   According to ayurvedic principles, what are the three basic functions of existence?

(a) _____ (b) _____ (c) _____

2   Name three main centres of energy:

(a) _____ (b) _____ (c) _____

3   The 'humour' that is concerned with maintaining and protecting the whole body is _____

4   What is the living goal of ayurvedic students?

To seek _____

9

Marma therapy

Essential Knowledge and Understanding NVQ Level 3 areas covered in this chapter are:

- **The principles and location of marma points in the treatment area.**

- **Note that specific marma therapies must only be given by qualified ayurvedic practitioners, as undue pressure on these points can be harmful.**

Practitioners of marma therapy believe in the existence of a series of energy channels running through the body, with centres located at specific points. This belief is very similar to the concept of a network of meridians and acupressure points found in the study of acupuncture and acupressure therapies.

Marma point therapy involves a search for a balance within the body, mind and spirit, seeking to achieve a calm flow of energy coupled with a strong feeling of connection with the five major elements and the universe, through massage techniques and meditation.

The five elements of earth, fire, water, air and ether follow the same order as these elements in the study of chakras,

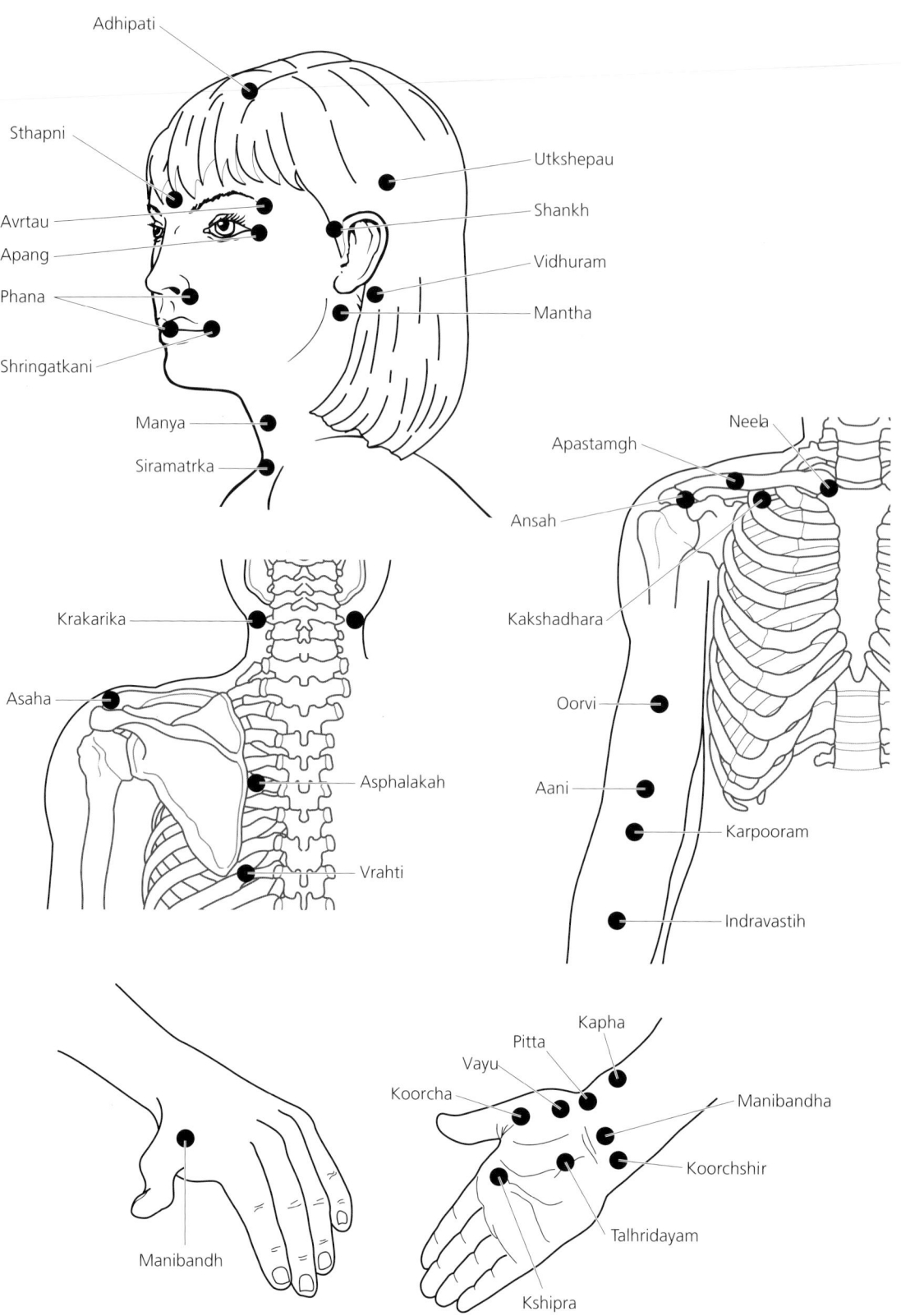

Marma points

but have a slightly different area of the body as their focal point. The five areas are:

- earth – from the ground to the knees
- water – knees to the anus
- fire – anus to heart
- air – heart to forehead
- ether – forehead to crown.

These areas can be grouped into three named regions:

- *Legs and feet*. Sankha marma, encompassing 11 marmas on each leg.
- *Trunk and arms*. Madhayamanga marma, encompassing abdomen 3, chest 9, arms 22 and back 14.
- *Head and neck*. Jutrurdhara marma, encompassing 37 marma points.

One of the principles of marma therapy is that the practitioner can control the various organs and bodily systems associated with each marma point. This is an extensive specialist study, as there are over 100 major and minor points on the body.

Marma practitioners use differing amounts of pressure on these points depending on the ailment to be treated, they also use herbs mixed to specific 'recipes', warmed and placed in a cloth bag on the relevant marma point.

The distance between marma points is measured in finger widths termed anguli or angula.

Massage application

The main marma points, their Sanskrit name, and specific location, found in the treatment area of an Indian Head Massage are set out in the following sub-sections.

Head, face and neck

- *Adhipati*. Measure eight anguli from the eyebrows to the highest point on the head.
- *Sthapni*. In the centre of the forehead (Third Eye chakra position).
- *Avrtau*. At the outer end of the eyebrow.
- *Apang*. At the outer corner of the eye socket.

- *Utkshepau.* Two anguli above the ear on the temporal–parietal border.
- *Vidhuram.* Behind the ear lobe on the occipital bone.
- *Mantha.* One anguli below the ear lobe.
- *Shankh.* Immediately above the zygo-manbibular hinge, in front of the ear.
- *Shringatkani.* At each corner of the mouth.
- *Manya.* On the neck, either side of the larynx.
- *Siramatrka.* At the base of the neck, above the medial end of the clavicle.
- *Phana.* Inside the mouth and accessed externally through pressure at the base of the nostrils.

Shoulder girdle and upper arm, anterior aspect

- *Neela.* The joint of the clavicle and sternum.
- *Ansah.* The joint of the distal end of the clavicle and the scapula.
- *Apastamgh.* Three anguli along the clavicle towards the sternum.
- *Kakshadhara.* Two anguli below apastamgh below the clavicle.
- *Oorvi.* The mid-point along the muscle between the triceps and biceps.

Shoulder girdle, posterior aspect

- *Krakarika.* Mid-point of neck either side of CV 3.
- *Asaha.* The point where the scapula articulates with the clavicle.
- *Asphalakah.* The inner wing of the scapula, at a mid-point.
- *Vrahti.* Either side of the spine at the eighth thoracic vertebrae.

Those therapists wishing to include forearm and hand massage in an Indian Head Massage will also cover the following additional marma points.

Arm

- *Aani.* On the inside of the arm just above the elbow hinge.

- *Indravastih.* On the inner forearm midway between the wrist and elbow.
- *Karpooram.* On the inner crease of the elbow.

Wrist and hand

- *Manibandha.* Centrally on the first crease of the inner wrist.
- *Koorchshir.* One anguli from manibandha, towards the little finger.
- *Koorcha.* Central point on the thenar eminence.
- *Talhridayam.* One and a half anguli from manibandha, between the thenar and hypothenar eminences.
- *Kshipra.* On the upper pad of the palm between the second and third metacarpals.
- *Manibandh.* On the back of the hand at the base of the first dorsal interosseous.
- *Vayu.* At base of the thumb, at the edge of the thenar eminence.
- *Pitta.* One anguli from vayu towards the elbow (over the pulse point).
- *Kapha.* One anguli from pitta away from the thumb.

Conclusions

The gentle flow of pressure over these points during an Indian Head Massage helps to relieve tensions and associated minor aches and pains. To have an influence on named conditions and the different systems of the body, a specific full course of study should be undertaken as this is a very extensive and involved subject demanding in-depth research and long course hours. Students studying ayurveda will find it a fascinating and sometimes frustrating study as many texts disagree due to the method of transfer of knowledge over many years through different routes of communication and a general unquestioning acceptance of the ideologies and beliefs rooted in it. The central theme of channels of energy and a need to balance the body within itself and with the spirit and the universe is, however, widely accepted and shared with other ideologies.

Knowledge review – Marma therapy

1   Marma therapy seeks to achieve a balance between

_____ , _____ and _____

2   What is the collective term for the marma points located in the head and neck?

_____ marma.

3   Which marma point is located at the same spot as the chakra Third Eye?

_____ marma.

4   Measuring eight anguli from the eyebrows towards the top of the head would bring you to the location of the

_____ marma point.

10

Chakras and Indian Head Massage

Learning objectives

Essential Knowledge and Understanding NVQ Level 3 areas covered in this chapter are:

- **The seven primary chakras in relation to Indian Head Massage.**

- **Basic principles and practices of chakras.**

Those who give Indian Head Massage will benefit from a growing understanding of the underlying theory. The study of energy forces around human beings, and the network of channels within the body known as chakras, is too extensive to be discussed in depth here, so this chapter provides a brief introduction only. As you practise the massage techniques, you are advised also to become more informed about the ancient Eastern thoughts, beliefs and therapeutic practices. You will find whole areas of self-awareness and healing opening up, both to yourself and to your clients.

Chakras

The ancient Sanskrit word *chakra* means 'wheel'. Another Sanskrit word, *nadis*, denotes the network of channels which converge at the chakra centres. Often this convergence is described as a spinning vortex: the vortex is believed to exist a few centimetres away from the body.

Chakras are also referred to as **lotus flowers**. Each has a specific number of petals, leaves or spokes; and each of these petals is a given Sanskrit letter. The lowest chakra, the **Root**, has four petals. The next, **Sacral**, has six. Then come **Solar Plexus**, 10; **Heart**, 12; **Throat**, 16; the **Brow**, with two divisions each with 48 petals (96 in total); and finally the **Crown**, with 1000 petals. Interlinking these seven major chakras are many minor ones, including the palms of the hands and the soles of the feet.

In Indian Head Massage we are specifically concerned with the Crown, the Brow and the Throat. These cannot be separated from the rest of the chakras, however: the whole system works together, each chakra sharing equal importance, and all linked to a central channel running from Root to Crown.

Balancing the chakras

The balancing of chakras is concerned with achieving a balance within each chakra; it is not concerned with balancing one chakra against another. Each chakra focuses on a different aspect of existence as detailed in the following sub-sections.

1. Root chakra – survival

The Root chakra is referred to as the prime chakra as it is concerned with survival, without which all else is irrelevant. The Root chakra is the focus of all consciousness, survival within the environment and a feeling of connection with the earth. This chakra is balanced by a feeling of oneness with the environment. To balance this chakra we should seek out somewhere in our personal environment where we can feel a sense of 'grounding one's being' – feeling the shared energy of the plants, trees and flowers around us. This may be in a public park or somewhere along a favourite local walk, or simply in our own garden. If none of this is possible in a physical sense, we can visit our chosen place in our imagination in order to feel this exchange of energy, through imagining roots going deep into the ground providing two-way channels.

2. Sacral chakra – sensations

The second chakra is the chakra of the world of sensations and the pursuit of pleasure. It is concerned with the pursuit of pleasurable sensations; it is easy to misplace the focus of this chakra and to emphasise the pursuit, rather than the sensations of pleasure.

Practise balancing this chakra though everyday experiences, slowly savouring your favourite food, consciously being aware of the pleasure derived from listening to music, viewing a garden or smelling a perfume. Drink in the pleasure of the moment by closing your eyes and feeling the deep sense of balance, satisfaction and completeness.

Nurture the 'feel good factor'; to experience interactive pleasures it is important that you feel alive and conscious of your inner attractions. To help you to recharge your inner brightness, try to allocate some time each week for a little self-indulgent pampering. Book yourself a relaxing massage using oils to suit your personality and needs, or set the scene in your own bathroom, with music, candles and a tub full of warm scented water. Relax, and put away all your worries and thoughts of 'jobs to do' in an imaginary basket outside the bathroom door. Focus your mind on the pleasurable sensations of soft lights, scented warmth and music – sink into them and fully enjoy this experience.

This awareness of pleasurable sensations balances the second chakra.

3. Solar Plexus chakra – will power, strength of character

The third chakra is the chakra of self-control and the drive for personal power. This chakra is where personal standards and ethics are formed; it is the seat of your will power, where choices are made and codes of honour developed. This is where courage and strength will be developed to support your own ideals and convictions.

4. Heart chakra – love in all its forms

The fourth Heart chakra is concerned with love in all its forms, personal and universal – love as a generous, joyful feeling reaching out to achieve harmony with those we interact with in our daily lives.

This is the first chakra where we move towards experiencing unity with all life, leaving the separateness of the three lower chakras. The Heart chakra is where the lower chakras of personal energy, identity and survival meet the higher chakras, connecting self to the universal energy. It is at the Heart chakra that the three upper and lower chakras merge into all-encompassing levels of reality.

5. Throat chakra – creative expression

This is the fifth chakra and it encompasses creative expression in all its forms, covering all aspects of artistic creation, appreciation and expression. It is through exploring this chakra that creative thought and ideas are formed and released, stimulating responses from those around us.

Learn to acknowledge your own creativity through balancing this chakra. This may be through the generally accepted routes of art, writing and music, or balance may also be achieved through creative thought and the expression and exchange of ideas. When the Throat chakra is balanced, creative ideas are born and trivial thought diminishes.

6. Third Eye

Located in the centre of the forehead, the sixth chakra is concerned with the desire for transcendence. This chakra looks for an awakening of a reality beyond that of everyday life.

On a lower level this chakra is balanced through simple escapism – a good book, film, play or television programme. Performed on a higher level a connection is sought with the divine, through spiritual quests and a meditative state of mind.

7. Crown chakra

This chakra focuses on the divine spirit of the universe. The belief that all things come from, and are returned to, the universe is held by many religions. Each individual will find their own pathway to seek out this oneness between the creation of the individual and the divine universe.

A useful general visualisation would be of the lower chakras developing and stabilising the person and their identity – gathering the energies of survival, character and purpose; flowing through to the higher chakras where the energies of love, sharing, meditation and creative awareness are developed through interaction with others around us; and, finally, to the Crown where the collective energies reach out to help and comfort those in contact with us through a feeling of calm exchange.

Relating massage to chakras

The relationship between effective Indian Head Massage and chakras starts at the beginning of the treatment. Clients are asked to adopt the recommended sitting position: as well as maximising muscle relaxation, this balanced position helps to open up the central channel of energy flow. Similarly, the therapist begins by emptying the mind of all thoughts except those centred on the treatment to be given. The 'rooted' or 'grounding' stance, and the light touch of the hands on the crown of the head, all contribute in opening up the channels of communication and 'healing' between the therapist and the client.

The therapist asks the client to take three deep breaths (*with* the therapist), in a controlled manner. This has a connection with the beginnings of chakra awareness and the first breathing exercise. After giving a treatment, therapists often experience a feeling of well-being and increased energy levels, but they may feel drained and tired. This is consistent with the view that when energy channels between people are indeed open, an exchange can take place, with strength being drawn where a need exists.

Working with the three higher chakras at the conclusion of an Indian Head Massage can help to restore harmony and energy, leaving clients feeling mentally alert, rejuvenated and peaceful.

To experience your own energy field, open and close your hands making a loose fist. Do this several times, then bring your hands towards each other with the palms facing. You should feel a slight resistance, or a tingling sensation. Try this with a friend – you can detect a response from *their* energy field.

It has recently been suggested that an eighth chakra may exist, between the Brow and the Throat. This has been given the name **Alter Major** meaning 'other rather than higher'. Note that terminology varies: you may find books that refer to the Sacral chakra as the Hara or Spleen, for example, and the Brow chakra as Ajna or the Third Eye.

The seven major chakras

The seven major chakras are associated with elements and colours.

Chakra	*Element*	*Colour*
1 Root – pelvis/coccyx	Earth	Red
2 Sacral – abdomen	Water	Orange
3 Solar Plexus – stomach	Fire	Yellow
4 Heart – chest	Air	Green
5 Throat	Ether	Blue
6 Brow – forehead	Mind	Indigo
7 Crown – very top of the head	Spirit	Violet/white

The colours given in the table are only a guide, as colours are not fixed with these locations – different colours, or combinations of colours, may be experienced whilst working with any chakra. Trainee therapists often record in their case studies the colours seen by their clients during treatments.

The seven principal chakras

Knowledge review – Chakras and Indian Head Massage

1 Which are the three chakras that Indian head massage is most concerned with?

(a) _____ (b) _____ (c) _____

2 The significance of the correct client sitting position with regard to chakras is _____

3 Which chakra is balanced through meditation?

4 The Crown chakra focuses on _____

11

Massage technique

Learning objectives

Essential Knowledge and Understanding NVQ Level 3 areas covered in this chapter are:

- **The importance of maintaining client modesty and privacy.**

- **The importance of allowing time for client questions and discussion during the consultation process.**

- **The importance of post-treatment advice and recommendations.**

- **The importance of not naming suspected contra-indications when advising clients to seek medical advice.**

- **The reasons why it is important for clients with a suspected contra-indication to visit their GP.**

- **Contra-actions are explained, plus care of the client who may experience a contra-action and the importance of recording contra-actions.**

Consultation

Tip

Consultation should not be hurried, but should be kept to relevant issues, allowing time for client questions and answers.

Before giving an Indian Head Massage, it is essential to consult with the client. This is the therapist's opportunity to establish a rapport with the client and to gain and to give information.

The consultation should only be carried out in a private area or room. It is important that your clients do not feel embarrassed or vulnerable, they must feel comfortable and able to relax; remember that clients with different cultural backgrounds and personal views on privacy must be respected. Assure clients of your concerns regarding client modesty and privacy at all times, particularly if clothing is to be removed. Explain your salon's policies and practices on confidentiality, in order to allay any concerns they may have.

As the therapist, you should discuss this treatment, explaining its benefits. An important part of the consultation process is to discuss the client's expectations and gain their agreement on the possibilitities and limitations of these expectations. You should also explain that **contra-actions** may be experienced after treatment. These are reactions to the treatment – for example, if oils are used, the client's skin could show a reaction such as irritation, swelling or sensitivity. Other possible contra-actions include sickness, dizziness, extreme tiredness, and in some cases fainting.

During the consultation, encourage the client to ask questions about the treatment and to voice expectations of this treatment. The consultation helps to give the new or the nervous client confidence in the therapist, and to allay any anxieties they may have about the treatment to be given. Many new clients will be unaware of the areas of the body covered by this treatment and the options available to them. The option of including the forearm and hand should be discussed and noted on the client's records. During this time you can make a visual check for any obvious skin conditions in the area to be treated.

Fill in a consultation form, checking all details carefully. The form should record the name, address and telephone number of the client, and of his or her doctor. It should also record recent relevant medical history, any localised contra-indications and any abnormalities in the treatment area. The form must also allow space for the client to acknowledge that a contra-indications checklist has been used and completed.

Tip

Before starting the
massage, you need to be
calm and relaxed. Try to
shut out anything that may
distract you, and to focus
on the client.

Tip

Fragrances may be
beneficial during the
treatment. For example, an
oil can be used in the
massage, burned in a
burner or in a perfumed
candle, or used in a room
spray.

During the consultation process, if a contra-indication is
discovered this must be handled sensitively by the
therapist who should allay any fears the client may have,
give him or her advice on the importance of visiting their
general practitioner whilst firmly assuring the client that
they will be very welcome for a treatment when the
condition has cleared or on the GP's recommendation. Note
that therapists must not be drawn into offering a diagnosis
of *any* condition which they think the client may have as
this could jeopardise future relationships with other
professionals, and could result in litigation. All suspected
contra-indications must be clearly entered in the client's
record file, dated and signed by the therapist.

On pages 131–133 you will find examples of a consultation
sheet, and of an accompanying contra-indications checklist
plus further examples of combined formats. You may wish
to use these as they are, or to compile your own based on
these.

After the treatment, allow a few moments to gain valuable
feedback from your client. All relevant points should be
entered in the client's records so as to enable repeat
performance of particularly enjoyable movements, and to
make adaptation or omissions of others. Client records
play an important part in the efficiency of the salon by
providing and improving the development of personal
treatments. They also guarantee continuity of individual
requirements should any future treatment be given by
another therapist.

Looking after yourself

When you deal with several clients one after the other, you
need to 'switch off' between them. You will then feel less
tired at the end of the day. Do not take on your clients'
problems. Listen to them, but try when they have gone to
lay aside what they have told you. Otherwise you will
become too involved, and eventually you will become
emotionally and physically drained.

INDIAN HEAD MASSAGE

Consultation sheet

Client's name .... Doctor's name ....

Address .... Address ....

....

....

Telephone number .... Telephone number ....

Occupation ....

Have you completed a contra-indications sheet? Yes/No

Have you received any hospital treatment in the last
six months? Yes/No

Have you experienced an Indian Head Massage before? Yes/No

If yes, how often do you have these treatments:

Weekly ☐   Twice a week ☐   More often ☐   Occasionally ☐

Client's signature   Therapist's signature
(confirming details and
permitting safe storage)

....

Date ....

INDIAN HEAD MASSAGE

Contra-indications consultation sheet

1	Any recent head or neck injury	yes/no
2	Severe bruising in treatment area	yes/no
3	Epilepsy	yes/no
4	Recent haemorrhage	yes/no
5	High or low blood pressure	yes/no
6	Migraine	yes/no
7	History of thrombosis or embolism	yes/no
8	Diabetes	yes/no
9	Spastic condition	yes/no
10	Dysfunction of the nervous system	yes/no
11	Skin disorder	yes/no
12	Scalp infection	yes/no
13	Cuts or abrasions in the treatment area	yes/no
14	Recent operations	yes/no
15	Chronic ME sufferer	yes/no
	Any other condition that may affect massage	yes/no

Client's signature   Therapist's signature
(confirming details and
permitting safe storage)

....

Date ....

INDIAN HEAD MASSAGE

CONSULTATION FORM

Client's name .... Date of birth ....

Address ....

.... Telephone ....

Doctor

....

Address ....

.... Telephone ....

ANALYSIS	PRECAUTIONS & CONTRA-INDICATIONS	
Occupation	Any recent head or neck injury	yes/no
Smoker	Severe bruising in treatment area	yes/no
Diet	Epilepsy	yes/no
Exercise	Recent haemorrhage	yes/no
Stress (0–10)	High or low blood pressure	yes/no
Energy (0–10)	Migraine	yes/no
Sleep	History of thrombosis or embolism	yes/no
General Health	Diabetes	yes/no
	Spastic condition	yes/no
	Dysfunction of the nervous system	yes/no
	Skin disorder	yes/no
	Scalp infection	yes/no
	Cuts or abrasions in the treatment area	yes/no
	Chronic ME sufferer	yes/no

Medical history/medication

....

....

Main focus of treatment

....

....

Declaration
I certify that the above statements are true and correct and that I have
been fully informed and advised of the treatment to be undertaken. I
agree to the treatment offered by my therapist.

Client signature .... Date ....
(confirming details and permitting safe storage)

Therapist signature ....

INDIAN HEAD MASSAGE

The lower section of this sheet can be detached and given to the client

CONTRA-INDICATIONS CONSULTATION SHEET

1	Any recent head or neck injury	yes/no
2	Severe bruising in treatment area	yes/no
3	Epilepsy	yes/no
4	Recent haemorrhage	yes/no
5	High or low blood pressure	yes/no
6	Migraine	yes/no
7	History of thrombosis or embolism	yes/no
8	Diabetes	yes/no
9	Spastic condition	yes/no
10	Dysfunction of the nervous system	yes/no
11	Skin disorders	yes/no
12	Scalp infections	yes/no
13	Cuts or abrasions in the treatment area	yes/no
14	Recent operations	yes/no
15	Chronic ME sufferer	yes/no
	Any other condition that may affect massage	yes/no

Details ....

....

Client's signature   Therapist's signature
(confirming details and
permitting safe storage)

....

Date ....

These are only some of the benefits you may experience

Stress relief   Relaxation
Psychological uplift   Improved sleep patterns

Aftercare for 24 hours – strongly recommended

Drink plenty of water or herbal teas   Eat a light diet
Relax whenever possible   Avoid alcohol

Salon's name   Therapist's name

....

Telephone ....

Massage procedure

Make sure that your client is sitting in an upright position on a low-backed chair. The chair back should be no higher than the base of the client's shoulder blades (the scapulae).

Sitting position

The spine should be straight, the legs uncrossed, and the feet flat on the floor. The arms should be relaxed and the hands resting comfortably in the lap.

If practicable, clients should be asked to remove their shoes.

Hygiene

Wash your hands.

Sitting position

Tip

The client's spine should remain in an upright balanced position throughout the treatment allowing for the maximum relaxation of the muscles and the free flow of energy through the nadi yogic/marma or meridian channels.

Preparing

1 Centring – mental preparation

Tip

Take this opportunity to clear your mind, opening up energy channels between you and your client.

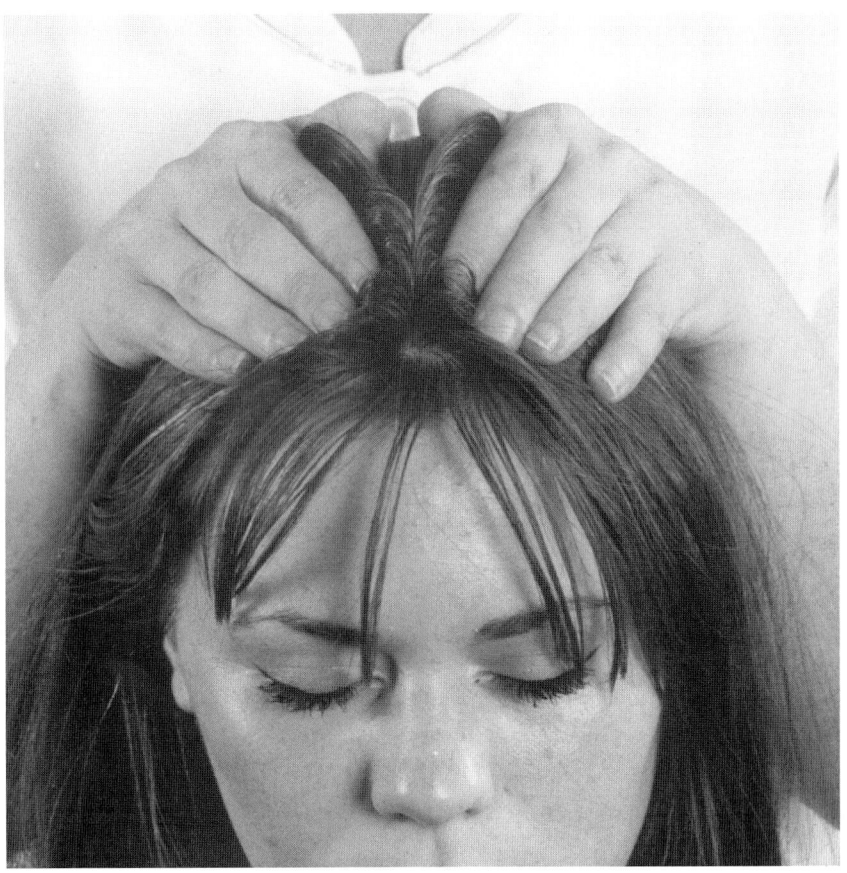

Centring

a When you are ready to start, stand behind your client, with your feet planted a hip-width apart.

b Take a moment to focus your mind. Relax, and very lightly place your hands on top of the client's head. Breathe slowly and easily.

Hold for approximately 10 seconds.

2 Head-rock stress detector

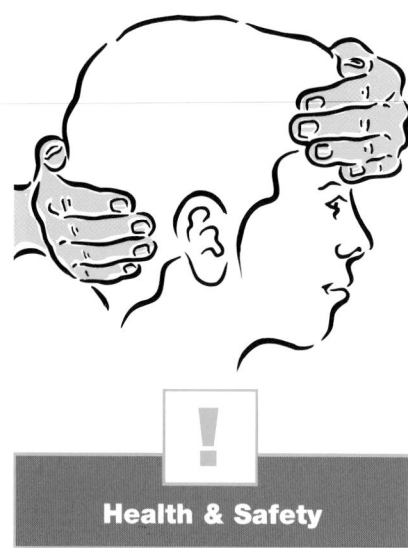

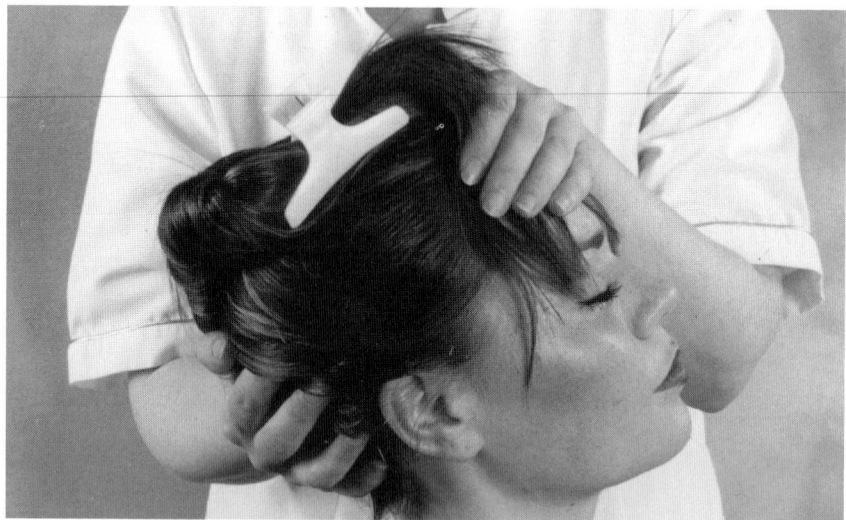

Head-rock stress detector

a Move to stand on the left of the client, moving your left hand to rest along the forehead and over the hairline, and glide your right hand into position across the nape of the neck.

b Gently move the head forwards and then backwards, returning it to the upright position.

c Invite the client to take three deep breaths with you, breathing in through the nose and out through the mouth.

d The head should move more easily now. If it is still stiff after this sequence this indicates muscle tension and signs of stress. Adapt the massage by increasing the number of repetitions whilst working on the shoulders.

One movement; three breaths; then two more movements.

Shoulder massage

3 Thumb sweeps

Marma points covered – vrahti, asphalakah and krakarika.

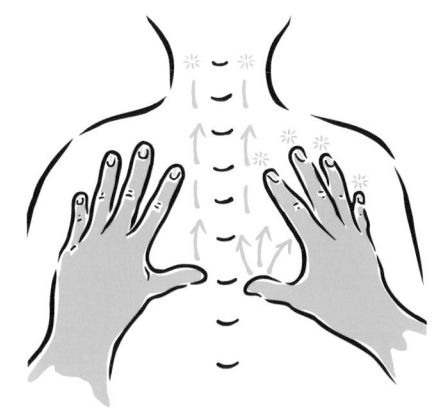

Tip

Check pressure with client at this point.

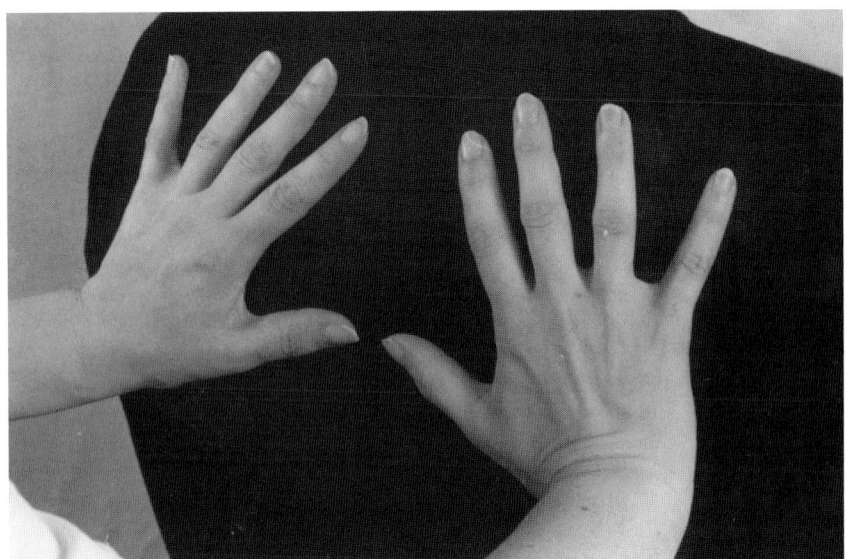

Thumb sweeps

a   Place the little fingers of both your hands on the outer corners of the top of the shoulders (roughly where the seam of a garment would be). Fan your fingers out and reach down the back as far as possible with your thumbs.

b   Draw your thumb to your little finger, describing a semicircle. Repeat, sweeping to the ring or middle finger, and then to the index finger. As you make these three sweeps, work towards the root of the neck.

c   Lastly, place your thumbs on either side of the spine, opposite the base of the scapula. Push upwards, ending at the occipital bone.

Carry out each movement three times using both hands at once. Gradually progress towards the spine and finish at the occipital bone. Increase your pressure with each repeat.

4 Heel rub

Marma points covered – vrahti and asphalakah.

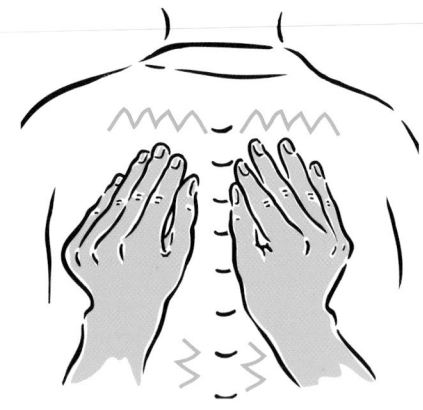

Tip

On very slight clients or children you may use the themar eminence and the length of the thumbs by turning your hands in order to carry out this movement.

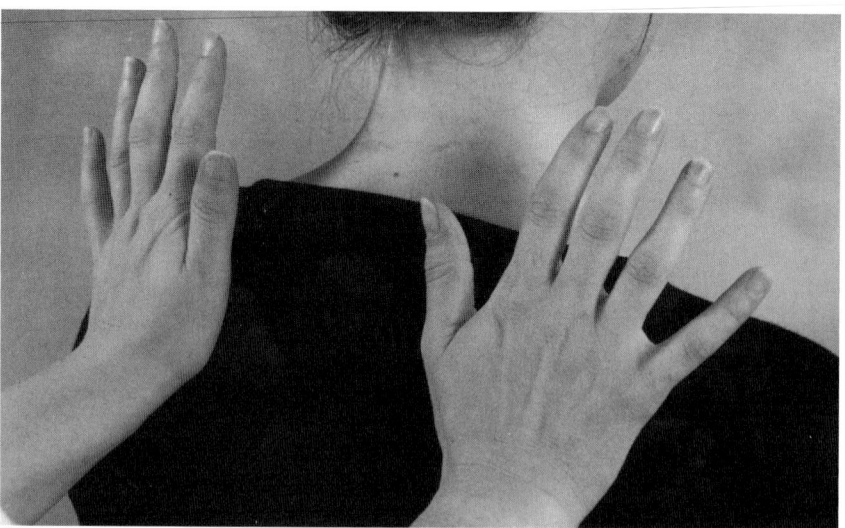

Heel rub

a Using the heels of your hands and starting at the base of the scapula, describe a horizontal zig-zag between the spine and the scapula. Change to vertical zig-zags along the area above the scapula, working out towards the shoulders.

b Relax your hands and glide smoothly down to the starting point.

This movement warms and relaxes the trapezius muscle.

Carry out the whole movement three times.

5 Thumb pushes

Marma points covered – ansah, apastamgh and neela.

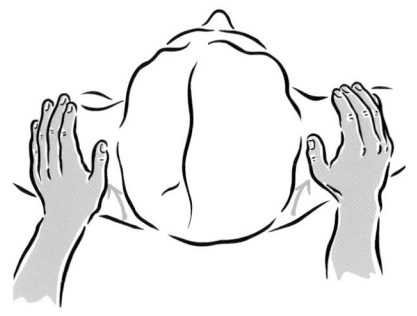

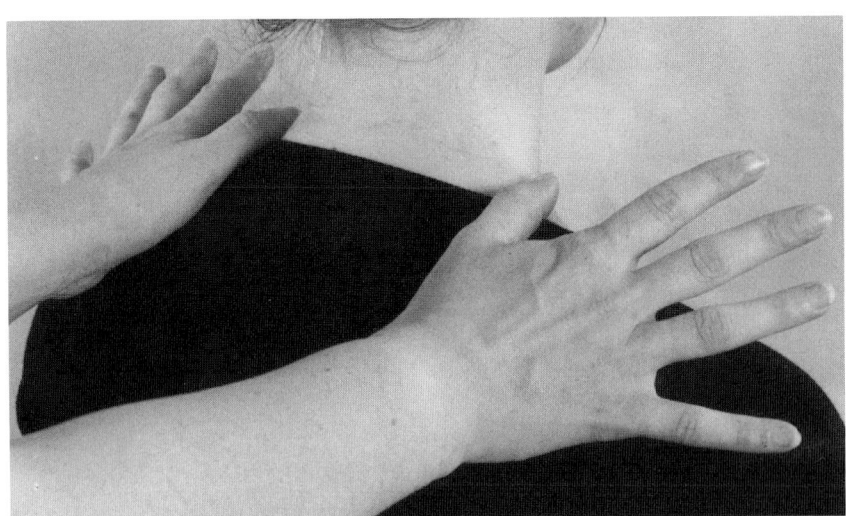

Thumb pushes

For this movement, work over the top of the shoulder (across the garment seam area) from the back to the front.

a Place your thumbs at the shoulder corners, above the scapula, and gently push forward over the ridge of the trapezius muscle.

b Carry out each movement three times before moving on to a mid-point, followed by the last series of movements at the base of the neck.

Use the thumbs only, with both hands together, working from the shoulders to the base of the neck.

Carry out each movement three times, then move on.

6 *Finger pulls*

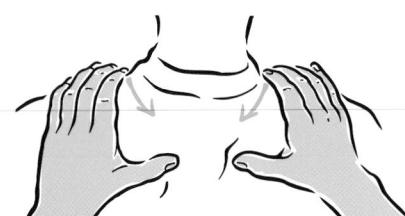

On larger clients you may prefer to use the heel of your hand instead of thumb pushes. If so, use the balancing movement of finger pulls to complete the sequence.

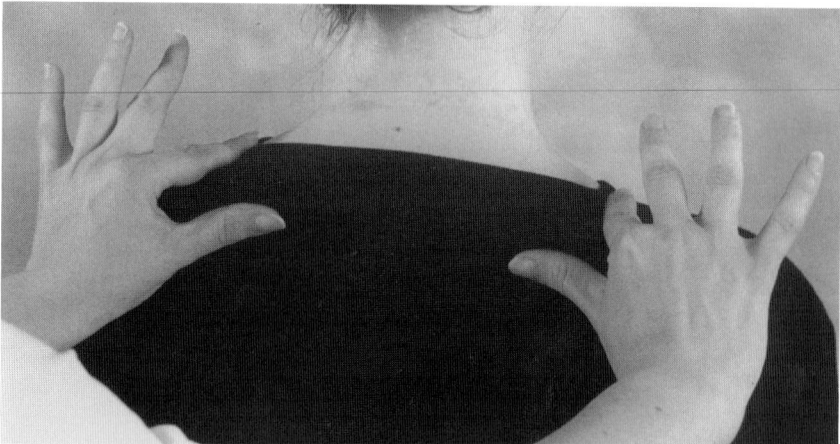

Finger pulls

a Using your index finger, perform the opposite movement to the thumb pushes, drawing your finger over the top of the shoulder. You may feel more balanced if you place your thumb behind the shoulder as an anchor, drawing your finger towards it.

b Move along in three stages, working your way towards the shoulder corners once again.

c Start at the base of the neck, and work in three stages towards the shoulder corners.

7 Champissage – hacking

Marma points covered – vrahti and asphalakah.

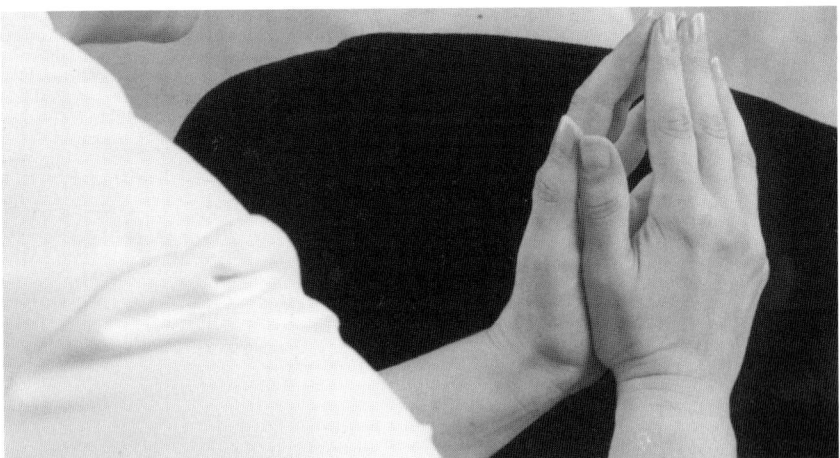

Champissage (hacking)

Health & Safety

Do not carry out any hacking movement over the spine.

Champissage is a gentle form of hacking. Hold your hands in a praying position, then relax them, leaving the heels of the hands and the fingertips in contact. Use this 'cage' of fingers and a loose wrist movement to gently perform this sequence.

a Starting at the base of the scapula, and following its shape to the shoulder corner, progress along the top of the shoulder to the base of the neck. Return along this path to your start position.

b Glide across the spine, and follow the same pattern on the opposite side.

Carry out each pattern three times on each side.

8 Pick up and hold

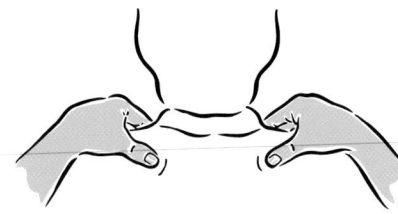

Tip

Muscle should be picked up as near to the bone as possible.

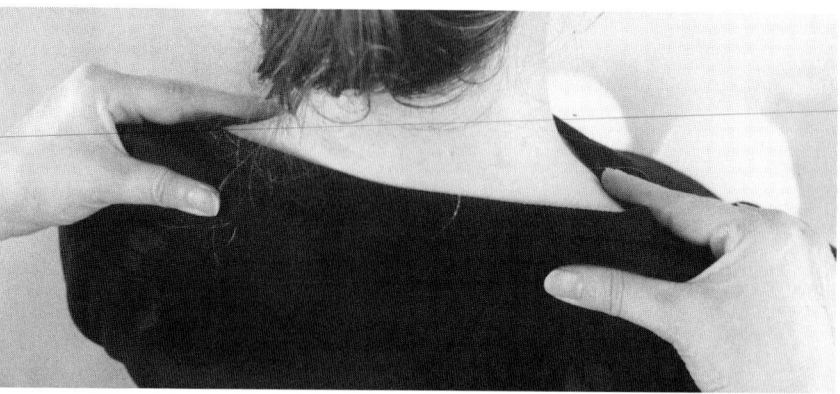

Pick up and hold

This sequence is performed over the top of the shoulder along the trapezius, taking care not to nip the skin.

a Pick up the muscle at the outer corners. Hold it for a few seconds, then release it and move along towards the neck to a mid-point between the outer corner and the base of the neck. Pick up the muscle and hold it again.

b Move to the base of the neck to perform the last movement.

Carry out this whole sequence three times.

9 Smoothing down

Marma points covered – mantha and asaha.

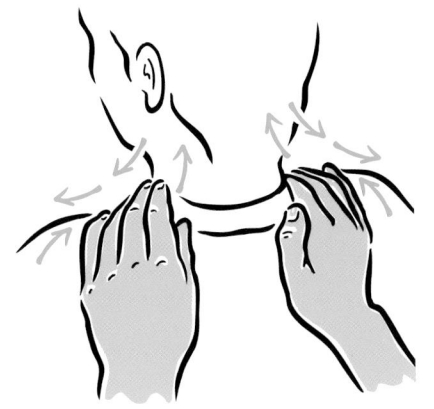

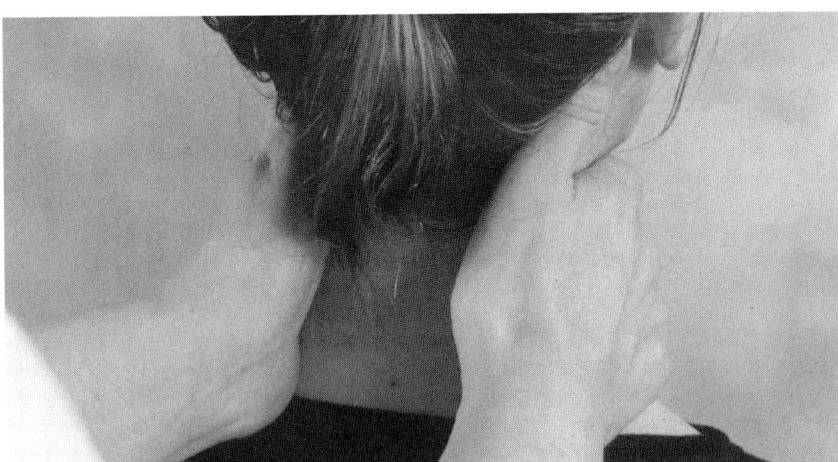

Smoothing down

a Starting at the shoulder tips, use the whole of your palmar surface to make a long sweeping movement, along the shoulder, up the neck until you reach the occipital bone (just below the ears), and back again to the starting point. Use a gentle pressure on the upwards sweep, releasing it on the way down. This movement should flow.

b You *may* also wish to smooth the trapezius across the back of the shoulder. With your forearms placed together, and the backs of your hands facing the client, make a loose fist. With a rolling movement, turn both arms together and move outwards towards the client's arms, ending with your palms facing the client.

Carry out this movement three times.

Upper-arm massage

Marma points covered when massaging the upper arm – oorvi and aani.

10 Ironing down

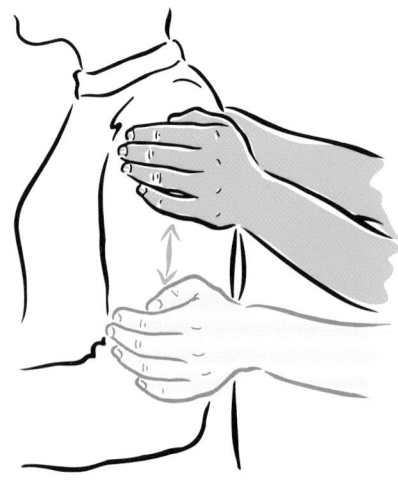

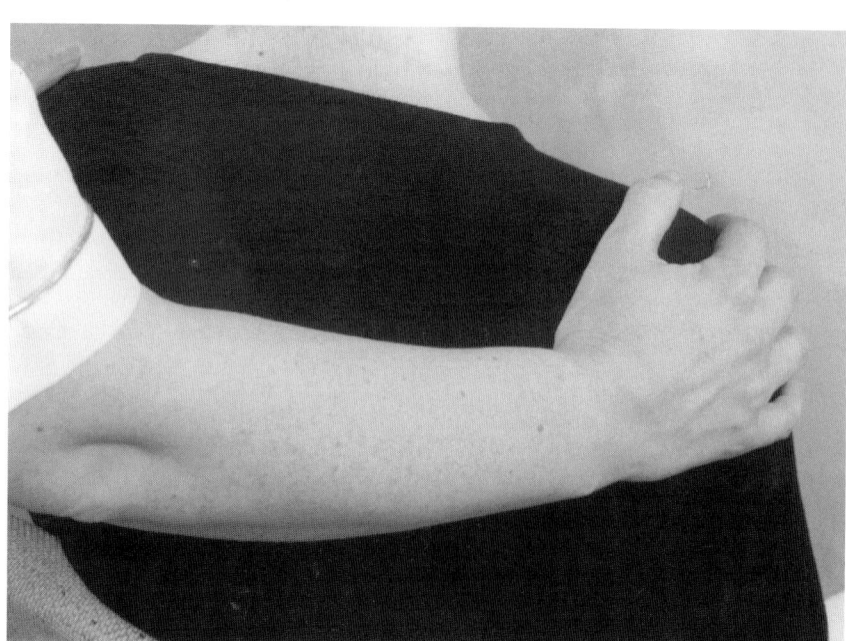

Ironing down

a Linking directly from your last movement, and still using the palmar surface of the whole of your hand, carry the movement down the arms to the elbow, and up to the shoulder again on the lateral line.

b Repeat on the anterior and posterior line of the upper arms. Use gentle pressure from the elbows up to the shoulders, releasing pressure as you go downwards.

Carry out each movement three times before moving on.

11 Heel roll

For this and the following movement maintain a wide stride stance; bend your knees as you work down the arms, keeping a straight back to protect from injury.

Tip

Try to keep your fingers fairly straight, so that your nails do not dig into your client's arms.

Take a wide, stride stance. This will make the movement easier to carry out.

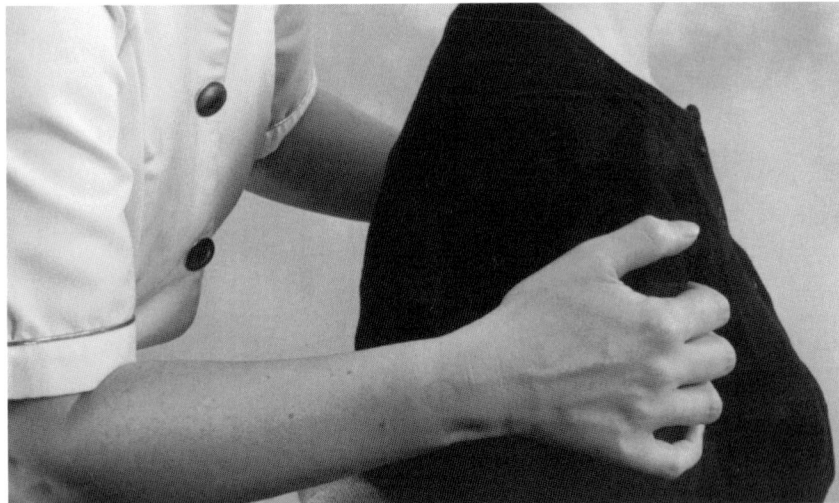

Heel roll

a Using both hands together, place your hands around the upper arms near the shoulder joint, with the heel of your hand behind and your fingers in front. Roll the heel of your hand around the arm towards the fingers.

b Repeat this at a mid-point, moving down the arm, and again just above the elbow.

Carry out each movement three times.

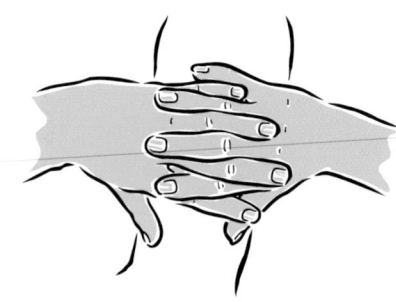

Tip

To avoid nipping the muscle, practise letting the muscle slowly slip out of your grip.

Bend your knees, keeping a straight back. This will allow you to place your hands correctly for this movement.

12 Squeeze and pick away

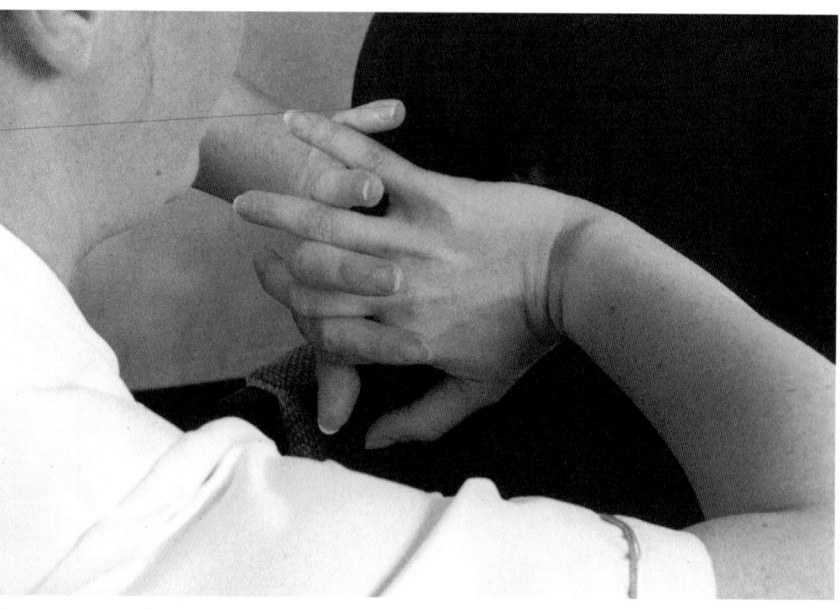

Squeeze and pick away

Clasp your hands, interlocking the fingers. Turn your wrists so that the palms face the client.

a Standing at the side of the client and facing the forearm, pick up the deltoid between the heels of the hands. Gently squeeze it and lift it away, letting the muscle slip out of your grasp.

b Follow the same pattern of movements as in **11**.

Carry out the movements three times at each point.

Optional forearm and hand massage

Therapists wishing to achieve an NVQ 3 qualification in Indian Head Massage will find that the massage routine now includes the option of extending the upper arm massage to include the forearm and hand. After qualifying the therapist will decide whether or not to offer this extended treatment as part of their services. The benefits of Indian Head Massage will be unaffected by the inclusion or exclusion of these additional movements.

However the decision should rest initially with the client, although therapists should be aware that the inclusion of these additional movements will extend the time of the treatment and this should be taken into account when costing this service. Therapists who offer a manicure service to clients may also wish to consider the economics of duplicating an important part of this service within another popular treatment.

Therapists wishing to include the arm and hand massage should do so after point 12 of the routine. Complete each arm and hand and replace it in the client's lap before continuing with the shoulder lift (routine 13).

12a Arm and hand massage

Marma points covered – forearm: indravastih and kapha; hand: pitta, vayu, koorcha, kshipra, talhridayam, koorchshir and manibandha.

(i) Effleurage

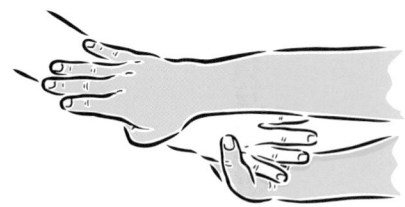

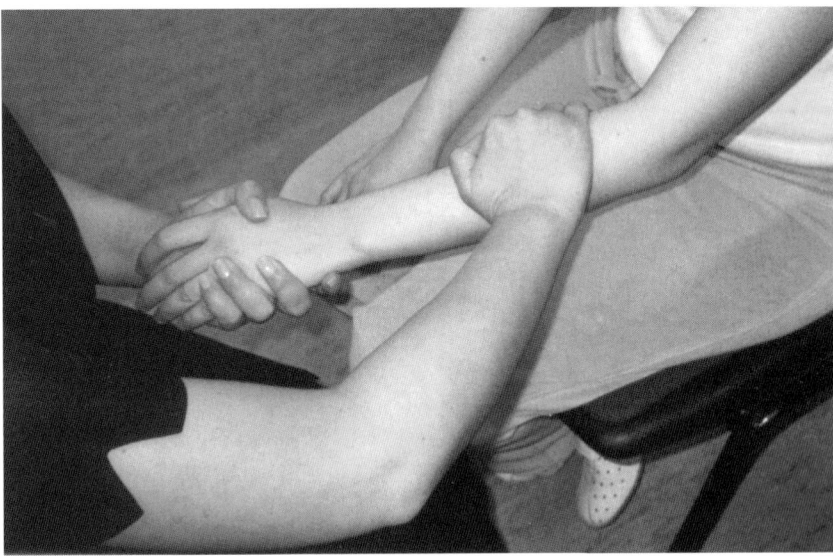

Effleurage

Standing facing, and to the side, of the client, hold the client's hand as though shaking hands, and with the opposite hand perform an effleurage movement on the whole arm. Repeat a minimum of three times.

(ii) Thumb petrissage

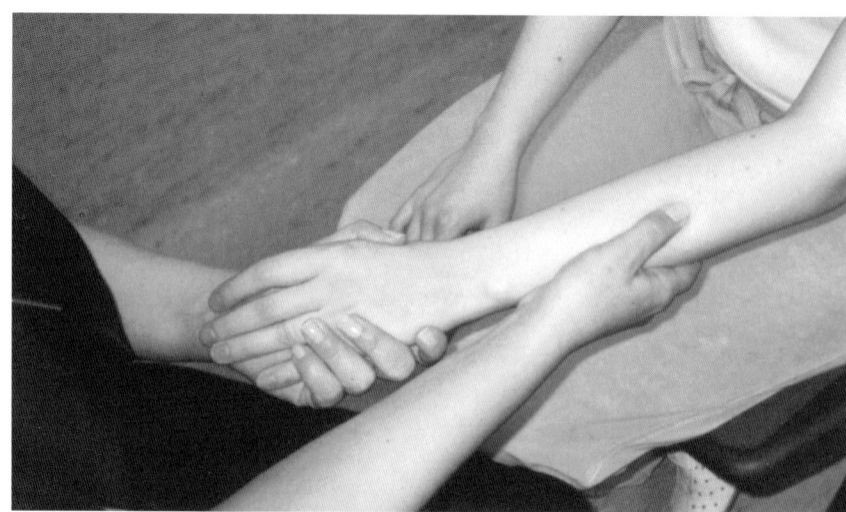

Thumb petrissage

Performed on the lateral surface of the forearm. Using your thumbs, perform a smooth movement with medium pressure from the wrist to the elbow, working between the extensors and flexors of the lower arm. Work your way down to the wrist using small circular petrissage movements. Repeat (i) effleurage

(iii) Wrist rotation

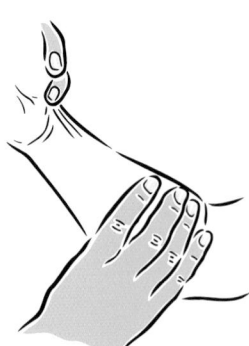

Wrist rotation

Using one hand to support the client's forearm, hold the client's fingers of that hand and gently rotate the wrist in a clockwise then anti-clockwise direction.

(iv) Frictions across the wrist

Frictions across the wrist

Perform brisk frictions using both thumbs across the pronator quadratus muscle of the wrist. Anterior and posterior surfaces.

(v) Thumb petrissage to the palm

Thumb petrissage to the palm

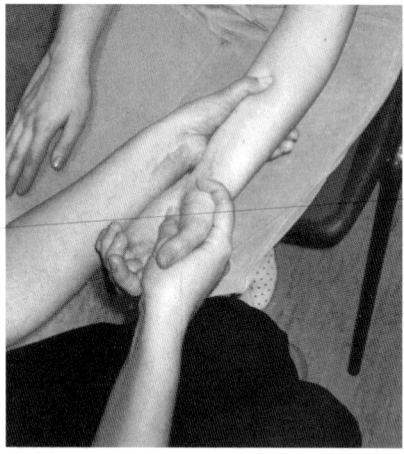

Repeat thumb petrissage

Using the thumbs, perform petrissage movements to the thenar and hypothenar eminences of the palm.

(vi) Repeat thumb petrissage (ii)

Repeat to the forearm on the anterior surface.

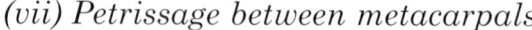

(vii) Petrissage between metacarpals

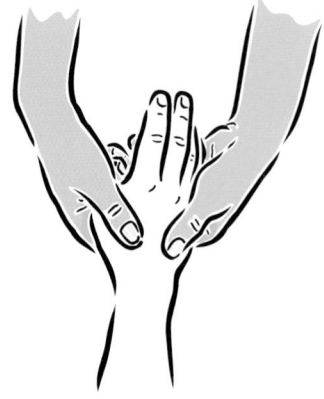

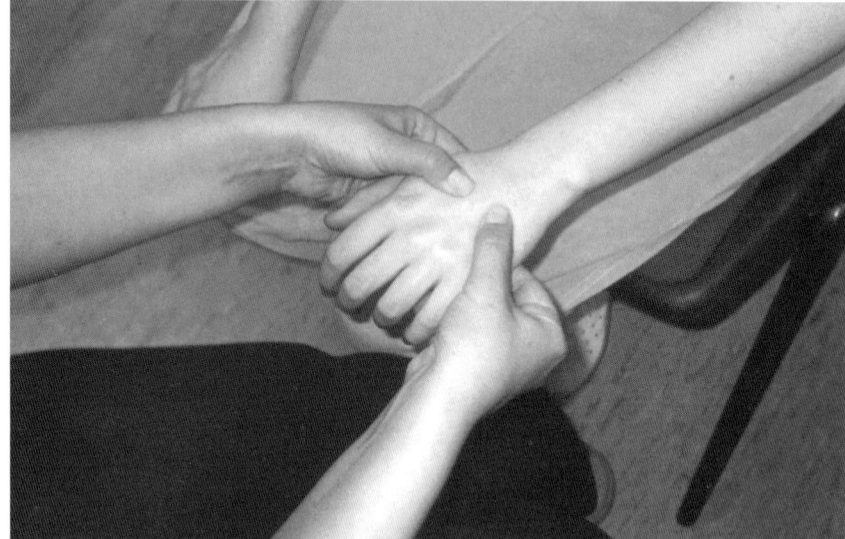

Petrissage between metacarpals

Using the thumbs and working between each alternate metacarpal, push up from the knuckles towards the wrist, and circle down using small petrissage movements.

Complete the movement by picking up and working down each digit in turn, using the index and middle fingers. With the client's finger held snugly at the base, work towards the finger tip with a rocking movement. Keep these movements smooth and continuous by gliding up the hand and picking the next digit up on the way down until all the fingers have been massaged.

(viii) Effleurage

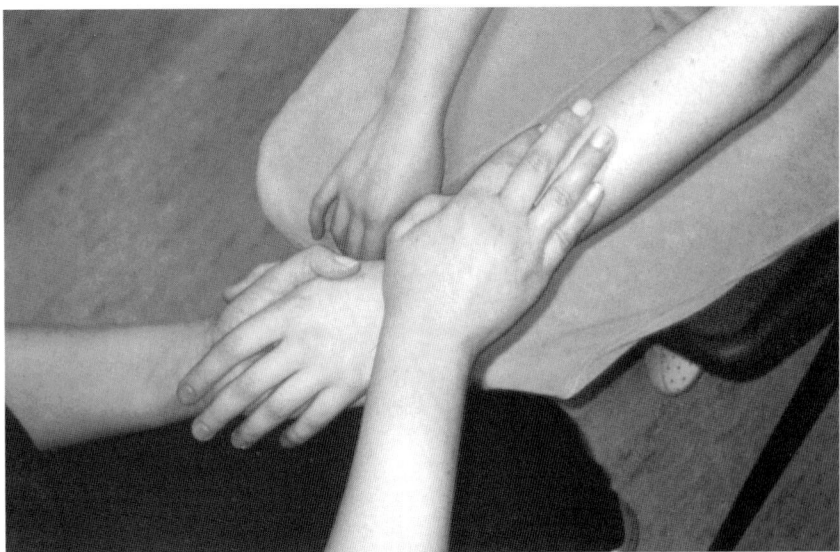

Effleurage

Finally, repeat a full-arm effleurage, replacing the hands in a relaxed position on the client's lap.

Maintaining continuity and flow

After completing the massage on one arm, lightly trail your fingertips up the arm along the shoulders and down the other arm ready to continue.

13 Shoulder lift

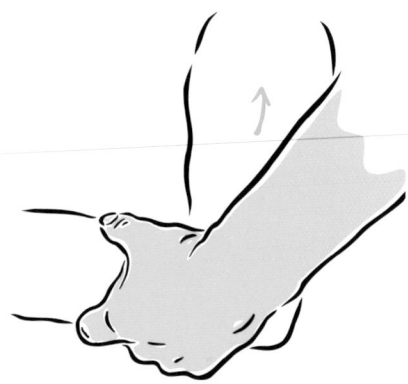

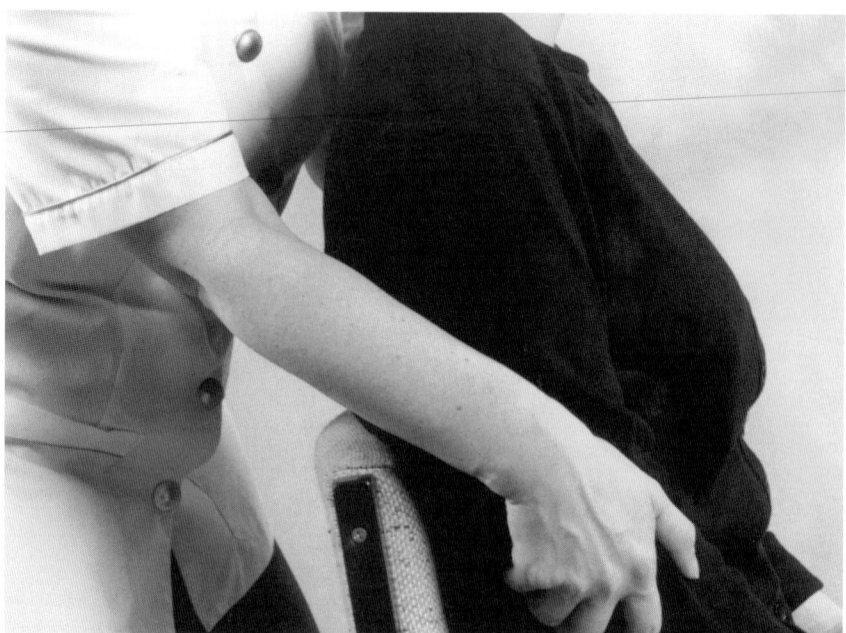

Shoulder lift

Tip

Keep the client's elbows in to the sides whilst performing this movement.

a Slide your hands down the upper arms and hold the forearms just under the elbows.

b Keeping the arms close to the side, lift the arms upwards as far as is comfortable, and gently return them to the resting position.

This movement helps to relax the shoulder joints.

Carry out the lift three times.

Neck massage

14 Grasp and pull back

Marma points covered – krakarika and mantha.

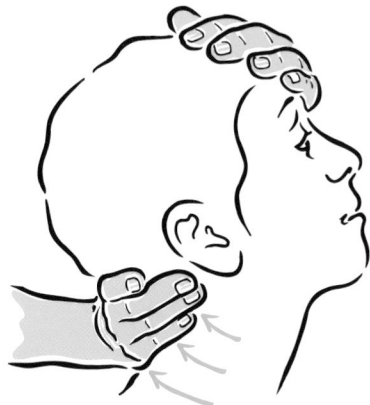

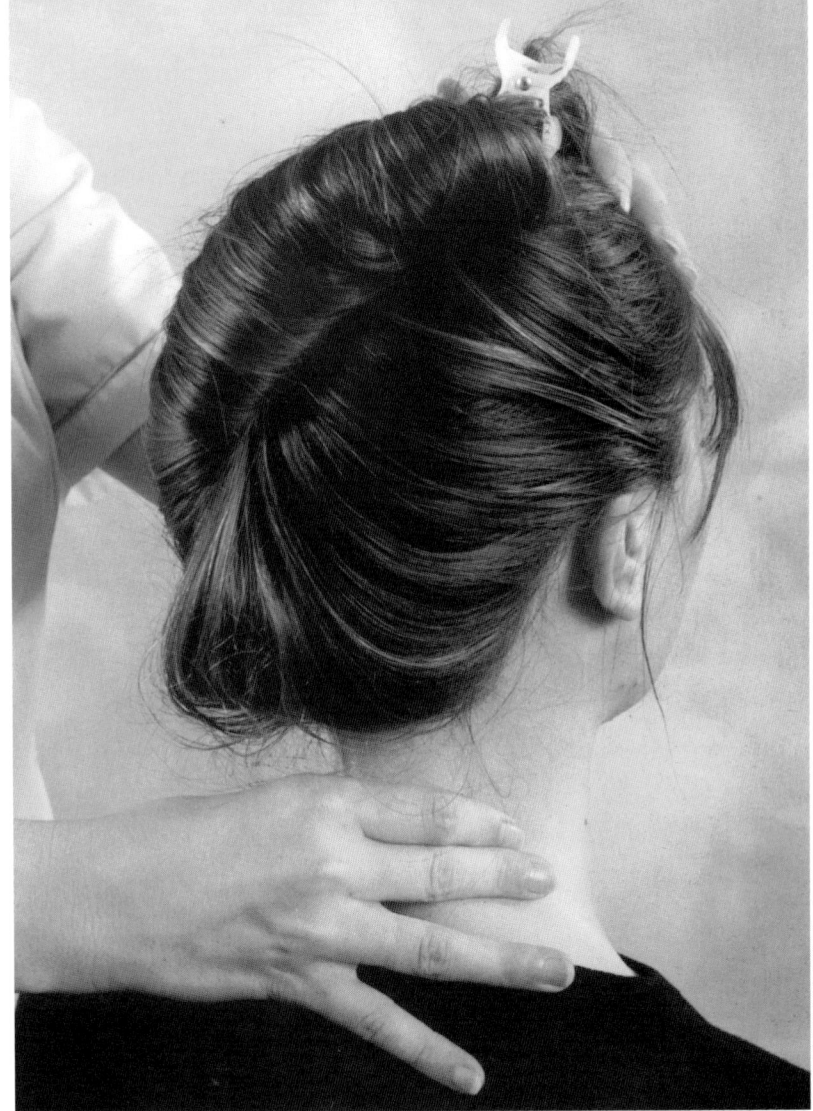

Grasp and pull back

Tip

For effective treatment it is important to keep the head tipped slightly backwards, as this keeps the upper part of the trapezius muscles relaxed.

a Stand to the side of the client, and place one hand on the forehead, just overlapping the hairline.

b Tip the head slightly backwards.

c With the other hand, grasp the back of the neck just under the occipital bone. Spread your hand as far as possible.

d With a slightly upward movement, draw your fingers and thumb together in a picking movement.

e Repeat at the mid-point and at the base of neck.

Carry out each movement three times.

15 Thumb pushes

Marma points covered – mantha.

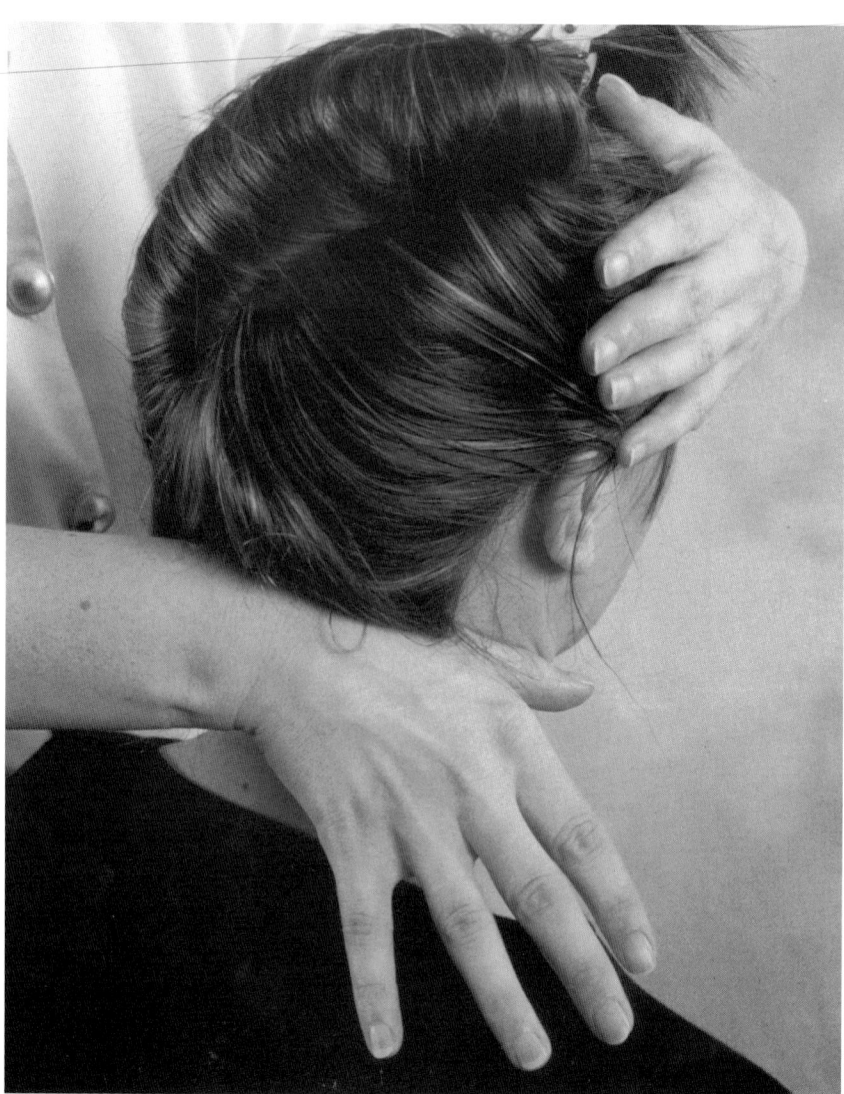

Thumb pushes

a Stand to the *left* of the client. Lean the head slightly to the *right*, supporting it with your *left* hand on the client's forehead above the *right* eye. (This will relax the muscles on the *right* side of the neck, where you are going to work using your *right* hand.)

b Using the pad of your thumb and firm, but not heavy, strokes, work across the side of the neck. Start just under the ear, then move to a middle distance, and lastly to the base of the neck.

16 Finger pulls

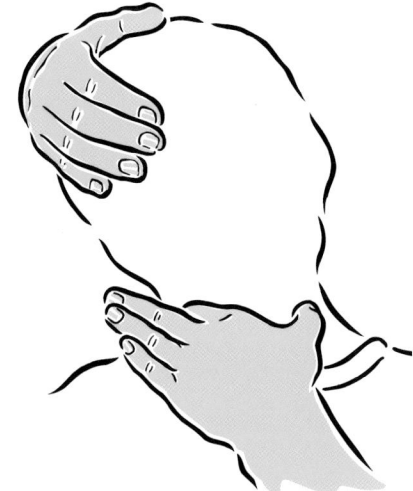

You may find it awkward at first working with the head held away from you, instead of towards you. However, it is important to maintain this position in order to keep the muscles you are working on in a relaxed position. Practice will soon help you to master these movements.

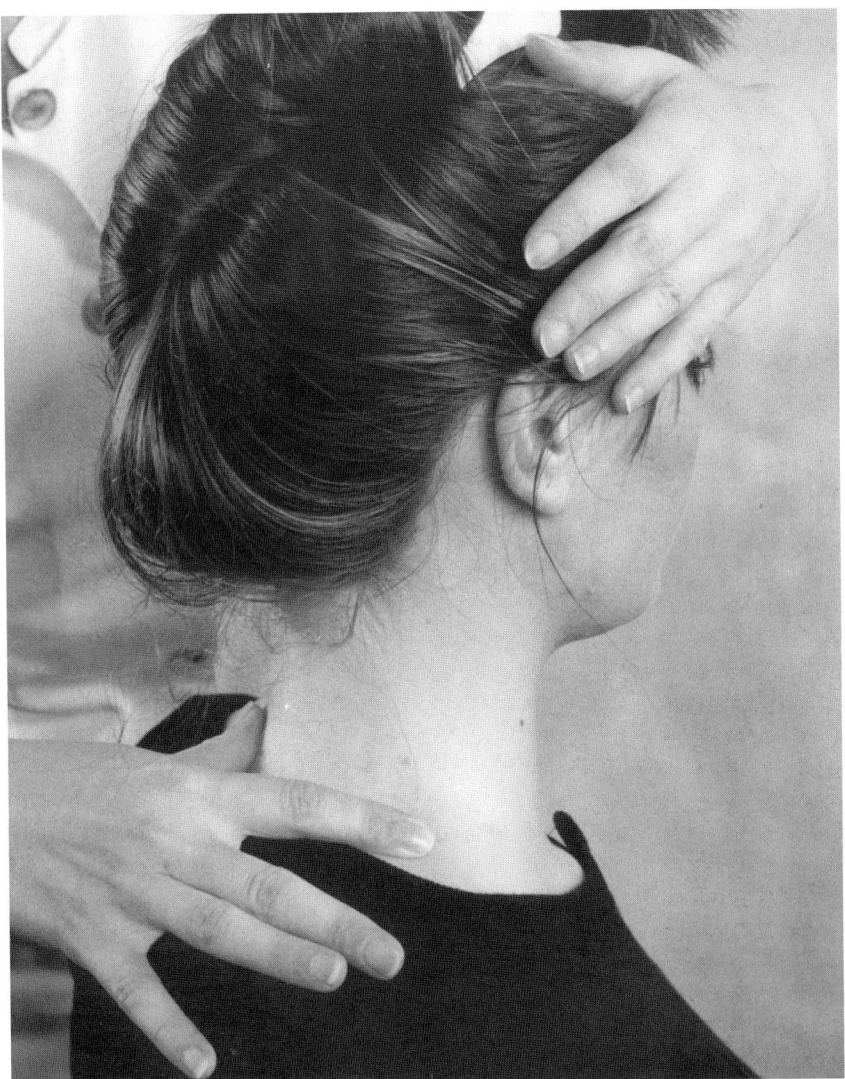

Finger pulls

a Maintaining your stance as for thumb pushes, complete the movement by drawing your index finger from front to back across the same areas of the neck as before. Start at the base and end under the ear. (You may find it useful whilst doing this movement to place your thumb at the back of the neck to act as an 'anchor'.)

Carry out each movement three times, before moving on to the next area.

17 Repeat thumb pushes and finger pulls: opposite side

a Repeat the movements **15** and **16** on the opposite side.

18 Friction under occiput

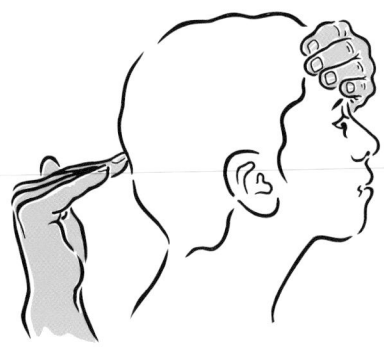

Marma points covered – vidhuram and mantha.

Use the pads of the fingers for this movement. Bend the hands at the knuckles, trying to keep your fingers as straight as possible. Let the movement come from a bent elbow, to resemble the movement of a windscreen wiper.

a Support the head along the forehead using the opposite hand.

b Using a horizontal friction movement, work across the back of the neck on the occipital bone. Move from ear to ear.

19 Heel-of-hand rub

Health & Safety

Keep this movement short and confined to the occipital ledge, as an extended action may result in striking the top vertebrae of the spine and causing injury.

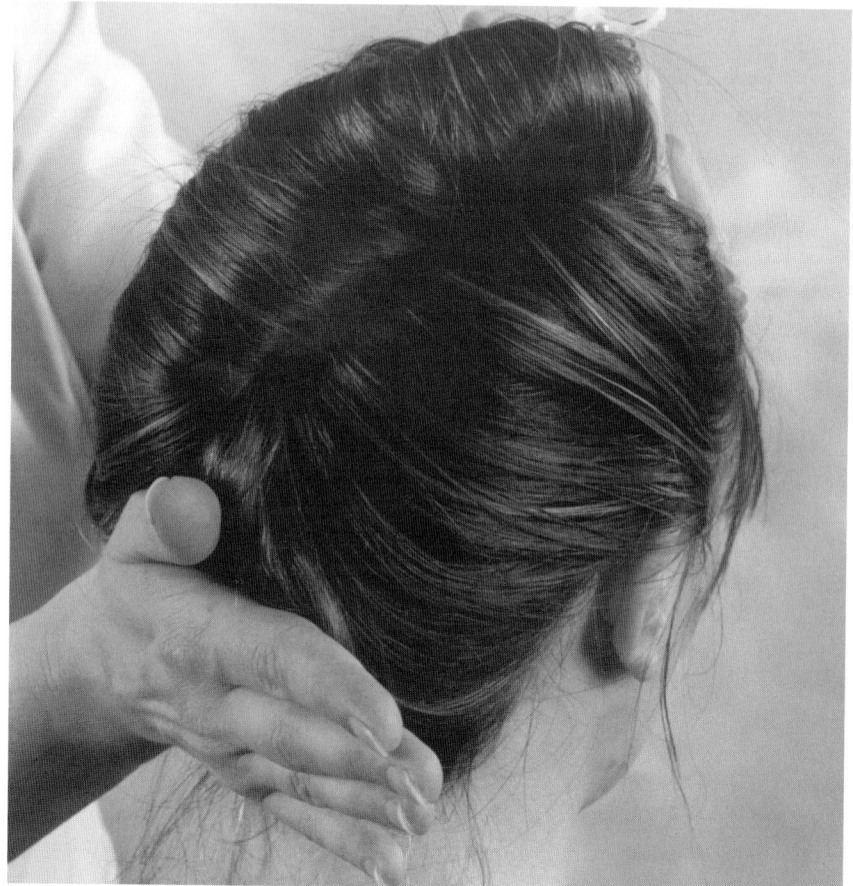

Heel-of-hand rub

a Stand to the side of the client, and support the head at the forehead.

b Use the heel of your hand to execute a vertical friction movement along the base of the occipital bone.

The friction movements carried out in steps **18** and **19** help to relieve congestion that can lead to headaches.

Scalp massage

20 *Windscreen wiper*

Marma points covered whilst carrying out the scalp massage movements 20–28 are shankh, utkshepau, vidhuram and adhipati.

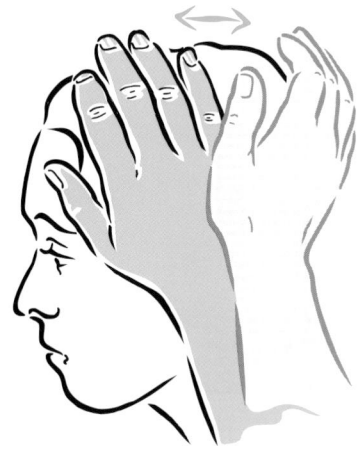

Tip

If long hair has been clipped up, remove the clip at this point.

Tip

This is a stimulating yet relaxing movement.

Windscreen wiper

a Stand to the side of the client, and support the head at the opposite side.

b Use the heel of your hand to describe a short, quick, wiping friction movement.

c Starting around the ear, make your zig-zag movement from the hairline to the nape and back again, describing semicircles as you move gradually up the scalp towards the centre of the head.

Change sides and repeat.

21 Whole-hand friction

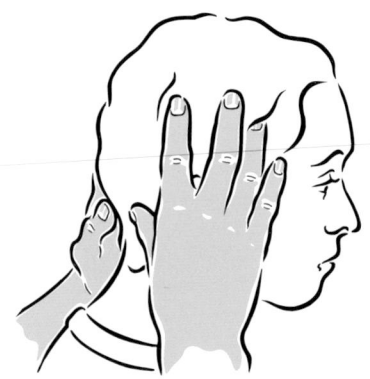

Tip

Friction is achieved by the movement of the skin against the underlying structure.

Tip

The hand should be resting on the scalp the whole of the time whilst performing this movement. Avoid pulling the hair.

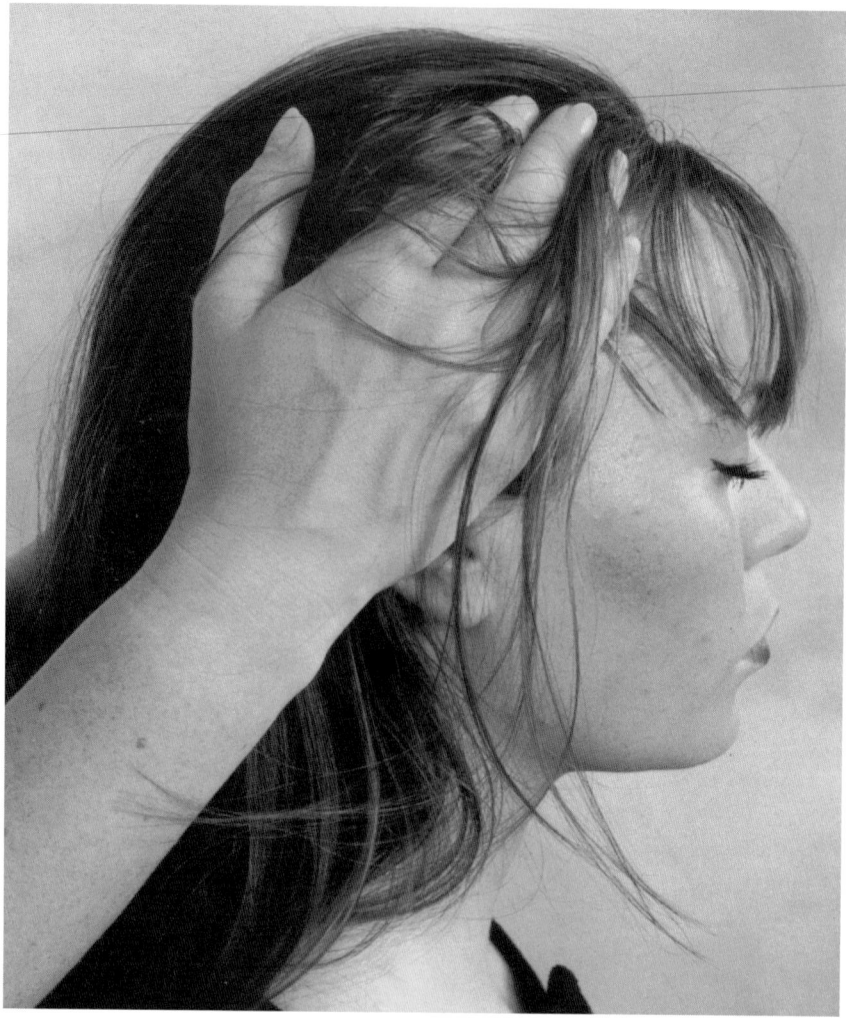

Whole-hand friction

a Stand behind the client and rest one hand over the temple area.

b Thread the fingers of your other hand through the hair at the opposite side of the head just above the ear with your fingers towards the top of the head; the fingers should be flat against the scalp over the temporal muscle, with the palms lightly covering the ears.

c Move your hand quickly up and down, using firm but gentle pressure.

d Move to the temple area and repeat. Reduce pressure in this area.

e Finally, move to a point slightly behind the ear and repeat. Pressure can be increased here if you wish.

The object of these movements is to stimulate and refresh, helping to increase the blood supply to this area.

22 Hair ruffling

Tip

This should be a brisk, scudding movement working all over the scalp. Increasing the speed of these movements will increase the stimulation.

Tip

The hand should be resting on the scalp the whole of the time whilst performing this movement. Avoid pulling the hair.

Hair ruffling

a Using the pads of your fingers and a loose wrist action, gently ruffle the hair.

b On short-to-medium hair, this movement can be done successfully using both hands together. With long hair, however, you may prefer to treat each side of the head separately.

23 Land and lift

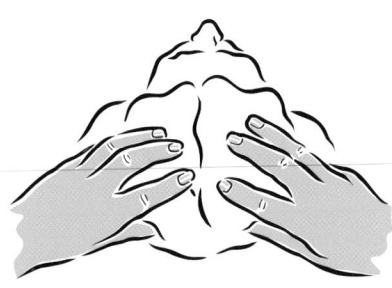

This is a light wrist movement allowing your hand to gently drop and lift away. Do not snatch the hands away.

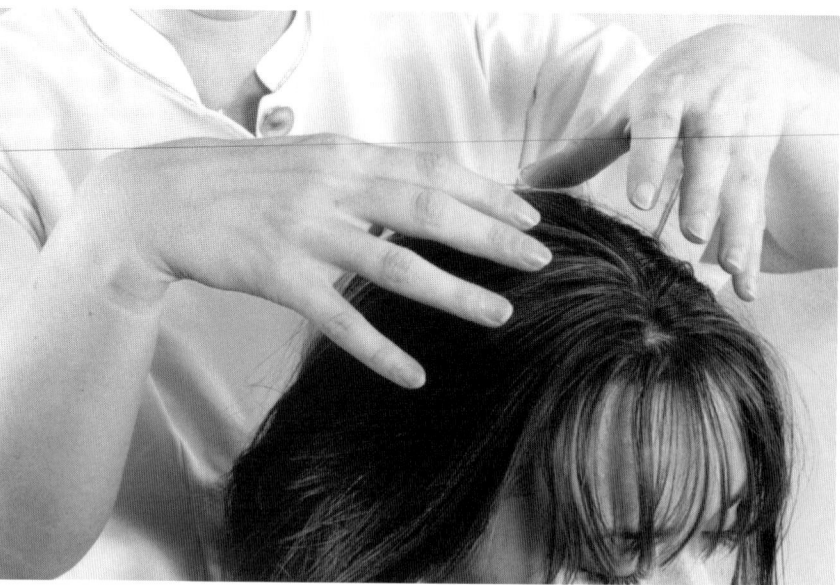

Land and lift

a Make a loose claw shape with your hands. Using the pads of your fingers, gently land on the scalp and quickly lift away.

b Repeat this movement lightly all over the scalp.

24 Raking the scalp

Raking the scalp

a Still in a claw shape, rake the fingers through the hair, running along the scalp. Use both hands together.

b Fingernails can be used, if the client wishes. Care should be taken to ensure that no scratching of the scalp occurs.

25 Tabla playing

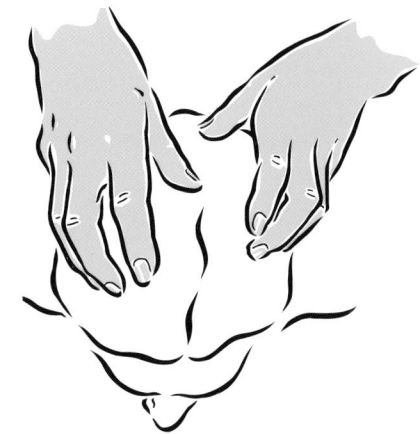

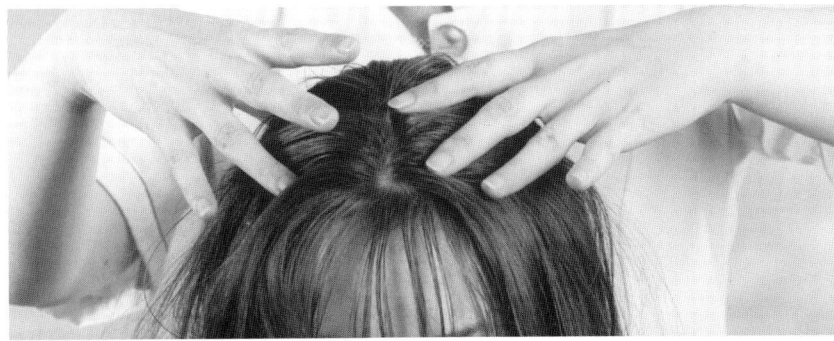

Tabla playing

a Using a drumming action, gently cover the whole head.

b If you wish, gentle champissage can be used across the *back* of the head, where tabla playing is difficult.

26 Squeeze and lift

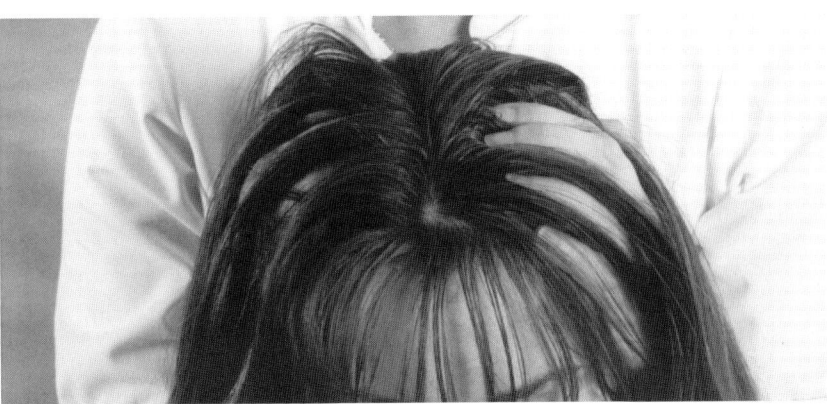

Squeeze and lift

a Stand behind the client. Place your hands on either side of the head, just above the ear. Thread your fingers through the hair if necessary, to ensure that your hands are resting on the scalp, your fingers should be pointing to the top of the head.

b Using both hands together, gently squeeze the head and move the scalp upwards, then release.

c Repeat the same movement at the temple area and just behind the ear.

d Close your fingers, gently trapping the hair between them, to help move the scalp upwards and down.

Carry out the movement three times in each area.

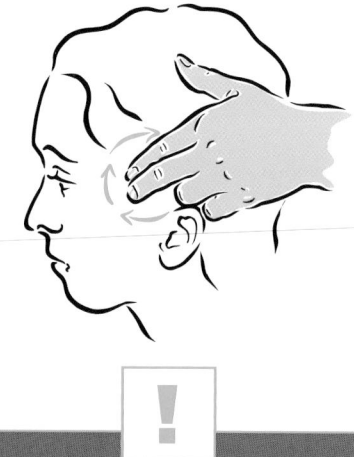

Tip

Perform this move lightly over the temples and with a deep pressure on the scalp. Increase the duration of this movement for clients suffering from tension headaches and for male clients.

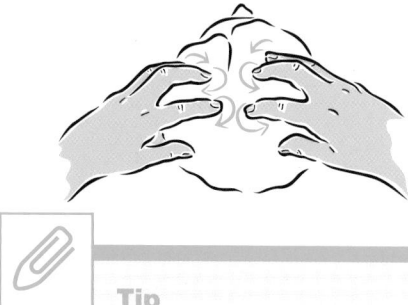

Tip

Make your circles in an upward direction when you are nearest the face. Use slightly more pressure on this half of the circle, and slightly *less* on the downward side of the circle.

27 Circular temple frictions

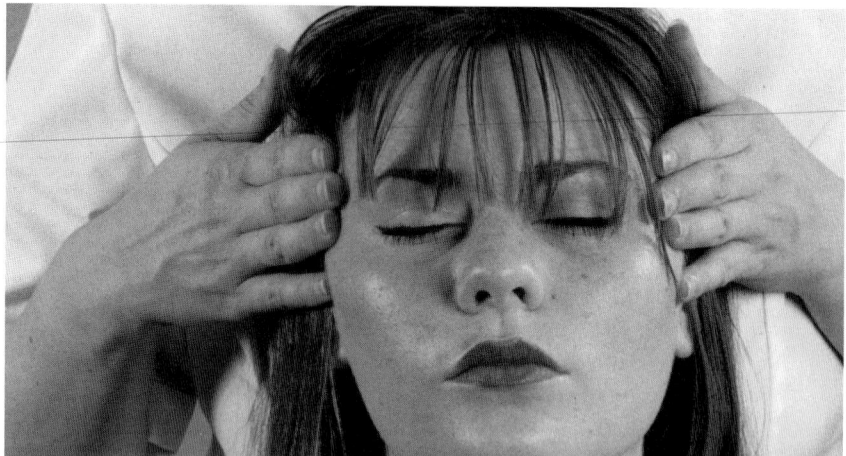

Circular temple frictions

a Using the pads of the index, middle and ring fingers, describe a circle around the temple area. For the best effect, the circles should go upwards as you pass over the temple, and downwards as you come through the hair.

This is a calming and soothing movement, and should be done slowly and with very little pressure.

28 Petrissage to the scalp

Petrissage to the scalp

a Holding your hands in a claw-like shape and using the pads of your fingers, make circular movements with your fingers.

b Try to keep your hands opposite each other as you work over the whole of the scalp. Apply medium pressure during this movement.

Tip

Increase the repetitions for clients suffering from eye-strain.

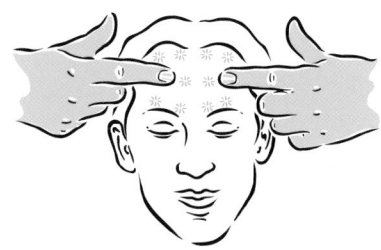

Health & Safety

Therapists must ensure that the client's head is not tipped backwards during the facial movements as this will result in pain and discomfort, which may last for several days. The small folded towel listed under 'Materials and equipment', used in the interests of hygiene to protect the therapist's overall, also plays an important part in helping to maintain the upright position of the head, especially for those clients with large muscle bulk in the shoulder area.

Face massage

Marma points covered while carrying out facial massage movements 29–37 and the final movement 38 are avrtau, apang, phana, shringatkani, shankh and asaha.

29 Pressure points – forehead

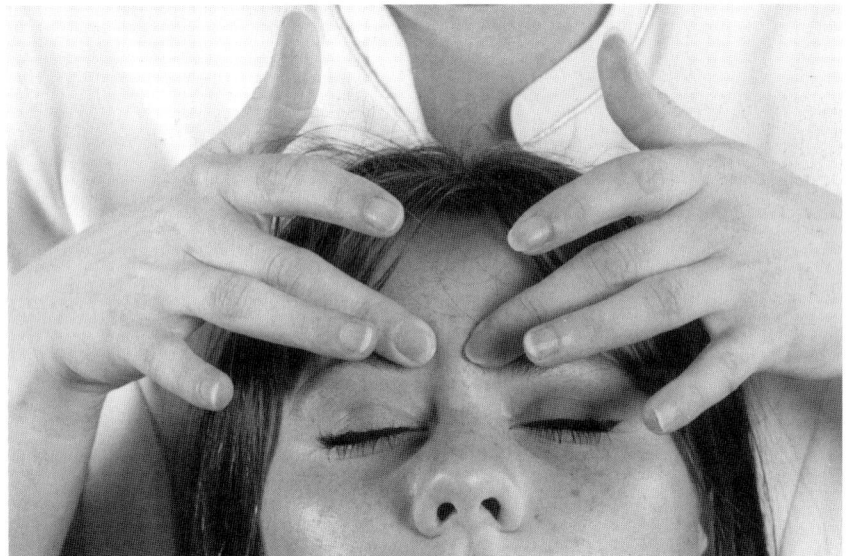

Pressure points – forehead

a Use the pads of the index or middle fingers, and start at a point just above the inner eyebrow.

b Apply medium pressure. Hold for approximately six seconds, then release.

c Move up the forehead to a mid-point between the eyebrow and the hairline. Apply pressure, hold and release.

d Glide up to the hairline. Repeat the pressure and release.

e Move outwards along the hairline about 12 mm, and work down to the eyebrows in the same three stages.

Carry out all six movements three times.

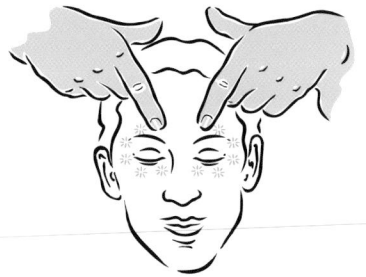

Pressure points – eye sockets

Tip

There is no set number of pressure points as you work your way round the eye socket, but a general guide would be 7–8.

!

Health & Safety

Clients suffering from sinusitis may find this movement painful. Check the pressure for client comfort.

Tip

This movement can be repeated more often to relieve blocked sinuses.

30 Pressure points – eye sockets

a This movement carries straight on from the last, moving to just under the eyebrow at its inner end, onto the inside of the eye socket, and following its shape.

b Carry on with your pressure release, and glide movements as you complete this sequence.

Carry out this sequence three times.

31 Pressure points – cheekbones

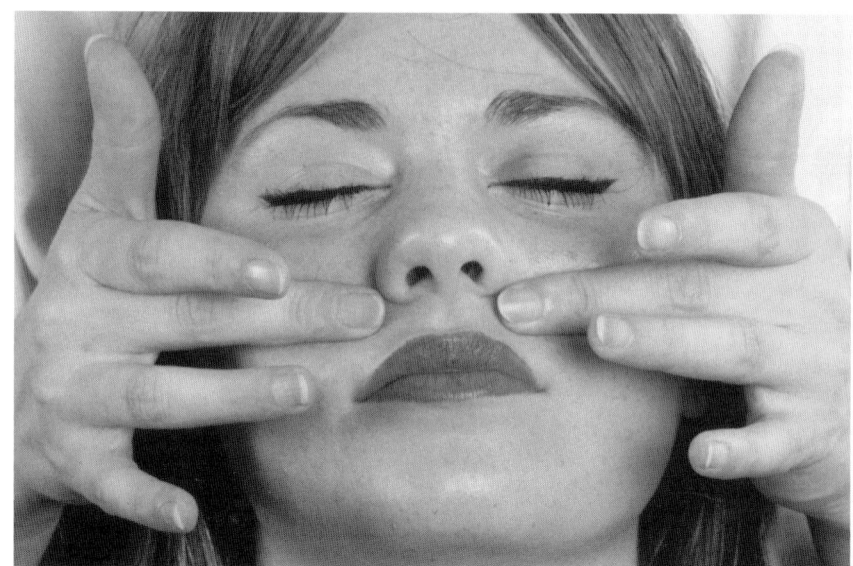

Pressure points – cheekbones

a Following on smoothly from the last movement, glide your fingers down the sides of the nose to the indent at the sides of the nostrils. Feel for a point at the end of the cheekbone and slightly under it. Continue to use the pads of either your index or middle fingers for these movements.

b Perform very small, quick friction movements here, using both hands simultaneously.

c Finish the movement by sweeping lightly along the cheekbone to the ear.

Carry out the movement three times, depending on the condition of the client's sinuses.

32 Pressure points – cheekbones (step two)

a Find the point at the end of the cheekbone where it hinges with the lower jaw. Make your final friction movement here.

b Finish with a gentle sweep over the ears.

Tip

This final sweep leads you into the next step, which is the ear.

33 Ear massage

Tip

This is not a common massage area. Although very relaxing to most clients, massage here may irritate others. Note your client's reactions and record them on the consultation sheet.

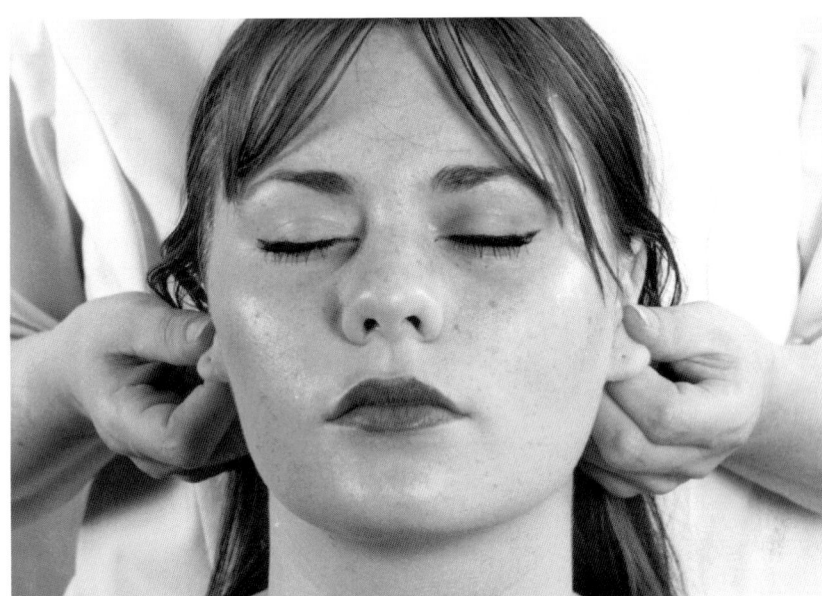

Ear massage

a Beginning at the earlobe, and using the thumb and fingers and small circular movements, work your way up and round the ear.

b Squeeze gently all round the ear.

c Pull the lobe gently down – diagonally outwards, and finally horizontally outwards.

d The ears can also be twiddled and flicked using the index finger and the thumb.

34 Palmar placing

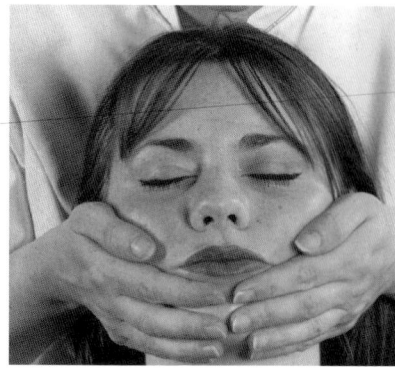 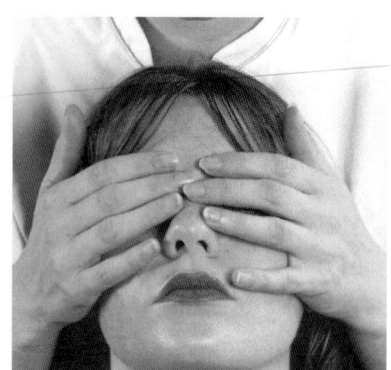

Palmar placing

a Place the heel of your hand gently over the ears, and cup the lower jawbone with the rest of your hand. Your fingertips should just touch in the centre of the chin.

b Swivel your hands gently round until the fingers lie over the closed eyes. Your fingertips should now be just touching at the bridge of the nose.

c Move your hands upwards to cover the temples and the forehead area.

d Move up again, covering the parietal and upper frontal area.

35 Palmar pressure placing

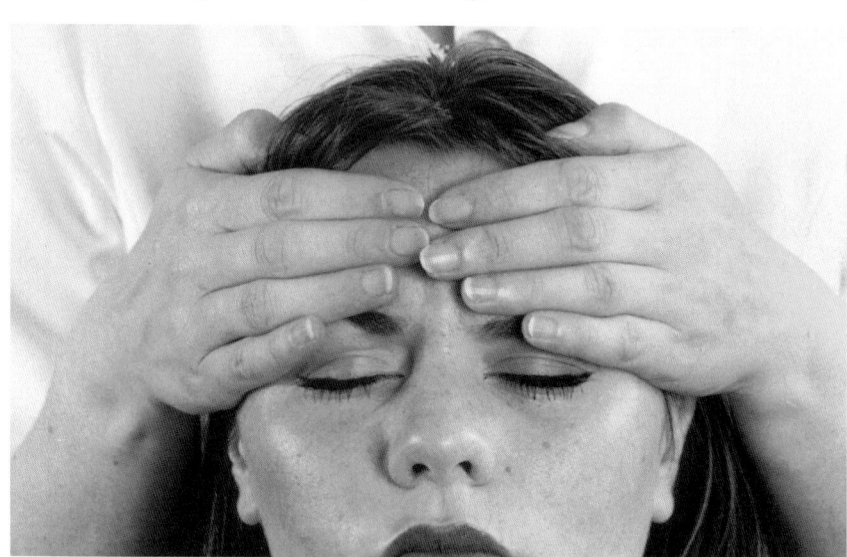

Palmar pressure placing

a Repeat stages **c** and **d** of step **34**. Use medium pressure and a lifting, squeezing movement each time.

Carry out each movement three times.

36 Feather fingertip stroking

Feather fingertip stroking

a Using your finger pads and feather-light strokes, work from the mid-line of the face towards the ears, then from the forehead down to the chin.

37 Palmar pressure placing

Palmar pressure placing

a Repeat step **34**.

38 Brushing down

Tip

Speaking quietly, tell your client that the treatment is complete and bring them back to full consciousness.

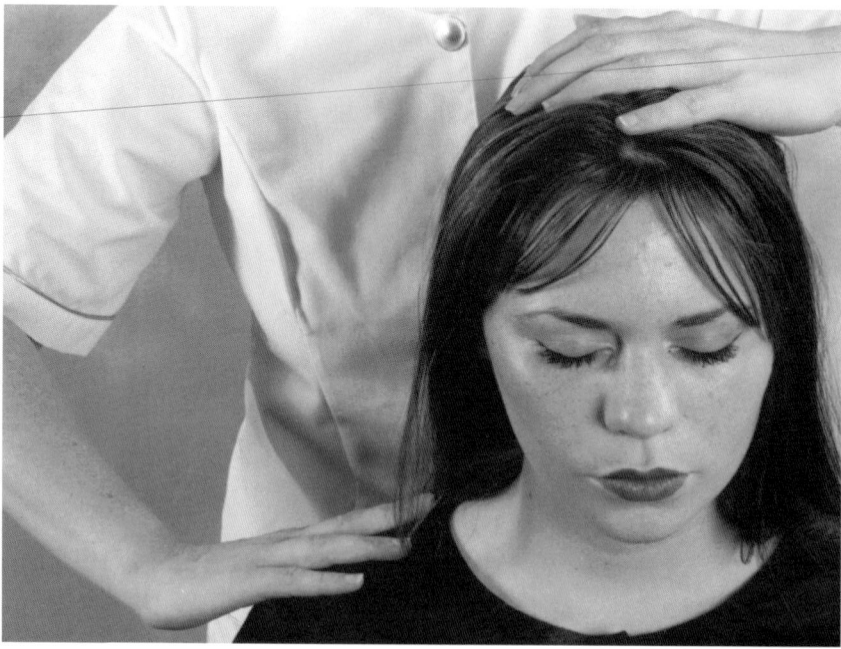

Brushing down

a Stand behind the client.

b Using your fingers, start with your right hand placed on the scalp above the client's left eye. Describe a long, flowing movement over the top of the head, down the neck and along the top of the shoulder.

c Lift your hand and repeat with the other hand on the opposite side of the head.

d Repeat these movements alternately several times. Finish by floating both hands off the shoulders together.

Adapting the massage

There are several reasons why the massage technique sometimes needs to be adapted. For example, when carrying out massage on men, therapists may need to use more pressure than they would when massaging women, as men's muscles tend to be firmer, larger and a lot stronger, and their skin tends to be thicker and have less fatty tissue. To be equally beneficial, therefore, the massage needs to be a lot firmer.

If the massage is intended simply to be relaxing, it should avoid any stimulating movements (any tapotement techniques). The pressure needs to be firm, and the movements slow.

On areas that are tense and where the muscles are tight and contracted, tapotement movements should be avoided. The movements should be slow, with a slight pressure applied to try and stretch the muscles, making the area more supple. On areas of slack muscles, stimulating movements need to be used to increase the circulation and help tone up the area.

Clients who are overweight will need the pressure to be increased. Clients who are thin and bony will need the pressure alleviated and tapotement movements avoided, otherwise the massage will become extremely painful and uncomfortable. It is always best to invite feedback from your client throughout the treatment: every individual's needs are unique.

Remember: if the correct pressure is not applied – if it is either too light or too heavy – the client will not relax and so will not benefit from the treatment. The massage movements should always be appropriate to the client's needs, and carried out in a rhythmical and continuous sequence.

Some clients may prefer to lean forwards on to a cushion or pillow placed on a couch or table while movements 3–7 are carried out. Therapists who adopt this starting position should remember the importance of sitting the client up into a relaxed upright position with head well balanced before continuing the treatment.

Adaptations for the whole treatment

It is possible to adapt the treatment to suit clients who prefer to add an Indian Head Massage on to other massage therapies carried out with the client in a prone position on a couch. Where the immediate treatment has involved the massage of hand, arm, neck and chest area, the movements in these areas may be omitted. Support the neck with a small-rolled towel and commence with the scalp movements, adjusting the hand positions as necessary, then complete the ear massage and facial movements. Remember to gain client feedback with regard to effectiveness and comfort in this position.

Aftercare

Immediately afterwards

Immediately after the treatment, the client should be encouraged to sit quietly for a few minutes. Offer a glass of water or some herbal tea.

For the next 24 hours

- Advise your client to try to spend the rest of the day in as calm and stress-free a state as possible.
- Encourage the client to avoid alcohol, which tends to dehydrate the body and introduces toxins to the body. Drinking water or herbal teas will help to clear the system.
- Recommend a light diet.

If followed, this advice will ensure that the maximum benefits are gained from the Indian Head Massage. Clients can expect to experience a good night's sleep, and to have improved concentration, clearer thinking and greater alertness the following day.

Indian Head Massage clears the sinuses and airways. There have been reports of persistent snorers experiencing up to three nights of trouble-free sleep after the massage.

Long-term aftercare

During a course of treatments clients with hair that lacks shine and vibrancy, poor hair growth, dry scalp and hair conditions, often see a marked improvement in these conditions due to the increase in the flow of nutrients to the scalp and hair roots.

All clients should be encouraged into a regular routine of shampooing and conditioning their hair and scalp, and should be ready to change their products as they experience these improvements. Clients should be advised of the necessity of thorough rinsing after shampooing, and of the avoidance of over-rinsing after conditioning, as the benefits are then removed from the hair. Hair should be left feeling silky, not slimy.

Clients with greasy hair conditions should be advised that this condition may worsen initially but should improve with time as the scalp adjusts to the introduction of increased nutrients and gains a better balance.

Advise clients that adopting a good regular hair care routine will help maintain an improved condition, and minimise everyday wear and tear. This should include regular cutting, shampooing and conditioning, combined with the daily use of high quality styling products and equipment.

Contra-actions

Usually the reactions immediately after the treatment are pleasant, as explained above in 'Aftercare'. This is not always the case, however. The treatment activates the body's own healing power to get rid of toxins, and in some cases a reaction occurs. Such a reaction, sometimes called a **healing crisis**, is really a cleansing process. The severity of the reactions will depend upon the degree of imbalance.

The most common reactions related to the cleansing of toxins within the body are these:

- depression, and an overwhelming desire to weep
- tiredness
- headache
- dizziness or nausea
- disrupted sleep patterns
- increased secretions from the mucous membranes in the nose and mouth
- aggravated skin conditions, if particular conditions have been suppressed.

The client should be made aware that some of these reactions may occur, and be reassured that if so they will only be temporary until the body's natural balance has been restored.

Knowledge review – Massage technique

Consultation

1   Name three important aspects of an effective consultation:

(a) _____

(b) _____

(c) _____

2   Having completed the client's details, what check must you then make before commencing treatment.

The _____ check.

Massage routine

1   Describe the sitting position of your client that will allow him or her to gain maximum benefit from the treatment.

_____

2   When performing champissage the _____

should be avoided because of the danger of _____

3   Care should be taken not to _____
when carrying out the picking-up and holding sequence.

4   The objective of carrying out the whole-hand friction movement

is to _____

5   Explain how you would adapt the massage to suit a client who wants only to be relaxed?

_____

Aftercare

1   You should always be able to offer your client

_____ after a treatment.

2   The most common reactions the client may have if he or she experiences a contra-action are

(a) _____; (b) _____; (c) _____.

12

Independent study

Answers to 'Knowledge review' questions

CHAPTER 2
Anatomy and physiology

Skin

1 (a) epidermis; (b) dermis; (c) subcutaneous tissue.
2 37 degrees centigrade.
3 Cuticle or scarf skin.
4 Finger-like projections interlocking the epidermis with the dermis.
5 Stratum corneum.
6 Keratinisation.
7 Stratum germinativum.
8 Melanin.
9 Form fine networks of connective tissue linking bundles of collagen fibres.
10 Subcutaneous tissue.

Bones

1 (a) Eight; (b) 14.
2 (a) Frontal bone; (b) two zygomatic bones.
3 (1) Nasal; (2) ethmoid; (3) maxillae; (4) mandible.

Blood

1 Carry oxygen to the muscles, tissues and organs.
2 Oxygenated.
3 Aorta.
4 Head.

The lymphatic system

1 (a) Parotid. (b) Buccal. (c) Sub-mental. (d) Occipital.

Nervous system

1 Sensory nerves receive information, motor nerves act on information received to trigger muscular activity.

2 Ophthalmic; maxillary; mandibular.

3 Nose; mouth; and skin.

Muscles

1 (a) Voluntary; (b) involuntary.

2 Frontalis.

3 Flex the elbow.

Respiration

1 Ventilation.

2 External respiration.

3 Cellular respiration.

4 Slowing the rate of external respiration.

CHAPTER 3
Health and safety

1 Control of Substances Hazardous to Health.

2 Workplace (Health, Safety and Welfare) Regulations 1992.

3 16 degrees minimum within one hour of employees arriving at work.

4 Straight back, bent knees, keep load close to the body.

5 (a) dry powder (blue); carbon dioxide (black); halon-gas extinguisher (blue).

   (b) water.

6 Any two from the following text:
   - Salons and workplaces must have a secure method of storing all records.
   - Information kept on records or files must be relevant to the treatments given.
   - All information must be accurate and, in the case of handwritten records, legible.
   - Salons must gain written consent for personal details to be kept.
   - Clients must be allowed access to their own records, failure to do this contravenes the Act.

CHAPTER 4
Stress

1 The autonomic and the voluntary system.

2 Carry messages across the gap between the end of the neurons and the organs.

3 Autonomic.

4 Close to the base of the brain.

5 False.

CHAPTER 5
Preparation

1 To remove rough or sharp areas on the nail prior to treatment.
2 (a) Hand wipes; (b) small towel; (c) comb; (d) hairclip; (e) water.
3 To keep the hands supple and flexible.

Contra-indications

1 Any injury, disease or disorder that indicates that you should not carry out a treatment.
2 I would defer treatment and refer the client to their GP.
3 I would use only soothing and relaxing movements.

Diseases and disorders

1 Harmful.
2 A disease is an infectious, transferable, pathogenic condition.
3 Abnormal skin pigmentation such as a birthmark.
4 (a) Bacteria; (b) virus; (c) fungi.
5 An infected hair follicle of an eyelash.
6 Herpes simplex.
7 No.
8 Dandruff.

CHAPTER 6
Oils

1 No.
2 Eight finger widths back from the forehead.
3 Crown whorl.
4 At the junction of the atlas and occipital bone.
5 Because of their ability to be partially absorbed through the skin.
6 (a) Almond; (b) coconut; (c) hazelnut; (d) apricot kernel; (e) peach kernel; (f) macadamia nut oil.
   Clients may have an allergic reaction to nuts.

CHAPTER 7
Massage benefits and manipulations

1 The benefits are (a) relaxation; (b) improved blood circulation; (c) improved lymphatic flow; (d) reduced muscular tension; (e) regenerated skin; (f) softer skin; (g) reduces stiffness in the neck and shoulder region; (h) stimulates nerve endings.
2 Sebaceous.
3 (a) Slow down evaporation; (b) retain moisture; (c) maintain elasticity; (d) increase resistance to infection.
4 It has a soothing effect on nerves and it increases blood flow and lymphatic circulation.
5 (a) Kneading; (b) picking up; (c) rolling; (d) wringing.

CHAPTER 8
Ayurveda and ayurvedic principles

1 (a) Creation; (b) organisation; (c) destruction.
2 (a) Kapha; (b) pitta; (c) vata.
3 Kapha.
4 To seek a true balance between personal mental and physical state and also with the common environment.

CHAPTER 9
Marma therapy

1 (a) Mind; (b) body; (c) spirit.
2 Jutrurdhara.
3 Sthapni.
4 Adhipati.

CHAPTER 10
Chakras and Indian Head Massage

1 (a) Crown; (b) throat; (c) brow.
2 To help open up the channels of energy flow.
3 The Third Eye.
4 The divine spirit of the universe.

CHAPTER 11
Massage technique

Consultation

1 (a) Chance for the therapist to carry out a visual check. (b) Discuss the expectations of the treatment. (c) Carry out a contra-indications check.
2 Jewellery.

Massage routine

1 Upright position, feet flat on the floor, hands relaxed in the lap.
2 Spine. Injury or displacement of vertebrae.
3 Not to nip the skin. Muscle should be picked up as near to the bone as possible.
4 To stimulate and refresh, by increasing the blood flow.
5 By using slow firm movements and omitting those using tapotement techniques.

Aftercare

1 A glass of water or herbal tea.
2 (a) Dizziness; (b) sickness; (c) extreme tiredness.

Revision questions

Student Name _____

Date _____

CHAPTER 2
Questions

1 How many main functions does the skin have? Name three.

2 What, if any powers of absorption does the skin have?

3 When is the stratum germinativum at its most productive?

4 What are melanocytes?

5 What qualities do collagen fibres have, and why are these important to the skin?

6 Name the two main layers of the dermis.

7 Which layer gives smoothness and shape to the body?

8 Which is the strongest facial bone?

9 Name the location of the maxillae.

10 What are the two vena cava?

11 How is backflow prevented in the veins?

12 Which massage movement helps to improve the venous flow?

13 The main sensory nerve endings in the skin are receptive to what?

14 State the action of the temporalis muscle.

15 What is the action of the pectoralis major muscle?

16 What action causes air to be pushed out of the lungs?

Student Name _____

Date _____

SHEET TWO

1 As a practising therapist, what are you legally required to provide?

2 When was the Data Protection Act 1984 updated?

3 What differences did the new Act make to the storage of records?

4 Why must regular health and safety checks be carried out in the workplace?

5 What do you understand by the following terms: (a) cross-infection; and (b) secondary infection?

6 What are the three stages of discipline?

7 Describe the procedure for clearing away broken glass.

8 Name the region of the brain responsible for correlating the information from the senses and triggering the remedial action.

9 How does the hypothalamus control the delivery of hormones to the necessary action sites?

10 Which system is responsible for the changes in activity produced to deal with stress?

11 The autonomic system encompasses which two other systems?

12 What is the location of the adrenal glands?

13 Where is the hormone cortisol produced?

14 What is produced in the adrenal medulla?

Student Name _____

Date _____

SHEET THREE

CHAPTER 5
Questions

1 Why is it important to remove your jewellery, and request that your clients also remove their jewellery, before treatment commences?

2 What hygienic procedures should you follow before and after treatment?

3 Why is it important that your client observes you carrying out hygienic practices?

4 Give three visible contra-indications to Indian Head Massage.

5 How would you advise a migraine sufferer seeking an Indian Head Massage?

6 What points would you need to clarify with an ME sufferer before making a decision regarding treatment?

7 Name three non-infectious skin conditions.

8 Describe what is meant by a contagious disease.

9 Name three pigmentation disorders of the skin.

10 What is meant by a localised contra-indication? Give an example.

11 What is an infestation?

12 What is a micro-organism?

13 Describe pediculosis capitis.

14 What is tinea corporis and how does it get its common name?

15 What advice would you give a prospective client suffering from dermatitis?

16 Is eczema classed as an infectious or non-infectious condition?

17 How would you recognise alopecia areata?

Student Name _____

Date _____

SHEET FOUR

Questions

1 Name three possible benefits of using oils for scalp massage.

2 List three traditional oils and state their main benefits.

3 Which oil would you recommend for a client suffering from skin disorders?

4 What precautions would you take before recommending oils with curative claims to clients?

5 Which oil has properties also found in the skin's natural lubricant?

6 What are the effects of tapotement movements?

7 State the benefits of vibration movements.

8 What are the effects of massage on the following: (a) muscles and joints; (b) nerves; and (c) circulation? Give at least two points for each one.

9 Name five types of massage movements used in Indian Head Massage.

10 When applying pressure in massage, should this be done working towards the heart or away from the heart?

Student Name _____

Date _____

SHEET FIVE

CHAPTERS 8, 9 AND 10

Questions

1 What is the traditional system of medicine in the Hindu religion called?

2 What does the centre of energy kapha represent?

3 Where is tarpaka situated?

4 Which centre of energy is concerned with digestion?

5 Where is pitta located?

6 Situated in the abdomen, which 'humour' is concerned with destruction?

7 What is the similarity between acupressure and marma therapy?

8 How can minor aches and pains be relieved using marma therapy?

9 Which marma points would you concentrate on to help a client who was suffering from eye-strain? State their location.

10 Which marma point is covered during effleurage to the forearm?

11 Suggest ways of balancing the Root chakra when trying to achieve a sense of oneness with the environment.

12 Which chakra is balanced through everyday pleasurable experiences?

13 The Heart chakra is the meeting point of which other chakras?

14 Why may therapists experience a feeling of well-being, increased energy levels or tiredness after giving a treatment?

15 What action can you take that will help to recharge your inner brightness?

Answers to revision questions

CHAPTER 2
Answers

1 The skin has six main roles: protection; heat regulation; secretion and excretion; absorption; respiration; and sensation.

2 The skin has limited powers of absorption.

3 Between midnight and four a.m.

4 Cells that produce melanin.

5 The protein elastin with elastic properties. They help to give skin its resilience.

6 The recticular layer and papillary layer.

7 The subcutaneous layer, which contains adipose tissue.

8 The mandible.

9 The upper jaw.

10 The main veins entering the heart.

11 By a series of valves.

12 Effleurage.

13 Temperature, pain and touch.

14 Raises the lower jaw.

15 Draws the arm away from the body and rotates it inwards.

16 The relaxation of the diaphragm and the intercostal muscles.

SHEET TWO

CHAPTERS 3 AND 4
Answers

1 A safe and hygienic environment.

2 1998.

3 Only relevant client details are to be kept. The new Act also requires businesses to register with the Data Protection Register whether they use computer or manual filing systems.

4 To ensure that safety is being maintained at all times.

5 (a) When infection is transferred from one person to another. (b) When infection enters an existing wound.

6 Informal discussion; formal verbal warning; formal written warning.

7 Wear suitable gloves, place broken pieces in a closed container, and place this in a waste bin.

8 The hypothalamus.

9 By organising nerve impulses to the organs.

10 The autonomic system.

11 The sympathetic and the parasympathetic systems.

12 On the top of each kidney.

13 In the adrenal cortex.

14 Adrenaline and noradrenaline.

CHAPTER 5
Answers

1 Check your answers against the text reference on page 82, 'The treatment'.

2 Personal: wash your hands before and after each treatment. General: check that all equipment and materials are hygienically clean.

3 It will improve client confidence and encourage return visits and recommendations.

4 Any three from the text on pages 83 and 84.

5 Discuss the frequency of attacks; advise that if these are infrequent, treatment may help; warn that in rare cases treatment may trigger an attack. Therefore the decision to treat must remain with the client.

6 Ascertain if the client is now gradually recovering; explain that the treatment could greatly assist this. But for those clients in the initial or severe stages of ME, treatment *may* reduce rather than increase energy levels. Advise these clients to delay treatment until the body is showing signs of rebalancing, then to try a treatment.

7 Check your answer with the information on page 91.

8 A disease which is spread by direct, or indirect contact with the infection.

9 Check your answers against the information on pages 90 and 91.

10 A small area contra-indicated to treatment i.e. small covered abrasion, or a bruise or pustule in the treatment area.

11 An invasion by a small animal parasite.

12 A micro-organism can be bacteria, or fungi, which lives on the skin. They can be pathogenic or non-pathogenic (harmful or harmless).

13 Head lice.

14 Starts as small red circular patches. Heals from the centre resulting in visible rings – hence its common name, ringworm.

15 Advise clients to seek medical attention.

16 Non-infectious.

17 Small areas of baldness on the scalp.

SHEET FOUR

CHAPTERS 6 AND 7

Answers

1 Refer to page 95 headed 'Using oils'.

2 Give any three from the following list: sesame; mustard; olive; almond; coconut; and jasmine. For benefits, see under each heading on pages 96 and 97.

3 Jojoba or evening primrose oil.

4 Check for allergies.

5 Macadamia nut oil.

6 To stimulate and tone the area.

7 To clear and stimulate the nerve pathways, and to relieve tension in the neck and back, producing a relaxing sedative effect.

8 Check your answers with reference to the sections starting on page 102.

9 Effleurage; petrissage or compressions; tapotement or percussions; frictions; and vibrations.

10 Towards the heart to assist in venous return.

CHAPTERS 8, 9
AND 10
Answers

1 Ayurveda.

2 Earth and water.

3 In the spinal cord protecting the nervous system and ensuring peace of mind.

4 Pitta.

5 The solar plexus.

6 Vata.

7 They share the belief in the existence of a network of energy channels running through the body.

8 By exerting gentle pressure over these points.

9 Avrtau – at the outer end of the eyebrow. Apang – at the outer corner of the eye socket.

10 Indravastih.

11 Sit quietly in the garden or park; take a walk in the country either physically or mentally.

12 The Sacral chakra.

13 The chakra of personal energy, identity and survival.

14 This is due to the exchange of energy between the therapist and the client.

15 Try to plan some time each week for yourself for a little self-indulgence; you can enjoy the sensations of relaxation through a massage with sweet smelling oils or a relaxing bath. Savouring sensations helps to balance the Sacral chakra.

Course evaluation questions A

Student Name _____

Date _____

SHEET A

1 Which traditional oil is used to help cool the head in the high temperatures of summer?

2 State the location of the traditional first point of application when using oil, in terms of marma therapy and chakra ideology.

3 How might massage affect the nerves in skin and muscle tissue? Name the movement that would achieve these effects.

4 Describe the massage movement used in the massage routine point 28.

5 Explain the term allergen.

6 Name and describe an infectious bacterial condition affecting the eyes.

7 What is the most common non-infectious skin disorder?

8 Describe the appearance of psoriasis and explain any adaptations to an Indian Head Massage treatment that you may make.

9 What treatment advice might you offer a client suffering from psoriasis?

10 What must always be carried out before giving any treatment?

11 Explain the term contra-action.

12 Name the deepest layer of the skin. (a) What determines its thickness? (b) In addition to giving shape and smoothness to the body, what other important function does it have?

13 Explain the term mitosis and state where this occurs.

14 When carrying out the facial massage routine 29, which bone are you working over?

15 (a) Which facial bone is bat-wing shaped? (b) Name the bone that forms part of the nasal cavity.

Course evaluation answers A

1 Sesame.

2 Adhipati; Crown.

3 (a) Light movements sooth and calm – effleurage. (b) Brisk movements stimulate – vibrations. (c) Pain relief and possible numbness – compressions/petrissage.

4 Petrissage – a circular deep movement performed with the fingers and thumbs.

5 A substance that provokes an allergic reaction.

6 Conjunctivitis – inflammation of the lining of the eyelid and the mucus membrane that covers the eye.

7 Psoriasis.

8 Dry raised scaly patches of stratum corneum, silvery in appearance. Adaptations to treatment could include the use of oils, gentle movements over the affected area to avoid accidental removal of thickened patches, and extending the movements of stimulation on surrounding tissue to increase the blood flow and nutrition to the affected area.

9 Treat with coal tar based products. Plan a programme of Indian Head Massage treatments to reduce stress levels (often a cause of psoriasis) and stimulate the skin's natural balancing activity in the affected area.

10 A full consultation.

11 A contra-action occurs when the body activates its process of rebalancing by getting rid of toxins. It is really a cleansing process.

12 Subcutaneous tissue. (a) Age, sex and general health. (b) It acts as a protective cushion against injury.

13 Cell growth and division, mitosis takes place in the stratum germinativum.

14 Frontalis.

15 (a) Sphenoid. (b) Ethmoid.

Course evaluation questions B

Student Name _____

Date _____

SHEET B

1 List the bones of the neck, chest, shoulders and arms.

2 Explain the flow of blood through the heart starting at the right atrium.

3 One of the main functions of the lymphatic system is to remove bacteria and foreign matter; name two other important functions.

4 Explain the route taken by lymphatic fluid after its collection into the thoracic and right lymphatic ducts.

5 Which cranial nerve passes through the temporal bone? Name the parts of the face which it serves.

6 Which surface muscle are you working across when carrying out massage routine numbers 15 and 16?

7 Name the massage movement/s which relaxes these muscles: (a) caninus; (b) temporalis; (c) occipital; (d) frontalis.

8 Explain what happens during cellular respiration.

9 Name two responsibilities of employees to the employer.

10 When working with clients' chakras and energy fields, what colours may they 'see' during treatment?

11 What is the link between bharahaka and oils used in Indian Head Massage?

12 While carrying out movement 8 – pick up and hold – which marma point is being worked on?

13 What advice would you give to a client suffering from marked symptoms of stress?

14 Name five major muscles of the lower arm.

15 In what ways does the Data Protection Act 1998 differ from the previous Act of 1984?

Course evaluation answers B

1   Spinal vertebrae
    - Hyoid
    - Scapulae
    - Clavicle
    - Sternum
    - Humerus
    - Radius
    - Ulna.

2   Right atrium venous blood; tricuspid valve; right ventricle; pulmonary semi-lunar valve; lungs; left atrium; bicuspid or mitral valve; left ventricle; aortic semi-lunar valve; aorta – to the body and, via the carotid artery, to the head. Returning to the heart via the superior and inferior vena cava into the right atrium.

3   (a) Helps to prevent infection. (b) Drains away excess fluids.

4   The lymph from these ducts is emptied into a vein at the back of the neck, which in turn is emptied into the vena cava. The lymph is mixed with the blood as it returns to the heart.

5   The 7th cranial nerve: tongue; palate; muscles of the face; and the ear muscle.

6   Sternocleido-mastoid muscle.

7   (a) Pressure points – number 31. (b) Circular frictions – number 27. Whole-hand frictions – number 21.
    (c) Friction under the occiput – numbers 18 and 19.
    (d) Pressure points – number 29.

8   An exchange of oxygen within the cells of the body used to 'burn' foodstuffs, thereby releasing energy.

9   To be responsible for health and safety in relation to fellow workers, the general public and themselves.

10 Shades of blue/violet and white light as the treatment balances the three highest chakras – Throat, Brow and Crown.

11 Bharahaka represents the organ of the skin and, as a subdivision of pitta, the digestion of bharahaka is interpreted as the absorption of oils through the skin.

12 Apastamgh.

13 Advise a course of Indian Head Massage treatments as massaging the head encourages the supply of oxygen to

the brain, which is one of the best ways of reducing stress. Try to find five or ten minutes a day to practise breathing and meditation techniques.

14 Any five of the following: bachioradialis; supinator; pronators teres; flexor carpi radialis; flexor carpi ulnaris; pronator quadratus; palmaris longus; flexor digitorum superficialis; flexor digitorum profundus.

15 (a) Clients' written permission must be gained before records can be kept. (b) Clients may view their records at any time. (c) Records must be kept in a secure place. (d) Only relevant details can be stored. (e) Record keeping regulations apply to manual filing and computer records.

Case study records

Case studies should consist of at least three consecutive treatments. Examples of case study log sheets are given on the following pages. Students who wish to devise their own case study log sheets should include the following:

- relevant treatment log sheet ie. 1st, 2nd, 3rd
- consultation sheets
- contra-indications list, if not included on consultation sheet
- pen.

Log sheets should include the following information:

- student's name
- client's name and address
- date
- space to write client's feelings and expectations of the treatment; any adaptations to proposed treatment; areas the treatment will cover – for example, inclusion or exclusion of the lower arm and hand; immediate post-treatment feedback
- space to write the therapist's personal evaluation of his or her performance.

Subsequent sheets should begin by eliciting feedback from the client on their experiences during the days immediately following treatment.

A final sheet should include the client's comments on the benefits and improvements experienced throughout the course of treatments. The final sheet should also have space for therapists to write a report on the progressive changes in client experience, and their overall self-assessment of the case study visits. This report may extend to accompanying sheets.

Case study log sheet

Case study log sheet – first visit

Student's name _____

Client name _____

Address _____

Client's feelings regarding this treatment. Previous experience of Indian Head Massage: yes/no? Nervous/relaxed/looking forward to it.

Contra-indication list completed and relevant notes made.

Treatment area and client preferences noted – areas of particular attention:

Client immediate feedback:

Any contra-actions experienced?

Aftercare advice given, general and specific:

Student's self-evaluation of his or her performance and the effectiveness of the treatment.

Case study log sheet – second visit

Student's name _____

Client name _____

Address _____

Client's feedback from the days immediately following their first treatment:

Contra-indication list checked and any alterations/additions made:

Any changes in the treatment area or client preferences noted – areas of particular attention:

Client immediate feedback:

Any contra-actions experienced?

Aftercare advice given, general and specific:

Student's self-evaluation of his or her performance and the effectiveness of the treatment.

Case study log sheet – third visit

Student's name   _____

Client name   _____

Address   _____

Client's feedback from the days immediately following their second treatment:

Contra-indication list checked and any alterations/additions made:

Any changes in the treatment area or client preferences noted – areas of particular attention:

Client immediate feedback – should include comments on the benefits and improvements experienced throughout the course of treatments:

Any contra-actions experienced at any stage in the course of treatments:

Aftercare advice given, general and specific. Include at this point advice on future treatments:

Student's self-evaluation of his or her performance and the effectiveness of the treatment.

_____

Students should next compile a written report on the progressive changes in client experience, and their overall self-assessment of the case study visits. The report may extend to further sheets.

13

Case studies

Assessing the benefits of Indian Head Massage

In the West, Indian Head Massage is proving to be a fascinating therapy with many differing benefits for people with varied needs. Because Indian Head Massage is relatively new, however, there are no formal lists of benefits. Instead, therefore, this chapter offers a selection of case studies which together give an insight into the kind of feedback you may expect from clients. Though representative, these experiences are by no means exhaustive. As more therapists train, and treat a wider section of the population, the range of benefits experienced is likely to expand.

Case studies

Case study 1

Gender:	Male.
Age:	34.
Occupation:	Warehouse supervisor.
Reason for treatment:	Ache in shoulders and back of neck. Uneven sleep pattern.
Frequency of visits:	Three, at weekly intervals.

Outcome

Gary found it difficult to relax on the first visit, but still enjoyed the treatment and felt less tense at the end of it. The second treatment was much better: he managed to relax at the beginning of the session. On the third visit he really enjoyed the treatment, and noted a much freer feeling in his neck and shoulders. He also reported that he was enjoying a full night's unbroken sleep, and consequently feeling more refreshed and relaxed generally.

General comments

After each visit Gary's wife noticed that for up to three nights he stopped snoring. (Note: This has been reported by several other case study clients.) Gary intends to continue with regular treatments.

Case study 2

Gender:	Female.
Age:	28.
Occupation:	Housewife and mother of three children.
Reason for treatment:	Irritable, short-tempered; feeling depressed.
Frequency of visits:	Four visits at weekly intervals.

Outcome

At the first visit Janine found the treatment a little strange and unusual. She enjoyed the second session and said she felt more relaxed. At the end of the third session she reported an improvement in her general feeling of well-being. She really enjoyed her fourth visit; she was sleeping better and felt she had benefited greatly from these sessions.

General comments

Janine reported that she had experienced a gradual improvement in her sleep pattern after each treatment, and was now sleeping better than for many weeks. There was also interesting feedback after these treatments from Janine's family, who said that she was calmer and much more patient, that there had been no temper outbursts, and that she had smiled a lot more!

Case study 3

Gender:	Female.
Age:	62.
Occupation:	Retired headteacher.
Reason for treatment:	Facial ache and painful sinuses.
Frequency of visits:	Planned weekly visits over four weeks.

Outcome

First visit: Heather enjoyed her first treatment – she found it easy to relax and was surprised how refreshed she felt after such a relatively short treatment. She particularly liked the fact that it was not necessary for her to undress.

Second visit: Heather was eager to discuss her experiences on the day following her first treatment. She needed to use a few more tissues than usual to blow her nose early next morning, but then said her head felt wonderfully clear and that the pain she had been experiencing from blocked sinuses had disappeared. She was very excited about a further benefit: the next morning she had played her best round of golf ever, and had improved her handicap.

Heather was looking forward to this improved level of concentration and alertness again after today's treatment.

General comments

It is interesting to note that the experience of improved concentration is not confined to those in the business world or the classroom.

Case study 4

Gender:	Male.
Age:	38.
Occupation:	Journalist.
Reason for treatment:	Curiosity! Mike had heard about Indian Head Massage treatments and was sceptical of some of the claims about the benefits, so when a relative undertook a course of study he offered himself as a case study.

Frequency of visits: The four requisite treatments were carried out over a period of four weeks.

Outcome

First visit: Mike admitted to having tension in his shoulder and neck area; the area proved to be very stiff, with some restriction of movement. He also suffered from eye-ache and concentration headaches in the spenoid and temporal areas of the head.

Second visit: Mike was surprised and pleased to notice that his headaches had improved for three days after treatment. This time his shoulders felt a little better after massage. Mike felt more relaxed, and actually admitted to enjoying the session.

Third visit: Mike was much more relaxed, and his shoulder and neck muscles were softer and easier to work on. He had a heightened 'feel good' sense after treatment.

Fourth visit: Mike enjoyed this session. After it, he felt relaxed and really able to wind down. He had noted a marked improvement in his tension headaches, which were much less severe, and felt more able to deal with his stressful job. As the father of three children he was enjoying his home life to a fuller extent.

General comments

After the fourth visit Mike had another benefit to report. Like many men he had been suffering from loss of hair over a period of time, but during these weeks of treatment he had noticed that his hair had stopped falling out. It is to be hoped that the scalp stimulation will continue to help with this problem, and progress is being recorded. Mike is now a regular client and fully committed to head massage sessions.

Case study 5

Gender: Female.

Age: 29.

Occupation: Unemployed careworker.

Reason for treatment: ME sufferer.

Frequency of visits: Four planned visits over a period of four to six weeks.

Outcome

First visit: Having discovered in my consultation that Sarah was an ME sufferer I was at pains to explain to her that it may not be a suitable treatment for her. (I unknowingly treated another ME sufferer on a previous occasion and she had not responded well – the treatment seemed to rob her of what little energy she had.)

Sarah pointed out that she was now experiencing signs of recovery, and would like to try at least one treatment. I used a light pressure throughout the treatment, and after a glass of filtered water Sarah said she felt nicely relaxed and not at all drained, so we agreed a further visit.

Second visit: Sarah was delighted to tell me that the day after treatment she had had more energy than she had experienced for years, and was sure that these treatments were going to assist her in her fight towards recovery.

(Note: Great care should be taken when treating ME sufferers as it has been found that only those recovering find this treatment beneficial. Medical approval should always be sought before treating clients with this condition.)

Case study 6

Gender:	Male.
Age:	7.
Occupation:	Schoolboy.
Reason for treatment:	Hyperactive. Short night's sleep. Poor concentration span.
Frequency of visits:	Weekly over a six-week period.

Outcome

First visit: Simon found it difficult to sit still, so the massage was adapted and concentrated mostly on the scalp.

Second visit: Simon's mother said that she wanted to try a full routine as Simon had calmed down towards the end of the last session. This treatment went much better, with only the facial movements omitted. Simon seemed calmer at the end and his mother was pleased with his behaviour.

Third visit: Mrs Bates was pleased to report that after the last treatment Simon had slept better and for longer. He had another full treatment with some facial work, but did not like having his eyes covered. He was only a little fidgety during this session.

Fourth visit: On the day following the last treatment, Mrs Bates had noticed improvements in Simon's hyperactive state. She thought his concentration span seemed a little better. He had continued to sleep longer after the treatments.

General comments

Simon sat much more quietly for this treatment, and went off happily with his mother afterwards. Mrs Bates is keen to continue the treatments and hopes for further improvements.

Case study 7

Gender:	Male.
Age:	35.
Occupation:	Labourer.
Reason for treatment:	Continual head cold, earache and sore throat.
Frequency of visits:	Once a week, over a six-week period.

Outcome

On the first session Mike was very unsure about the whole situation. His wife had persuaded him to come along as antibiotics no longer helped.

His nose started to run and his eyes to water before the treatment had finished. By the second treatment Mike's head cold wasn't as bad, but his throat was quite sore. By the third treatment and fourth treatments, his throat was a lot better, his head cold nearly gone, and his ear only slightly sore. At the last sessions he felt 100 per cent better.

General comments

Mike reported that as the treatments had progressed he had begun to feel better. Usually that evening his nose would run for a few hours, and his throat and ears would be particularly sore, but the next morning he would have no symptoms at all. His senses of smell and taste had vastly improved, and he no longer needed the antibiotics or the painkillers.

Case study 8

Gender:	Female.
Age:	45.
Occupation:	Full-time factory worker.
Reason for treatment:	Suffering from sinusitis.
Frequency of visits:	Once a week, over a month.

Outcome

On the first visit the client, Fiona, was very apprehensive and unsure about the treatment. She found it hard to relax, giggled a lot, and was clearly uncomfortable with the situation.

By the second treatment, Fiona was a little more in control than at the previous session. She did not seem as embarrassed.

By the third treatment, Fiona was looking forward to the treatment and dozed near to the end of the session.

On the fourth visit, Fiona was quite eager to get started, and relaxed straight away. Her tension zone was almost supple, with no nodules, and halfway through the session she fell asleep.

General comments

After the first visit Fiona felt very tender around the nose, eye and cheek region. She found it hard to sleep that night, as she could not stop blowing her nose – she said it was like a tap. She reported that the following day the constant dull ache in her face, which she had seemed always to have, was a lot better. As the treatments progressed she reported that the dull ache had disappeared completely; since having the treatment she had not taken any tablets to relieve the pain.

Fiona no longer feels 'silly' about having the treatment, and has since recommended it to her friends.

Case study 9

Gender:	Male.
Age:	60.
Occupation:	Retired.
Reason for treatment:	Hair loss.
Frequency of visit:	Once a week over 12 weeks.

Outcome

Bob had been losing his hair over the last 12 months. He was feeling extremely down and conscious of his condition.

Over the 12 weeks I carried out the Indian Head Massage concentrating particularly on the head area. I used rosemary and cedarwood essential oils, diluted with jojoba as a carrier oil. I feel that hair loss is a difficult condition to treat and this was rather new to me, so I became as anxious as Bob as the weeks progressed, wondering from week to week whether there would be any improvement.

For the first few weeks there was no improvement. Bob was not put off, however, as he enjoyed the treatment, and had found that his hair loss did not take over his life as it had been doing – he was not as obsessional about it as before. After 10 weeks the hair seemed to feel thicker, and Bob felt there was a definite improvement. The hair had not continued to become thinner.

General comments

The treatment will take months before there is a substantial improvement. Bob is quite happy to continue; already he feels a lot more confident in his appearance.

Case study 10

Gender:	Female.
Age:	50.
Occupation:	Full-time lecturer (maths and science).
Reason for treatment:	Completely run down; no energy; 'burnt out'; can't concentrate.
Frequency of visit:	Once a week, over a four-week period.

Outcome

On the first session the client relaxed completely and fell asleep after the first five minutes. No tightness or tension nodules were found. Gill seemed to be suffering rather from mental exhaustion.

At the second treatment Gill was very eager to get started, and again a few minutes into the massage she was sound asleep.

The third treatment and fourth treatments were exactly the same, although on the last session she snored very loudly. It was always the same that she slept through the sessions, but the moment I removed my hands she woke up. Gill would wake up very groggy, so after the first session we decided that it would be better to offer the massage at her home, so that she would not need to drive afterwards.

General comments

Gill said that she went straight to bed after each session, as she felt very drowsy and unable to do anything. The following morning she would wake up feeling refreshed and on a high, her mind clear and alert instead of the usual heavy, dreary feeling.

As the treatments progressed, she reported that she had not slept as deeply in years, and had ceased to have vivid dreams. She felt more positive about work, and is now contemplating a degree course in management. As long as she can continue to have her weekly session, she feels she will cope well.

Case study 11

Gender:	Female.
Age:	40.
Occupation:	Full-time secretary and housewife.
Reason for treatment:	Suffering from insomnia and bad headaches. Feels very depressed, chiefly because of not being able to sleep. Leads a very busy lifestyle; works full-time; has two teenage children.
Frequency of visits:	Once a week, over a month.

Outcome

On the first visit Mary found it hard to relax, tended to talk all through the session, and was extremely tense and uncomfortable with the situation. Her shoulder and neck area was very tight, with many tension nodules; these hurt when pressure was applied.

At the second treatment Mary was very tired and irritable and close to tears, but towards the end of the massage she started to relax slightly. Her neck and shoulder region was still as bad, although she managed to tolerate the pressure. This time she talked only at the beginning of the treatment.

By the third treatment she was more cheerful, and seemed to relax almost straight away. The tense areas seemed to be slightly better. By the end of the session she was nearly asleep. The tension region was more supple, with very few tension nodules.

At the fourth visit Mary was quite eager to get started and relaxed straight away; her tension zone was almost supple, with no nodules. Halfway through the session she fell asleep.

General comments

After the first visit Mary felt very tender around the neck and shoulder region, and found it hard to sleep that night. She therefore felt rather reluctant to come for the second treatment. As the treatments progressed, however, she reported that she had not slept better in years. She felt less irritable and more positive about her lifestyle. The headaches were now less frequent.

Mary's family stated that she was a different person – more relaxed, far happier, and with much more energy. Mary continues to have the massage on a weekly basis.

Further reading

Beck, Mark. *Milady's Theory and Practice of Therapeutic Massage*, 2nd edn. (Milady, 1999).

Bennett, Ruth. *The Science of Beauty Therapy*, 2nd edn. (Hodder & Stoughton, 1995).

Cutting, P. and R. Ross. *Hairdressing – The Complete Guide* (Addison Wesley/Longman Higher Education, 2000).

Goldberg, Audrey and Lucy McDonald. *Body Massage for the Beauty Therapist*, 3rd edn. (Butterworth-Heinemann, 1996).

Joari, Harish. *Ancient Indian Massage* (Coronet, 1974).

Nordmann, Lorraine, Lorraine Appleyard and Pamela Linforth. *Professional Beauty Therapy: The Official Guide to Level 3* (Thomson Learning, 2001).

White, Ruth. *Working With Your Chakras* (Piatkus, 1993).

Index